All of the above are available at your local bookshop or may be ordered by visiting:
Hay House UK: www.hayhouse.co.uk
Hay House USA: www.hayhouse.com
Hay House Australia: www.hayhouse.com.au
Hay House South Africa: orders@psdprom.co.za

Smart Spending

with Jane Furnival

HAY HOUSE

Australia • Canada • Hong Kong
South Africa • United Kingdom • United States

Published and distributed in the United Kingdom by:
Hay House UK, Ltd • Unit 62, Canalot Studios • 222 Kensal Rd, London W10 5BN
Tel: (44) 20 8962 1230 • Fax: (44) 20 8962 1239 • www.hayhouse.co.uk

Published and distributed in the United States of America by:
Hay House, Inc. • PO Box 5100 • Carlsbad • CA 92018-5100
Tel: (1) 760 431 7695 or (800) 654 5126 • Fax: (1) 760 431 6948 or (800) 650 5115
www.hayhouse.com

Published and distributed in Australia by:
Hay House Australia, Ltd • 18/36 Ralph St. • Alexandria NSW 2015
Tel: (61) 2 9669 4299 • Fax: (61) 2 9669 4144 • www.hayhouse.com.au

Published and distributed in the Republic of South Africa by:
Hay House SA (Pty), Ltd • P.O. Box 990 • Witkoppen 2068
Tel/Fax: (27) 11 706 6612 • orders@psdprom.co.za

Distributed in Canada by:
Raincoast • 9050 Shaughnessy St., Vancouver, B.C. V6P 6E5
Tel: (1) 604 323 7100 • Fax: (1) 604 323 2600

© Jane Furnival 2006.

Cover images: Champagne bottle © punchstock/stockbyte
A glass of sparkling champagne © punchstock/foodcollection.com
Gift bag © punchstock/photodisc
Toy vintage convertible car © punchstock/Corbis
Dualit Vario 4 slice bread toaster in petal pink supplied by Dualit
Pink stiletto, price tag © Leanne Siu.
Design: e-Digital Design.

A catalogue record for this book is available from the British Library.

ISBN 1-4019-1029-7

Printed and bound in Great Britain by T J International, Padstow, Cornwall.

Contents

Preface

Who do I think I am?

'I heard you on Radio Four today. Who do you think you are, telling other people how to save money?' demanded a mum I met on the school run.

My answer was – and is – I am an ordinary mother of three who nearly went bust, but pulled herself back from the brink of bankruptcy and has survived. There is nothing I suggest or ask you to do in this book, that I have not done myself, or inflicted on my husband and three children, dog, three cats and hens. Nor has anyone ever paid me, directly or indirectly, for recommending their company in my books. I pay my way and speak as I find.

I don't live like a miser, nor am I personally mean. We *Smart Spenders* like our comforts. My version of thrift is to save on the boring bits that we all grudge spending money on, to have fun with the rest. This book passes on my secrets to help you.

So you really want to know the dirt? Cue violins. Near Christmas 1991, I was heavily pregnant and with a five year-old son when the newspaper I worked on as a freelance, *The European*, went bust, thanks to the international fraudster Robert Maxwell. I was out of a job and owed thousands of pounds in back-pay and travel expenses for flying all over Europe.

We were already 'running on empty' as my husband had just started a new business and we had put our home up as security for his business loan. Sometimes I would work free as his receptionist while writing at the same time.

During the worst times, I recall bitterly cold days when I looked round our home and took anything I could out of drawers and off the wall, went out to sell it – at car boot sales, anywhere – and came back delighted with £30 which would feed us for the week. Instead of eating, I had a 'meal' by looking at food in shop windows. Once, we found £10 in the street and had fish and chips. No meal has ever tasted as good.

I had never been in financial trouble before. Before leaving work to look after my first baby, I had been creative director of an advertising agency and earned a reasonable salary – not massive, as I was a girl and this was the early 1980s, but good. I was innocent about any need to save money. When my cleaning lady asked me to buy a bucket, I sent a bike messenger from my office in Covent Garden to Habitat several miles away, to bring back 'a selection of the prettiest colours'.

I adopted a thriftier lifestyle when we had to think what to give our son William for Christmas that year. We went to the local dump for a rattlebanger bike, hoping to do it up. But we found a pram chassis. This we transformed into a splendid go-kart. William became the envy of his friends and I realised that there was a world of alternative, and more interesting, solutions to life's problems, apart from just throwing money at them.

My first book, *Mr Thrifty's How to Save Money on Absolutely Everything* (Michael O'Mara), inspired the BBC to ask me to become thrift guru to save six familes from financial trouble in the recent BBC-1 series *Smart Spenders*.

This new book is larger, more wide-ranging and more personal. You don't have to read it in any particular order but you can dip in anywhere and find something useful. It is based on my years of experience in helping individuals to lift themselves out of debt or simply to improve their lives with the minimum of hassle.

It fills you in on the inside knowledge I learned during my years in advertising, selling everything from mortgages to face cream, about how to make people buy things. Armed with this information, you can understand yourself better. And once you master your own foibles and deeper impulses, you can become a smart spender too.

Jane Furnival

Acknowledgements

A book is really a team effort. Under the acrobat at the top, where the spotlight shines, is a pyramid of support.

Ruth Higham is an astute researcher, checker, rock and good friend, sharing my daily ups and downs even at dead of night and weekends. I can't thank her enough.

Hay House Publishers are my dream team. Editor Michelle Pilley, text editor Ruth Jeavons, Megan Slyfield, Jo Burgess, Jo Lal, Leanne Siu, Giovanni Ceroni, and Paul Disney... all have been delightful and helpful.

Jacqueline Burns, my literary agent at Free Agent, made brilliant suggestions, especially about psychology, and gave me the kind of care that most authors only fantasise about. Nicola Ibison, Jo Wander, Julia Chapman and Dawn Astill at NCI-Management, my TV agents, have all been fantastic supporters.

Individual experts have generously given me their knowledge and time. Christine Northam, counsellor for Relate; Dr Cosmo Hallström Consultant Psychiatrist; Nicola Williams from accountants Wilson Wright & Co; Anne Redstone, spokesperson for The Chartered Institute of Taxation; Dr Dorothy Rowe, psychologist and author; Mark Ritson, Associate Professor at the London Business School; Dr Steven Reiss, Professor of Psychology and Psychiatry; Frank Furedi, Professor of Sociology at the University of Kent; Greg Philo, Professor of Communication at Glasgow University; Mike Hepworth, Honorary Reader in Sociology at Aberdeen University; Francis Lilley, Cognitive Behavioural Therapist; Malcolm Hurlston, Chairman of The Consumer Credit Counselling Service

(CCCS); author Jonathan Aitken; Yvonne Ridley, independent financial adviser from Pearson Jones PLC; Stella Egert, family counsellor; Lionel Hilary Qadosh Fanshawe of The Chap magazine; and fashion adviser Sheila Warren-Hill. Also thanks to everyone who allowed me to use their real-life examples, even when your name was changed as requested.

For help with surveys and statistics, I am grateful to The Office for National Statistics (Family Spending Report), and to Helena Bakunowicz for helping to type it; MSN, Mintel, The Henley Centre, The Prudential, Philip Hale of the RAC and Barclaycard.

TV development producer Miriam Akhtar first pinpointed my potential to be a TV 'thrift guru' and deserves my thanks.

Big thanks to my husband Andy Tribble for his suggestions about men and tools. William Tribble, Charlie Tribble and Henry Tribble (they like their names written in full!) gave up Mum-time to allow me to write this book. Jacqui Bakunowicz talked me through the sticky bits. Jacqui Cobb and Sara Leyser looked after Henry. Ekaterina Petrova made coffee and Oliver Gardner drank it with me in the vegetable patch. Clive and Jeanne French poured out wine liberally as did David and Barbara Nadel.

Special thanks go to Rose Leonard of insurance brokers Stackhouse Poland, loss adjusters John Bickley and HSBC insurers for taking a headache away when, during the writing of this book, five small foxes invaded my home through the cat door and five rooms had to have the carpets replaced. Accolades to Sylvia Smith for suggesting I made the claim in the first place and Steve Watling, my bank manager at NatWest, for carrying the cost until the claim went through.

I hope I haven't left anyone unthanked but if so, forgive me. Oh, Flash the cat for keeping the computer warm.

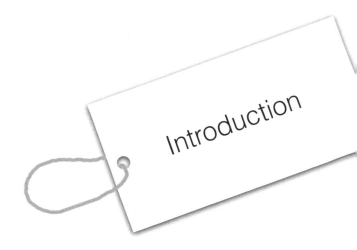

Introduction

Everybody wants to save money. And, these days, everyone needs to. If you would like to make your money go further, or have trouble making ends meet, it is pointless feeling ashamed to admit it. Everyone's in the same boat today.

It does not mean that you are a bad person or a failure. You are actually a success – because you are taking steps to remedy the problem by reading this book. And I will sort out your problems as painlessly as possible!

I aim to show you every possible way to save money, from hard-headed practical tips to help you slash your outgoings – but not your lifestyle – to psychological techniques you can use for the rest of your life, to stop you overspending again.

It has never been quicker or easier to get into debt. Increased taxes, rocketing fuel bills and massive motoring fines chomp away at our hard-earned money like caterpillars eating cabbage. An entire family's weekly food budget can be wiped out when you get an £80 fine for something trivial like driving in an empty bus lane that you didn't notice. It's ridiculous.

On top of this come unexpected expenses: unemployment, illness, setting up home or a new business, parenthood, single parenthood or retirement. Of course, some people do buy too many things too ...

Economists claim that interest rates would have to halve, to help many of us repay our borrowings sensibly, rather than just plod along repaying the interest and waiting for Father Christmas to repay the lot. That drop in interest rates isn't going to happen, despite the fact that credit cards can cheerfully charge interest of three or four times the Bank of England's base rate.

Each home owes an average of £2,272 according to the latest figures. More than one in ten people have problems repaying their credit cards.

Average borrowings, like yours, can include any or all of the following:

Personal loan from loan company	£5,538
Student loan	£5,168
Car loan	£4,439
Credit cards	£2,203

Loans from friends or family	£2,121
Rent arrears	£1,100
Overdraft	£928
Store loans	£848
Repayments via debt management companies	£727
Catalogue purchases	£410
DSS loan	£304
(Source: FSA Financial Risk Outlook, 2003)	

That is why you need this book. I help you to understand yourself and those around you, to resist typical temptations – and I reveal the secret strategies that make marketing and advertising so hard to resist for ourselves and our children. I show you how to say 'no' to those you love, too!

Here, you will find hundreds of names and contact details of organisations that save you money in every way, and even help you earn a few extra pounds without too much bother. Plus loads of facts you didn't know, that will help you become comfortably off.

This is no ordinary book. It's an investment in your future, and your family's.

'What you do is really liberating.' Happy client Megan, whose income was £26,000 a year and whose spending I cut by £800 a month.

The checklist on the next page is based on the experience of lots of people from debt advisors to self-help debt groups – people who are probably well in at the deep end compared to you. So don't feel overwhelmed. You will be delighted to find how quickly and easily you can turn your life around.

How seriously are you out of control with your spending

1. Did your parents have problems with debt?   Yes/No
2. If you are feeling low, do you go shopping?   Yes/No
3. Once you start spending, do you feel powerless to stop? Yes/No
4. By spending, do you feel you are making yourself more acceptable to others?   Yes /No
5. When spending, do you 'compartmentalise' other debts, as if they are not there, and tell yourself that you will pay everything off overnight when your lucky break happens?   Yes/No
6. Have you spent more in the past two years?   Yes/No
7. If you do receive unexpected extra money, do you buy something rather than paying off existing credit cards?   Yes/No
8. Does your shopping make your home life unhappy and cause disagreements?   Yes/No
9. Do you hide bills from your partner or family?   Yes/No
10. Have other people commented on your spending?   Yes/No
11. After spending money, do you feel guilty ?   Yes/No
12. Are your credit card balances increasing but your income staying the same?   Yes/No
13. Are you paying basic expenses like food or fuel by credit card, because you don't have the cash?   Yes/No
14. Can you only afford to pay the minimum towards your credit card bills each month?   Yes/No
15. Are all your credit cards near the limit?   Yes/No
16. Are you dipping into savings or retirement funds to pay bills?   Yes/No
17. Are you working overtime, or at a second job, and still not paying off more than the minimum of your credit card bills?   Yes/No

18. Are you too scared to work out how much you owe? Yes/No

19. Do you take a long time to open bills, or never open them? Yes/No

20. Have you received a bailiff's letter, court summons or justified debt collection agency letter? Yes/No

21. Do you sometimes feel that you are so much in debt that you might as well spend more and enjoy yourself until it all catches up with you? Yes /No

22. Does the stress of having debts make you lose sleep or worry, so you can't concentrate during the day? Yes /No

23. Do you fear what others might say if they knew how much debt you are in? Yes /No

24. Have you ever got drunk or taken drugs to relieve the stress of feeling in debt? Yes /No

25. Have you ever lied to get credit? Yes /No

26. Have you applied for new loans to pay off your old ones, without considering whether you could afford the interest rate? Yes /No

27. Have you considered running away, going bust or suicide because of your debts? Yes /No

If you answer 'yes' to three or more questions up to and including question 9, you have a moderate problem.

From 9-19, you'll be fine, but only after I have tied you to a tree and duffed you over a bit.

From question 20 onwards, if you answer 'yes' to anything, I urge you to read what I say and try it for a few weeks.

You are not alone. About a third of us lose an hour's sleep a night, worrying about paying bills.

(Source: Survey, Orange, 2005)

You did not run up bills overnight, and the solution won't happen overnight either. You are working on solving the problem. You can only do your best. When you chip away at something, sooner or later, a big chunk will fall.

You will be richer, happier and sleep better by the end of this book! (And have better sex as a result, if you're lucky.)

If you do even some of what I say, you can save money immediately and stay richer for the rest of your life.

I'm not an airy-fairy theorist who doesn't know how hard it can be to save money. Nor am I a grey, self-satisfied and dreary maths brainbox. I ogle gorgeous things in magazines, and struggle with my self-control in shops. I can't stand minimalism, empty rooms and empty lives, and no one is happier to have a glass of champagne and open a box of chocolates, preferably fresh cream truffles.

But stuff – whatever it is – is only worth having if you can afford it. If you can't, you will feel very low. You might even go bust and lose the lot.

If you are feeling depressed about debt and bored with bills, anguish and arguments about money, and if you wake up at night worrying about how you are going to repay your borrowing, read on.

Why am I so certain I can help you? Because I first tried these techniques on myself, when I was left penniless and heavily pregnant after my employer went broke. They worked for me and they work for others. I have helped people to save hundreds of pounds in as little as three weeks, and some have saved over a thousand. Nearly five million viewers saw this happen in the

BBC1 TV series, *Smart Spenders* – which dealt with six really hardened over-spenders.

I know a lot of people think that 'reality' TV programmes fake success – and I feared the same when I began working on the series. I worried that I would fail to rescue my 'clients' (as I called them) from their self-imposed financial nightmares, caused by chaotic over-spending on luxury cars, holidays, ball-gowns and even trainers!

One of the problems with over-spenders is that they have more than their fair share of charm. That is how others around them let them get away with their endless 'presents' to themselves. They would show me around their homes and, as the evidence of extraordinary amounts of overspending came to light, they fluttered their eyelashes, expecting me to let them off the hook and say they could go on with their 'naughty' habits.

Of course, I never did. When I had straightened them out, and told them what to give up and cut out, I think they all went through about ten days of resentment and anger with me.

I didn't care what they thought. I didn't need them to like me – I've got friends to do that. My attitude was that if they needed to be scared witless and needed some very tough talking, to shock them into facing financial reality, so be it.

Then something magical happened. They all started saving. Then they began smiling and welcomed my visits. By the end of a month, some were incredibly high on success, bubbling with a new energy and determination. They had rediscovered life beyond materialism and felt free of their worry, sometimes for the first time in years. They were having more sex – they had more time to have sex, as they weren't at the shops or exhausted from shopping! – because they felt better personally, and closer as couples. This could be you.

Thrift – an old-fashioned word for saving money – is nothing to do with meanness towards others. It is a re-balancing of your life so that you don't automatically head for the shops because you need new things.

Of course, I won't be there swinging my leopard skin handbag and stamping my red stilettos to check up on you as on the TV – you hope! But if you do what I say – even half-properly – you will save money quickly.

This book is for general information. The facts contained in it are accurate to the best of my knowledge. I am a thrift expert, not a professional financial adviser and I am not giving you investment, tax, legal or other forms of advice. You must rely on yourself or get personal independent professional advice when making or not making decisions for your own situation.

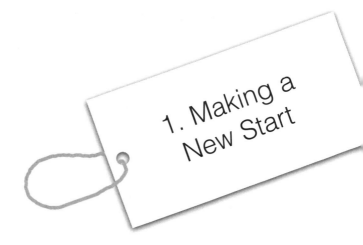

1. Making a New Start

Start today. You will feel better immediately. If you put it off, you will feel worse as you have now wasted good money on this book, to add to all the rest of your spending – and that is a shame as I know I can help you.

You may not be a big spender in the sense of splashing out £300 on a bottle of vodka in a club, driving a Maserati or buying a Gucci bag to match each outfit. But if you're reading this book, the chances are that you know you have some sort of problem with spending.

Most people keep a watch over their spending in many areas, but have specific 'problem' areas where their emotions overrule their commonsense. These emotions could be pride, guilt or good old-fashioned self-indulgence.

Proud parents, for instance, think 'Nothing but the best for my baby'. They blow mind-boggling sums on tiny designer outfits and exquisite little shoes for a baby that can't walk.

Guilt is another feeling that makes us overspend. Many women will know it. An eminent lawyer I know works hard, and seems a sensible person. But in her lunch breaks, she shops at over-priced touristy shops buying trinkets for her children. Her behaviour means that no present is special to her children. Gifts are everyday occurrences so she then has to spend super-duper sums of money for birthdays and Christmas.

There are also people who have swallowed a self-love manual and need to 'reward' themselves by buying flimflam all the time, as if they were martyrs or doing us all a favour by just getting through the day. To them I say: the world's work is mainly done by people who aren't 'feeling good about themselves' that day but manage without buying themselves presents.

If any of the above sounds like you, don't worry. That was then. Don't waste time beating yourself up (or reproaching your partner) about past regrets and extravagance. This is now.

Don't expect yourself to be perfect or you will never start, but just sit there fantasising about a future golden time when every-thing will be OK. Aim to be 'good enough' and you will achieve your goal. Take your goal seriously though.

And while we're about it, stop thinking that none of this applies to you as you will wake up one morning to find yourself a million-aire.* Yes. And I'm the Fairy Queen. The odds of winning the Lottery are one to fourteen million, and zero if you don't do it. My methods, on the other hand, have 100 percent success rate.

If you gamble, you will lose money, so don't start.

> Mick thought he was a natural winner. When he was made redundant, he gambled away his pension. Only when the bailiffs seized his furniture did he realise how much he had spent. He had to sell his home, to the distress of his wife and family, and his current mortgage runs until he is 80 years old.

I have also experienced 'clients' who say that they are just on the verge of a business breakthrough and need not heed my advice. I say I'll believe it when I see it.

You are also unlikely to become a well-paid footballer or marry the same, especially if you are a lap-dancer who reveals all to a Sunday paper.

This is not about denying yourself all treats and luxuries. A little of what you fancy does you good. However, if you feel like a treat, make it a small and cheap one, even if it is symbolic of your future aspirations. Before I bought my first car years ago, I bought a red Dinky toy and put it on my desk while I saved up for the deposit. Have a chocolate, cookie, tin of beer or whatever, but don't treat it as a free-for-all. It is not free. You have paid for those things.

Don't go on a 'last ever' spending spree just before you begin. This is not a golden opportunity to acquire a sun tan machine, set of fondue forks and remote control Dalek. The following story is a tough analogy but I will make it anyway. A friend of mine decided to give up smoking and before she started, smoked her way through her considerable store of cigarettes three at a time. She became more hooked on nicotine than ever, never gave up and died of throat cancer, aged 52.

* If I am wrong and you do, in fact, become a millionaire, I will come to the tax-haven of your choice, with my family, three cats and large dog, and drink your champagne to celebrate in your new luxury house. I am partial to Krug at £120 a bottle and Godiva chocolates if you're paying.

Take one day at a time. Concentrate just a little ahead. Think of yourself as playing a game, to win. Tell yourself that if you feel like splashing out, you will do it tomorrow. And tomorrow. Do your best to avoid temptation. But if you fail today, don't throw in the towel. Like a rider falling off a horse, get back on that beast and master it immediately before you lose your nerve.

Get a friend to act as a mentor and monitor your savings at an agreed time each week. Not your nicest friend, nor a bubble-head, but someone you feel a little scared of. You might even need two friends: one mentor and one checker-upper at the end of the week. One to confide in and one to be tough. Or one to hold you and one to hit you. Arrange a specific time to discuss your progress. That gives you a target time to work towards, where you can take stock of how the week has gone, and someone to impress, to give you a pat on the back.

Tell people what you are doing. Ask for their support in not suggesting shopping trips. Friends or family members who say, 'What the heck? Just give up,' when you are having the slightest difficulty, don't have your best interests at heart. You can email me at jane@smart.spending.co.uk.

You may only have one or two problem areas to tackle. Here's how to find out.

The ultimate personal budget planner

Here is my ultimate personal budget planner. It will give you a good overview of where your money is going and therefore how you can save it. You have instantly saved a fortune on computerised budget planners which are no more than glorified checklists.

How to use this planner

Fill the planner in quickly, rather than putting it off until you retrieve your bank statements and check them off. Later, you can check your guesstimates against your real spending via your bank statement. It will probably be revealing.

> *Jane's absolutely and totally golden rule,*
> *so golden it should be platinum.*
> *If you lie, you are only cheating yourself.*

Do you think you will lie? Can't face filling out the list? Get someone else to do it for you. In return, offer to do the same for them, or payment in kind, like babysitting or making early-morning tea for a week.

Don't forget to include irregular or one-off items like insurance in your budget.

Here is exactly what I do when allocating a budget to all my clients, including the *Smart Spenders* clients you saw on TV.

Look at your budget sheet.

Take a pencil (always use one if possible: it's cheaper than a pen) and *halve* every figure on it, apart from utilities, insurance, pension payments and mortgage. We'll deal with those later.

Now go through it again. Rub out the halved figures and halve them again.

Now show your cutbacks to your partner or family, and get their comments. It may be more productive for you to suggest their outbacks, and vice versa

The Ultimate Personal Budget Planner

COSTS	£ expenditure per month
Mortgage	
Top-up mortgage or second-property mortgage	
Mortgage saving vehicle/endowment policy 1 2 3	
Council tax	
Credit card/Store card payments 1 2 3	
Hire Purchase Agreements/Car Loan (remember any catalogue repayments)	
Loan repayments (incl. loans from friends and family)	
Property/garden maintenance (incl. roof repairs, new fixtures, plants, landscaping – over 12mths)	
House insurance: • buildings • contents • any additional/specialist insurance cover	
Water rates	
Gas	
Electricity	
Oil	
Coal/Logs	

Landline telephone	
Mobile phone 1 2 3 4	
Internet connection/dial-up fees Ink cartridges/paper/stationery/home office costs	
TV licence/rental Cable/Satellite/Digital fees	
Life Assurance and Private Medical Plans incl. Denplan 1 2 3	
Life Insurance	
Pension contributions 1 2 3	
ISAs/Saving Scheme/Stamps/Commitments Overdraft set-up fees/Interest on O/D/annual credit card fee/banking charges	
Car Tax 1 2	
Car Insurance 1 2	
Breakdown cover 1 2	
Car MOT/maintenance 1 2	
Running costs • petrol/oil/antifreeze • car-wash/hoover/valet • parking, plus congestion charges and speeding or parking fines	

Train/bus fares/season tickets 1 2 3 4	
School uniform	
School meals/work lunches	
After school clubs/Music lessons (per child) e.g. dance, Scouts, Guides, swimming, drama, judo, etc.	
Pocket money	
Child maintenance payments 1 2	
Childcare costs, e.g.: • nanny/aupair plus their living costs • nursery fees • pre-school fees • private school fees • tutor fees • student loans • kid's activities/birthday parties/presents for other kids/teachers • courses during school holidays. • misc. costs for books/school trips/PTA, etc.	
Clothing 1 2 3 4	
Shoes 1 2 3 4	
Beauty/Hair/Spa treatments (incl. products)	

Housekeeping • all shopping (food and non-food) • drinks • window cleaner • domestic cleaner • ironing service/dry cleaning/laundry • milkman • florist (incl. any special deliveries to friends) • newspaper/delivery boy charges • Xmas tips for bins/milk/ postman, etc.	
Pets • food • maintenance/classes (grooming, etc.) • equipment/shows • vets bills • insurance	
Club/Society subs	
Mag/Newspaper/Online subs	
Hobbies • specialist activities • weekend activities	
Socialising • eating out • drinking/going out • smoking • trips out/admissions/snacks etc • weddings/funerals/christenings, etc. incl. outfits/gifts • hiring films/music incl. online downloads	
Private Healthcare/Nursing Home 1 2 Dental costs 1 2 Medical prescriptions	
Charitable donations (regular and collections)	

Holidays • cost plus travel insurance • taxi transfers/hanging about airport • specialist equipment • spending money • excursions and outings • food/drinks/snacks • souvenirs	
Seasonal: Gifts and Entertaining (Xmas, Easter, summer bbq, halloween, etc., incl. decorations)	
Miscellaneous: sweets, crisps, coffees, chewing-gum – you'll be surprised how much you spend each time you stop for petrol or pop in a newsagents!	
Anything else ...	
And the other stuff ...	
Are you sure there's nothing else? ...	

THE BOTTOM LINE   TOTAL £.............................

Expect to take several hours filling in the form if you are being scrupulous – you'll need to hoik out bank statements, policy documents, shopping receipts and really rack your brain to provide honest answers in all the applicable spaces. Now add up all the figures. There you have it – your total monthly expenditure. Hopefully less than your monthly income.

This level of honesty will enable you to see which areas need to be cut back and also pinpoint flashpoints for further attention. If you need extra copies of my budget planner you can find a printable version at *www.smartspending.co.uk.*

You might like to complete two planners – one with your real figures and the other with revised target figures. Just slashing a few pounds off three or four of the items, especially the luxuries, will greatly affect the bottom-line and there is nothing more satisfying than beating your target.

If your expenditure is way ahead of your income and you feel overwhelmed there are a several debt counselling organisations that might be able to help. Never do nothing. Seek advice sooner rather than later as debt soon escalates and ruins lives.

Beware of private or professional debt/loan companies who charge extortionate interest rates and often resort to unpleasant methods of doing business when they want their money back. See the list of consumer advice associations on p.314–318 at the end of the book.

Keep it real. Debt counselling agencies get fed up with people in debt who persist in thinking it's OK to allow themselves £100 a month for their mobile phones and £200 on nights in the pub.

If you can't complete the form, get someone else to do it for you.

At this point you may have an argument. If you need someone to resolve it, email me at *jane@smartspending.co.uk*. Use this for good, never for evil …

Press on regardless – or you have wasted your money on this book and the opportunity to deal once and for all with your debts.

> **SHORTCUT.** Can't be bothered to do all the figures and budget? You can achieve goodish cuts by just figuring out your seven biggest bills and work on cutting them. In most cases, they are your mortgage, transport, entertainment, gas, electricity, phone and food. Cutting these is almost a no-brainer using the strategies on p 118–121.

The sacrifice section

How low can you go?

Decide what you don't need.

When I removed many people's 'absolute necessities' for a month, (i.e. the usual old self-indulgent rubbish) they realised they didn't need them at all and didn't want them back. This has happened with trainers, make-up, golf clubs ... you name it.

One of the most enduring images in the *Smart Spenders* TV series, which people in the street stop me about and mention, was Karen Holley's Saab being taken away on a large lorry. After some time without her must-have car, she resolved to sell it.

Do you need several mobile phones? Can you put teenagers on pay as you go contracts and make them responsible?

Check your TV if you have cable or digital. Do you need film channels? Cut out the extra at least for a little. You can go back later.

Nights at the pub. You don't need to buy everyone else a round. Show them this book. Ask them to buy the drinks.

Think how you can substitute something else for a must-have

If you want to become a smart spender, you must think around the problem. There is always a way of getting what you want. See the rest of this book for more inspiration.

'But I can't do without it.' Martha could not do without a cake from the baker's bought daily, although the cost mounted up. We settled on half a cake instead. Her children kept hiding her cake and she gave up and lost weight.

> **ANTIDOTE.** If you pay for lunch at the office each day, and you can't bear to give it up everyday, take sandwiches three days out of five. You will look forward to your 'days off' more.

If you buy a paper every day, take a library book for the train in the morning and ask to have someone's paper that they have finished with for going home. Or read papers in the library, which are free.

'But it's my looks.' Jean 'needed' expensive monthly hair-shining treatments at a salon, not to mention costly beauty aids. I told her that she was beautiful anyway – had she really looked at herself in a mirror? I told her husband to tell her how lovely she looked a lot more frequently. Then I took all but six of her potions away. After a month, she didn't want them back. She realised that these things made little or no difference. She looked more beautiful because she was happier and more relaxed because she had not overspent!

'These are trivial sums.' I don't see the point of saving. Steve spent lots on buying coffee during his breaks, including for his friends. I gave him a funky flask for him to make his own – and his friends were so impressed that they bought flasks of their own. They saved pounds in weeks.

'But this is my health.' Taki was obsessed with expensive American vitamins, assuming that if he did not take them, his food would not give him enough nutrition. As he refused to budge from his convictions, I introduced him to his local allotment and growing his own vegetables.

You may hate me for doing this to you for the first week. It's OK. Blame me, hate me. I don't care. Because afterwards, you may well become almost euphoric, as you discover that you can live within a tight budget without pain.

If you continue to buy stuff you don't need, you lock yourself in a prison of despair because you carry all that guilt around with you – and sooner or later, you pay back the money anyway.

This is the beginning of freedom. You are taking control of your life again. It won't take more than a month. Once you have lived on the minimum and repaid what you owe, then you can be easier on yourself.

Think you've got no self-control?

Find your willpower

It is somewhere there inside you. Here's how to find it. If you like chocolate, buy yourself a small bar. If you prefer something else as a treat, substitute this: biscuits, nuts, smoothies, beer, wine or whatever. Not cigarettes, drugs – and nothing expensive.

Are you back with me? Consume one section of your chosen choccy bar, or take a sip of the beer or whatever.

HELPFUL HINT

A little of what you fancy does you good. It does not have to be a case of 'one out, all out' to enjoy things.

Put the treat away. If necessary, give it to someone else to keep for you.

You will have another chocolate later and enjoy it more than the first. You have learned your first lesson in re-orientating your spending.

Now decide on your new cash-crashing budget.

Shortcut if you can't be bothered to do the maths

Most people can survive on £50 each a week for everyday expenditure, including food. Some people have to survive on less every week. If you do this, you will probably save hundreds of pounds in a week. I have personally spent under £5 in a week, but I grow food.

Get some disposable cups from a machine or use jam jars or mugs. Get scrap paper and rubber bands which you can pick up from the ground wherever the postman has dropped them. Write on each label, your budget for various items you buy during the week: transport, food, newspapers etc.

Take your weekly budget out of the bank. Put the money in the cups.

Give your friend who is going to check up on you each week, your cash card, credit cards (not your PINs) and cheque book. Or lock them up and give someone else the key. If it makes you feel better, keep one credit card for emergencies.

This concentrates the mind wonderfully. There is simply no room for spending on so much as a bag of peanuts.

Find a small book and pencil. Carry it with you and write down everything you spend, immediately you spend it. Total it up. Keep your receipts in one place. All of them. You will see how much you have frittered away in the petrol station shop alone. Check handfuls of small change rather than just putting them in your pocket, for rogue coins, etc.

How to stop spending on nothing much

1 **Do not spend anything this month on:**
- Clothes
- Shoes
- Anything else you wear or carry or do to yourself for that 'look at me' effect
- Takeaways
- Ready meals from the chiller or frozen cabinet of food shops
- Toys (except if your children have a birthday)
- Tickets to shows (see page 260 for how to have a free night out)
- Videos and DVDS
- CDs and games
- Your collection of anything
- Sports kit
- Gambling
- Drugs and cigarettes if at all possible
- Vitamins unless medically prescribed for you
- Bath or shower gels and toiletries, except basics like toothpaste which I expect you to buy only when you see a two-for-one offer

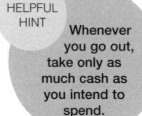

HELPFUL HINT Whenever you go out, take only as much cash as you intend to spend.

2 **Spend a limited sum only on:**
- Going out
- Alcohol
- Transport

If you fail one day, tomorrow is another day. Can you cut back and get even the following day? Think how much time you are spending telling yourself off, feeling guilty or concealing what you have done from others. It just isn't worth the emotion and guilt, is it?

At the end of each week, have a meeting with your mentor and go over your highs and lows. If you feel your willpower slipping at any time, consult the SOS section at the end of this book, see p.311).

Remember Paula Radcliffe, the runner tipped for a gold medal who lost confidence and stopped racing suddenly in the Olympics race? That's how crucial the right mindset is.

How to transform your attitude to spending

The two assumptions you need to change.

Here are two common ideas which have probably damaged more lives than anything else. Do they lurk somewhere inside you? If so, tell them where to go.

> 1. An overdraft is a limit, not a target you are supposed to hit each month.
> 2. A fistful of credit cards does not tell everyone that you are rich and successful, even if they are platinum-plated and studded with diamonds. These simply mean that the companies who issued them are becoming rich at your expense.

Don't be mean to others. I don't encourage people to be petty in a Scrooge-like way to others. It is not good for anyone's spirit. Stay generous, but if necessary, explain that you are 'doing Jane Furnival's book for a bit' and can't splash out. Hopefully they will buy you a drink.

Don't fritter. For instance, some women buy lipsticks and nail varnish each week as a small treat. Before they can wade through it all – if ever – their mascara and lipsticks will have gone off. They develop a funny smell. The products, I mean, though the women will too, if they use them.

Don't binge. Saving money on one area of life does not mean you have 'extra' to spend elsewhere, if you have debts to pay first. Pay them off.

Don't go shopping as a hobby. Hands up who goes to the shops and DOESN'T come back with more than they intended? Yeah well. You can go to the naughty step for lying.

Pre-empt the urge to go to the mall. Plan your weekends, evenings, and lunchtimes in advance so that you always have something more important to do. Make concrete arrangements rather than vague promises to yourself. Invite yourself to see friends, offer to walk someone's dog or babysit, go and watch your son play rugby, do the garden or clear out your wardrobe.

- **If you need anything, write a list, and give a friend the money to buy the things for you.**
- **Destroy all credit cards except one to be used for emergency only.**
- **Avoid discount warehouses or sales.**
- **Never go shopping in your lunch hour. Window shop only after stores have closed.**
- **Throw away catalogues within a few minutes of looking at them.**
- **Don't phone-in catalogue orders.**
- **Don't internet shop.**
- **Don't watch TV shopping channels.**
- **If you go to see friends, take gifts ready-wrapped. You will get a holiday feeling when shopping outside your normal neighbourhood and be tempted to spend more.**
- **If you get a sudden urge to shop, call a friend, go swimming, read a magazine, walk in the park, go to the gym or sit in the library.**
- **If you are tempted to go shopping at a particular time each week, like Saturday morning when you feel vaguely**

celebratory that you have got through the week, make other arrangements in advance.

End each week in your little spending book with an assessment of how you did – and I hope it shows very little spending. If you are saving money as a family or part of a group, this can be a hoot but also provides productive new ideas.

This is as important as sorting yourself out. 'Peer pressure' doesn't mean being touched up by a lord in the back of a taxi, but an urge we all have to imitate others who we think of as socially similar to us or just ahead of ourselves in some way – the Joneses who are richer, socially more adept, or whatever. How many of us have looked at someone else's baby, pet, car or home and thought, 'I'd love one like that'? It is not a bad thing in itself. It is natural and neutral. Like drink, it all depends how you use the impulse.

Dealing with other people

Explain to your friends and family that you are trying to cut back, or that you're giving this book a try – because you'd be daft if you didn't want to save a thousand pounds, right?

Don't be too specific about why you are embarking on this adventure with me. Keep your dignity and your financial secrets. I am always amazed at how plain nosey some people can be. If they're real friends, they may invite you over to theirs for a meal or two, saving you money!

Saving money while being surrounded by people who are richer than you

It may only be your feeling that others are better off financially than you. (A good example – personally I am sick of being told as a fact by silly-billies that I must be a millionaire because I was on the telly.) Whether or not that is true, if you seriously want to save money, the first thing to do is stop competing and start enjoying.

> ' I moved into a lovely old manor house, and several months later, a young family bought the prettiest house next door, the kind of house we could never have afforded at their ages. However my new neighbour greeted me with, 'WE could have bought your house, but decided not to.' I thought, he would soon stop envying us if he saw the size of the heating bills.'
> *Susan, Cornwall*

As Jane Austen remarked, in any family, one person's success is everyone's. The way to cope with family and friends who are better off than you, is to accept their invitations without feeling looked down on or patronized. Admire their lovely homes, smile and enjoy yourself, say nice things about their children and pets, swim in their pool, sip their wine and eat their meals. Don't forget to send a thank you card afterwards and then you can enjoy it all again.

The best thing about this is you are not paying for the whole shabang. I hope you become fonder of each other as a result of time spent together.

Never try to keep up with your wealthier friends. This is a game you will not win and it is probably how you started running up bills in the first place. You will simply end up with more bills and you will still not feel better off than them. If they boast about their spending and lifestyle, be pleasant and say, 'Yes, it's a lovely pool/car/boat/helicopter. Thank you so much for inviting us – it's been great.' Again, feel relieved that you don't have to pay for it.

As they say at school during exams, keep your eyes on your own work. Focus on what you are doing for yourself. Other people's lifestyles are not a reflection on you, nor can you measure yourself by what they have. People waste emotion on useless envy. If only they turned that emotion into a determination to do their best for themselves and their families!

If you feel that someone is trying to belittle you and you can't take any more of it, shoot the ground away from under their feet by reverse boasting about how much you have saved or emphasising what a simple life you lead. 'I try not to go to the shops these days. But I'm very pleased with my charity shop purchase – only 50p.' Very rich people are fascinated by bargains and love saving money. They will immediately want to know your secrets.

> **JANE'S GOLDEN TIP.** *When conversing in really posh and rich circles, anything you have which is home-made, home-grown or antique scores ten posher-than-thou points over anything bought from a shop.*

Many people assume that the way to 'get on' is to acquire more possessions. To me, such people are like children at an entertainment park: weepy and demanding, always wanting another ride, another thing. If that sounds strange, let me explain. When I have taken my children to mega-places created to give families 'fun', I have noticed that the more manufactured 'fun' you give them, the more they want – and yet they remain unhappy. They get trapped in a circle because they think they should enjoy it, because they think everyone else is, but it is essentially an empty experience. They are not learning much, nothing is 'real' and nothing is enough.

Now, can we think about where you are going in life?

I believe that the same is true of people who buy lots of things. You think 'Once I have these heated hair tongs/cashmere top/open-topped sports car, I have gone up a notch in my estimation and will feel fantastic'. That is as transparently untrue as the old story of the emperor's new clothes.

The brief, but highly addictive, feeling of exhilaration, improved self-worth and supremacy caused by buying things is like eating popcorn all the time. Great for a bit, but empty in the middle. It won't make up for the basic needs of life. So why are you trying to buy everything you 'need'? You're pouring water into a bottomless pit, so stop it.

A recent survey by thinktank The Henley Centre revealed that someone earning £7,500 a year is probably as happy as someone on £70,000.

TV programmes showing stars living in luxurious homes have given many of us a false sense of what is 'normal' to have. Once, people aspired to a gas cooker with an eye-level grill. Now it's a fitted kitchen with an Aga, steam oven and built-in coffee maker. They lose all sense of – well, just sense – and buy stainless steel fronts which show every fingerprint, because they have fallen hook, line and sinker for a magazine feature.

Don't seek to become like your favourite celebrity. Many of you probably already have the thing that rich celebrities want most.

What rich, famous and high-achieving people want most

I have spent years as a journalist working for national newspapers, and interviewed hundreds of rich, powerful and beautiful celebrities, business moguls, aristocrats and the odd royal, meeting them in their homes with their pets, partners and family.

Journalism is a funny job. You have to establish a warm friendship with someone in half an hour, in order to ask them the most prying questions above love, life and death. I have discussed a duchess's diarrhoea attack on her wedding night, the size of a famous sex symbol's body parts and heard about rape, incest and murder from the most unlikely quarters.

These celebrities could have any material thing they wanted. I observed that no matter what their age or background, everyone wanted the same – health, a good future for their children and a loving partner.

If these people who are at the top of the tree in life, had lots of fashionable material things, they were always in competition with others. How exhausting to be looking over your shoulder and feeling jealous of your friends, always in a race to be first with a particular handbag or hairstyle!

Occasionally, I read sadly of the deaths of people I have interviewed. Depression and alcoholism account for quite a few, not to mention the one who told me how much he loved buying fast cars, and years later, was killed in a famous tragic car crash with one of the world's most desirable companions.

Few of them seemed as content as ordinary people I meet daily: the retired lorry-driver I meet in the park when I walk my dog, or a young mum with her hands full. Having lots of money brings problems such as drug-taking teenagers and unfaithful partners, not to mention paying for the upkeep of a huge house and entourage which the main earner rarely enjoys because they are working all hours to fund the whole lot.

Bear this in mind and treat your quest to save money as an achievement. Accept that there will always be someone better or worse off than you in life.

When I worked in advertising, I had to help to choose models to appear in TV commercials I had written for hair or beauty products. I must have seen hundreds of the best-looking girls in the world close-up. Over time, I realised that finding one girl with a beautiful face and good legs was impossible. Many top models had noticeable moustaches and the team and I found ourselves discussing whether we could hide their five o'clock shadow under the bright lights of the studio!

My point is that we are all given our good and bad points in pretty equal measure. It is the same with money. You can have that; but you may not have health and happiness too.

Now I will show you how to understand yourself and your buying behaviour more and find hundreds of practical, hard-hitting ways of cutting your costs.

Where you live affects your spending

Spending in London, the South East and East of England is higher than for most of the country, but incomes are also higher. Spending in the North East is 17 percent lower than average. However this is where the lowest average incomes are recorded, followed by Wales and Northern Ireland.

If you live in the country, expect to spend more than average – £75 on transport, £47 a week on food and non-alcoholic drinks, £63 on recreation and culture and £37 on household goods and services.

Bringing up a child costs £5,888 each year until the age of 18 according to a survey by the Prudential. Others claim that children cost most between the ages of two and five, averaging £9,993 per year – presumably including the cost of childminding. Childcare for working parents is a great expense, at around £3,217 per year for an under-11.

The official cost of children

Having two children runs a coach and horses through your budget. The average weekly expenditure for families with children increases from around £531 for those with one child to £611 for two children, but only to £627 for three or more.

School and university costs £1,646.71 per year up to age 21. Private school fees cost £7,000 on average per year, usually doubled for boarding school and tripled if the boarding school is a bit swish, or caters for special needs. Girls' school fees are slightly cheaper than boys'. From 2006, a three-year university course costs up to £30,000 with £18,790 for subsistence over and above a student loan. (Source: Prudential.)

It may be that your overspending is driven by some economically suicidal urge or silly habit, such as a desire to paper your bathroom with Penny Black stamps or similar. I do hope not, because if that is the case, stop sticking those stamps to the wall now before you get a) broke; b) bored; and c) GTS, or glue tongue syndrome in which your tongue develops little stamp-like perforations round the edge.

Am I weird?

HELPFUL
HINT

Save money by avoiding going to uni in London, which costs up to £2,000 above the average over three years.

For those of us who are perfectly normal, thank you, and just trying to make savings, it can help to see how other people with similar incomes to ourselves spend their money.

There are some typical examples of spending for different groups of people at the end of the book in the Appendix. They are taken from '*Family Spending*', the latest Government statistics report compiled by the Office for National Statistics (Crown copyright).

On the principle that human beings don't always tell the whole truth, especially when anyone official is asking, and things are always more expensive than we remember. I suspect some people spend more than they admit, especially those who earn cash and whose bank is their back pocket.

The category 'other expenditure' covers mortgage interest and council tax or its Northern Ireland equivalent.

2. Who are you?

Define your spending personality

'It wasn't me. It was me when I was different, AGES ago.'
(My four year-old son, when one of his pieces of
monkey business was discovered.)

If you want to save effectively, first understand your Shopping Self.
A survey by Mintel placed shoppers in the following categories:

- **Addicted**
- **Happy**
- **Purposeful**
- **Reluctant**
- **Obstinate**

Recognise yourself? Our aim is to get you out of the first two states of mind when shopping and into the 'purposeful' or even 'reluctant' category.

Most of us fancy saving money and pay lip service to this ideal – until the next seductive purchase presents itself. Then all those good resolutions go out of the window. There comes a time when you must admit your problem – and then you can really work on it. I want to help you to do this before your credit cards explode.

Acknowledging the truth is the most difficult thing you can do. Most of us overspend. Deception and self-deception, fantasising and telling ourselves and others comforting stories are natural ways to avoid uncomfortable facts. No one wants to lose face. When I worked in advertising, I sat in on research discussion groups and noticed that the people who concealed their true feelings or behaviour most, were the ones who were – or aspired to be – from a high social group. They didn't want to look stupid to their peer group, those they considered their social equals.

Mia asked me to help her repay £30,000 of credit card debts, blamed on her divorce. Later, I found that the split had happened 15 years earlier, and she had quickly remarried. She couldn't blame the divorce. Other aspects of her life did not make sense. Whenever I suggested any savings strategies, she claimed she had already tried them. If she was REALLY so canny, how had she got into this pickle? Mia was 'in denial' so strongly that when facts were presented to her, she flew into a rage.

One of the best ways to economise is to be realistic about why you spend money.

Are there particular events, feelings, or moods that trigger your overspending – or what spending psychologists in their lovable way prefer to label 'excessive buying'? These triggers could be:

How to pinpoint your personal spending 'triggers'

- a feeling of temporary frustration with the world
- worry
- an empty feeling
- irrational optimism
- tiredness or boredom
- a need to escape everyday cares
- a need to win and look or seem smarter than someone else – perhaps someone in particular
- the weather, or seasonal affective depression (too little light)
- the time of the month or the menopause – male or female

You are keeping a daily spending diary, aren't you? I would like you now to keep a diary of your emotions.

Any time you feel like shopping, or buying something, as soon as you feel this urge, I want you to write down:

- what it is or was
- its cost
- when you felt the impulse to buy the item – did it creep up on you, or did you mull it over for several minutes, hours or days?
- where you were at the time – on your way to work, say, or at lunchtime
- events which happened on the same day as this impulse
- events which happened earlier in the week
- any other events you feel are important, whether or not directly related to the item or that spending urge

Even dreams count! Write them down if they stick in your mind. They can be powerful 'sifters' of your preoccupations, bringing the day's hidden impulses to the top of your mind.

Then note:
- **How you felt before buying the item. Happy, anxious, sad, frustrated, depressed, optimistic?**
- **How you felt immediately after buying the item or if you walked away from buying the item.**
- **Whether that feeling changed a few hours later.**
- **Whether you felt the same the next day.**

Mull over your diary. Or show it to your money mentor, if you have chosen to have one. Often, other people can see things that are glaringly obvious but which we ourselves fail to spot.

Are there any patterns that you can spot after a week? Look for particular times of the day, emotions, frustrations, people you encounter that set off irrational and unwanted spending. Are you binge spending instead of confronting a problem at work, say?

Are there any things that you can substitute for 'mood' spending? Not drink or drugs or self-destructive behaviour! See my section on happiness (pp.51).

HELPFUL HINT

If one category description makes you feel really cross, think why. Could it just be that it hits the nail on the head about you?!

Don't give up – I'm still here for you. Set yourself reasonable goals. Otherwise you'll be like the person on a diet who breaks it and then gives up immediately.

CONFESSION CORNER ... (I won't tell if you don't!)

Here are some typical temptations which cause ordinary people to feel their credit card is putting its hand up and shouting, 'Me, me!' like the class swot at school.

Do you recognise any of these? Tick for yourself, for your partner and even your teenagers ...

- [ ] Shoes
- [ ] Tools
- [ ] Party clothes
- [ ] Beauty potions and lotions
- [ ] Vitamins
- [ ] Gadgets

Add your own temptations to this list. If necessary, cut it out and stick it on your wallet. Or fridge door. (You have my permission to cut this book up in the interests of science.)

> **Dear Self, I am making a pact with you to avoid spending another penny this month on**...
> ....
> ....
> ....

JANE'S TRUE CONFESSION. I have to control my desire to go into junk shops that might just contain undiscovered undervalued antiques! Twice last year, after painful conversations with my husband about what I had done, I had to go back to shops and confess that I could not afford to buy stuff I wanted. They weren't best pleased, but fortunately in one case, I had only put down a deposit and I still agreed to buy part of my order. With the other, I just said my stuff and slunk away.

Some over-spenders have got into a fix because they have got into a behavioural rut. They have made assumptions about life that don't do them any good.

You might recognise yourself, or aspects of your behaviour, in the personality patterns I list below, which are based on psychological research into over-spenders. You may fit into one category, or several.

Then, once you understand yourself, unfortunately, you have to do something about it before your bank does. Believe me, and the independent financial experts I talk to: financial institutions can lend you anything you ask for and cheerfully wait for the outcome.

Some types of overspender

I have added my suggestions as to what you can try to do to lever yourself out of this mindset – apart from read this entire book!

Ozzymosis, or 'If it's good enough for Ozzy, I'll get that too.' You read magazines of the kind which invite you to gawp at celebrities' gold-plated bath taps and toothpaste-white sofas. You would like to believe that everyone lives like this, and bingo! It *IS* true, courtesy of your credit cards – at least for a time. Your fantasy life outstrips reality until you assume that everyone has a 'right' to a home cinema system, Mercedes and handmade shoes.

Nick, a freelance designer, was distraught when his wife Daisy left him saying that he could not provide the material things she wanted. Then he discovered that she had left him thousands of pounds of credit card debt and they would have to sell the house to pay it. 'She worked in a Mayfair hairdresser and seeing all those rich clients made her imagine that we should live like that, and she became angry with me when I could not earn enough,' he confided.

I SAY: If you are trying to enter the fantasy world of the rich and celebrated by getting the things they have, you have not understood the connection between talent, luck and hard work, and wealth. You have probably also confused the fact that people have a right to be treated equally, with the idea that people are born equal.

People are not born equal. Look at the disabled, those without a sensible parent around them, or those in horrible and oppressive countries.

People should be treated equally, with respect, but that does not mean that everyone has the same income, abilities or a 'right' to luxury without the income to pay for it. People who have earned lots of money usually do so because they work very long hours and give up the leisure time and family life that the rest of us have, or they are extraordinarily talented. They are seldom rich by chance.

FUNNY MONEY. *27 percent of us don't save, but 53 percent of these have satellite TV and take two holidays or more a year.*

Hello **magazine, Goodbye money.** You want to look like your favourite celebrity. You trawl the pages of magazines to get the 'right' look, spending, on average, £713 a year on designer accessories, fake tans and hair extensions (Source: Virgin Money). We're talking about women and men.

Advertising and magazines sell ideal images of people. You buy those ideals, ripping out magazine pictures of models and at the beauty counter of Boots, asking for the exact shade of lipstick they are wearing and the same shade of foundation, even if it is not right for you. You even buy clothes in an ideal size. Not your real one.

I SAY: Psychologists Wicklund and Gollwitzer coined the term 'symbolic self-completion' for this mindset. You feel inadequate in some way, so you buy a disguise. Aggressive masculine items like black leather jackets make a young man look more manly than he secretly feels – and tells everyone else too.

Why do you want to look like someone else? Are you not happy with yourself? You need to think why – perhaps with a counsellor's or a friend's help. Celebrities sell you an image of perfection, but like the rest of us, they have big bums, spots, and are usually more unhappy than the average non-famous person. Quite a few sex goddesses have body doubles on film, even if they are famous for their bodies. Improve what you don't like about yourself inside. Long-term talents are more important. Remember, kissing doesn't last. Cooking does. Or the equivalent. You're probably a nice-looking person. And personally nicer than your celebrity hero or heroine.

Breaker-Outer. You can economise for just so long. You're doing well, then something happens to give you a crumb of optimism. It only takes a £10 Lottery win and on a wave of optimism, you buy yourself several new pairs of Blahniks.

You tell yourself you can control your spending whenever you like. You just don't choose to, yet.

I SAY: You are like a person on perpetual holiday from reality – but it can all come crashing horribly down one day. Use the methods I am outlining to get yourself some real control. Only you can make your fantasy happen. At the moment, your state of mind is similar to binge eating, deciding that you don't need to join Weightwatchers for another month but you can sort it all out when you do.

I once worked with a hugely fat woman who told me that once a year, she shed all her weight and turned into a perfect size

12. I worked with her for four years and never saw it happen. Try to indulge your cravings for luxury or fun with small treats, not expensive ones.

Label lover. A very small number of people are dedicated to labels, but they are busy buying an awful lot of them.

I SAY: Label obsessives like structure and order but lack confidence in their own judgement. You think that if you just wear clothes with an expensive name, everyone will accept you as a 'valuable' kind of person. Actually, they are more likely to laugh at you behind your back for wasting all that money. And rather than being impressed, people do snigger about the money you waste.

Great Provider. You probably have several freezers full of food. You like to have a full set of everything and hate saying, 'We don't have that.'

I SAY: Great, as long as you can afford it. But you can't, so stop now. People will still love you even if you don't have every kind of cheese and biscuit known to man. Avoid turning into a martyr which is the other side of the Great Provider's personality. Denying your basic needs in order to pay your bills and telling everyone about it will not disguise the fact that you spent the money in the first place.

Unique Chick. You are usually female (or gay), creative and not very materialistic. You have a strong sense that everything around you, from clothes to the look of your home, tells your unique 'life story' or projects an image about yourself to others, boosting your status. It's not true, but that's not the point. This leads you to buy things not because you need them, or even use them, but because they say the 'right' things about you to others.
You also have a strong competitive streak. You don't care about

keeping up with the Joneses – you want to leave them behind choking on your exhaust fumes. To do this, you have to buy the latest things. Once someone else has that must-have item, you go on to the next thing. Kitchen, garden decking, hair extensions – hang the expense, you rip them out and get the next new must-have.

I SAY: You're a style leader and other people copy your looks. Why on earth should you care what they do? REAL leaders do their own thing and ignore the rest. They don't look over their shoulder at the herd. Don't discard things you really like, just because someone else has them. Make your belongings part of a real you simply by saying to yourself, 'I'm an attractive person, people will follow my taste and *this* is what I like.' You can make a pair of fluffy slippers, curlers and a housecoat trendy that way! Guard against being manipulated by the media into thinking you've made your own decisions, but in reality being a fashion victim. Also be wary of making yourself uncomfortable just to be in fashion, as so much designer stuff is badly designed for living.

A survey by *Virgin Money* concluded that the most common reason for feeling such keen competition was jealousy between neighbours about social lives, personal appearances and nicer-looking homes.

I heard a wonderfully funny DJ called James O'Brien confessing that he felt competitive when a younger couple moved in next door to him. He looked at his neighbour's wife and felt complacent because Mrs O'Brien was better-looking – until he smelt the Sunday lunch cooking next door. Then he thought, 'When I'm older, I may not be so keen on sex. But for the next thirty years, that man will have something nice to look forward to – great meals, twice a day.'

> Me-money: What women spend on keeping up their image
>
> Scottish women spend £4,214 annually.
> Women in the North East spend £3,837.
> Londoners spend £3,538.
> Women in the North West spend £3,436.
> Women in the South East spend £3,334.
> Women in the Midlands, £2,882.
> Women in Wales and the West of England, £2,653.
> Spending priorities, in order:
> Homes and gardens – just over half the budget
> Clothes and accessories – close to half
> Beauty products and treatments
> Hair styling
> (Source: survey, Virgin Money)

'I deserve it'. Well-known phrase or saying justifying an outrageous or expensive purchase which you know in your heart you do not need. 'Deserve' is the worst word in the language – the key to giving yourself permission to do silly things. Any grievance, large or small, from the past is seized upon as a good reason (or excuse?) for spending.

I SAY: Dissociate buying things from other emotional rewards or losses.

If you have worked long hours, for instance, what do you deserve? A good night's sleep in the short term; thanks from those you have worked for in the medium term; and success, in the long term.

If you have had a bad experience, been injured, or lost someone, you do not 'deserve' a material purchase if it pushes you into debt. You will end up more depressed. I don't want anyone to misunderstand me. If you want to, and you can afford it, use money to give yourself pleasure or to escape, like a neighbour of mine who bought herself a fabulous red sports car just after her dearly-loved husband collapsed suddenly and died. Take a holiday after a trauma, but don't expect too much too soon: you take your troubles with you. When I miscarried after being stalked, the police suggested that I claim criminal injuries compensation. I refused. For me, nothing material would make up for the loss of that baby.

Make a list of people, events or situations that you feel angry about and why. What you can do that doesn't involve injuring yourself or them?

Life's a party. Live for today. Viv Nicholson, the first big football pools winner, vowed to spend spend spend. Five husbands and a lot of heartache later, not to mention a book and a musical about her, she admits it was a huge mistake. You, and your closely related personality-type the Hobbyist Shopper, are hooked on adrenaline. Don't plan to pay taxes, or for the future … then when predictable bills come, feel surprised or that the world has given you a very poor bargain.

> *Mike took his wife to New York and gave his credit card to the hotel doorman telling him to buy tickets for a show at any price. $1000 later, he had no right to be upset, though he was – plus he footed a huge bill for the stretch limo he ordered to take them to the theatre. A year later, he had to sell his business to pay his debts.*

I SAY: If you spend to boost your self-esteem, the adrenaline high of being a big-shot 'look at me' spender will soon wear off. You will be left unsatisfied because you are taking the wrong 'medicine' for your condition.

If you spend to boost your self-image in other peoples' eyes, you get the kind of friends whose esteem is based on bribes.

As another of my 'clients' found, the people you treated to a £300 bottle of whisky at a smart club aren't your friends when the money runs out. Please follow the advice in this book and develop some interests and activities that keep you away from the shops.

Discount Diva. A stalwart of Matalan, T.K. Maxx or the local pound shop, you consider yourself queen or king of the discount dump bins, a Cleopatra of cut price know-how, high priest or priestess in the High Street, so canny you can barely contain the details of your latest low-price purchase before you are out of the shop door with it. But because it's a bargain, that gives you loads of extra money – to spend on other bargains.

I SAY: You are a fledgling spendaholic, even though you don't buy your things at full prices. This is both boring and annoying for your friends. Constant stories of how much you saved imply that their 'life-skills' are poorer than yours. Let someone else find a bargain more brilliant than yours for once. Get a bit of balance about life. Ask people how they are, not what they have bought.

Bank of Fairyland Shopper.
> 'I know I don't have the money but when I go to the shops, something turns off inside me. I still go and spend anyway.' *Anne, Rotherham*

You are an extreme impulse buyer, normally young, professional, and materialistic. When you see something you like, even if you can't afford it, every other consideration goes out of the window. The future, and payback time, does not exist. When you see the bill, it's the opposite: the charm of the item you bought has evaporated and you wish you had never bought it.

If it's put on your card, it's not real money, is it? When you're spending on your credit card, it puts you above ordinary people.

You feel accepted, one of a club, smarter than those who pay with mere cash. A close friend of this mindset is, 'If you're spending foreign money, it's not real, is it?'

You think that by re-christening your out-of-control spending habit as 'retail therapy', it becomes a medical necessity, everyone does it, and you can laugh away the bills together.

I SAY: Your brain is able to turn off the natural link between a benefit for now, and a benefit for the future, and you have to stop this dissociation. So when you're shopping, you can only see the benefits of the purchase. When you get the bill later, you can't think why you made the purchase and regret it. You will benefit most of all from keeping a spending diary, right there, in your bag or pocket, to remind yourself of this month's saving goals. If you can't control yourself, stop shopping completely. Ask a friend to do your shopping to a list and a budget.

What is feeding this is a feeling of emptiness inside. There is a gulf between your pay, your looks, your social standing with your friends, and what you want to be. Buying something – clothes, trainers, jewelry that is an extension of your body – will disguise you from prying eyes of others who might notice your shortcomings.

You need to do some thinking about yourself. See below.

Panic shopper. I am not referring to the panic of a Christmas Eve shopper, but a deeper panic to do with yourself. Suddenly, the sky falls in. You feel worthless, unwanted – almost that you don't exist. It can be to do with the loneliness or empty nests. Perhaps your ex-husband has got the children for the weekend and you are going home to an empty house. My late mother would shop for a family's Christmas food, although she was staying with me for the holidays and had no one to feed, for example. You shop to assure yourself that you exist and are worth something. 'I shop, therefore I am.' You need to try some of the happiness techniques I list below. Psychologist and author Dr Dorothy Rowe first told me about this condition.

Experience seeker. You don't buy things. You want experiences. You travel, take courses, read books. Because these are educational, they don't count as money overspent but put to good use, even if you throw your credit cards to the winds.

You have chosen one of the most expensive hobbies. Are you sure you're not using travel and education to run away from life's uncomfortable realities? Only you can tell. Use the techniques in this book to rein in your impulses.

Waiting for Father Christmas.

Over 600,000 adults
rely on 'pocket money' handouts from mum and
dad well into their thirties.

You wouldn't know a budget from a budgerigar. You never know what you have in the bank – that way you can't accuse yourself of overspending. One credit card pays off another, and cheques bounce like balls around you. You may borrow books, pens or small sums from friends and forget to return them.

You were always meant to be a millionaire, weren't you? Money to pay for the accumulated debts will just drop from the sky one day, without effort.

I SAY: You never wanted to grow up and you think that if you continue to behave like a dependent child, you will be treated like one. People like you have driven their families to worry and distraction as elderly parents are being asked to pick up the bills.

If you don't know how much you owe, I'll tell you who does. The people you borrowed it from.

The numbers of people who consider they are addicted to shopping has reached around 29 percent of women and 15 percent of men. You may be a compulsive shopper if you:

- [ ] **Have racks of clothes or possessions with the price tags still attached.**
- [ ] **Have things you have bought hidden in cupboards, still in their carrier bags, untouched.**
- [ ] **Can't remember everything you bought.**
- [ ] **Regularly bring home bags and bags of things.**
- [ ] **Consolidate several carrier bags of things into one to fool your family that you have not bought so much.**
- [ ] **Are also addicted to gambling, alcohol or drugs.**
- [ ] **Use Christmas or other holidays as an excuse to spend every last moment and penny in the shops.**

A decade ago, people made jokes about how much they drank. Now it's less socially acceptable. Overdrinking is a serious problem almost everywhere in Britain. I think, in another few years, we will stop joking about shopaholics.

Compulsive or addictive shoppers make for the mall at the first opportunity, or as a reaction to setbacks, each day. They feel comforted and then excited as buying things – nothing they particularly want or need – gives them an adrenaline rush and with it, a sense of freedom and control. When this chemical high recedes, they are left low, guilty, hopeless and pathetic. As debts mount, they may consider suicide and go to extremes to deceive their families and friends. To escape the bad feelings, they go shopping...

Friends and family try to help. When they fail, they feel useless and angry with the addict for bringing their trouble on themselves.

Seek treatment. Talk to your GP and ask to be referred to a counselling service or psychiatrist. Or contact *www.debtorsanonymous.info.* 020 7644 5070.

Let's find you some alternatives to spending.

You're not going to the shops to 'happy yourself up' any more. Because we've already said, this is an empty happiness, like a temporary sugar fix which plays tricks with your bio-chemistry, sending you sky-high and then leaving you down and worse off.

So what can you do instead? *Forget shopping and acquiring things!*

Many overspending problems result from low moments when life has given you a knock, or your low self-esteem or depression.

These are the real key factors that determine most people's happiness. How many of these do you have?

Tick here.

- [ ] **Happy family relationships**
- [ ] **An involvement with children**
- [ ] **A circle of friends**
- [ ] **Pets**
- [ ] **Roles, careers or jobs that make you feel either financially rewarded or personally valued (tick twice for both!)**
- [ ] **Health**
- [ ] **Health among those you care for**
- [ ] **A spiritual life – church, temple, religion, meditation, beliefs**
- [ ] **Involvement with the arts**
- [ ] **Contact with the natural world**
- [ ] **An interest in sports, games, crafts, hobbies or activities**

Some things cannot magically change. You can't have better health or cure your friends. However, the glass is always half-full or half-empty. Considering this list should serve as a jumping-off point for you to work out what is missing from your life – and whether you can change that. This is where you need to channel your energies – not strolling around the shops buying the next trendy 'must-have'.

When I am, occasionally, asked what my ideal day would be, it's a no-brainer. A walk in the woods with my family and the dog.

The most important factor in happiness is not what you have, but how you feel about what you have.

What kind of person are you?

Now let's try to sort out the things that motivate you.

Eminent psychologist Steven Reiss, when ill with a life-threatening disorder, first devised the principles which form the basis for this test.

Place these things in their order of importance to you. Be truthful or you are robbing yourself of insight into your personality. You might do this questionnaire once, then a second time the next day to see if you agree with yourself.

I am keen on:
- [ ] Acquiring new knowledge or skills
- [ ] Being accepted and not criticised by others
- [ ] Tidiness and order
- [ ] Sport and fitness
- [ ] Integrity, honour and loyalty
- [ ] Righting social wrongs
- [ ] Control, power and leadership
- [ ] Independence and self-reliance

☐ Having a laugh with friends
☐ Caring for my family first
☐ Getting even with people who wrong or offend me
☐ Romance and/or sex
☐ Food and eating
☐ Saving, conserving and recycling
☐ Seeking calm and tranquil surroundings

The first six are your strongest-held values.
Are they doing you any good?
Are you doing others any good by holding them?
Work on eliminating any which make you feel bad or that you
are letting yourself or others down. Find other values in this list
which are at least neutral and substitute them.

Use your self-knowledge to make yourself happier. Here are
some suggestions.

A lot of pop psychology talks about putting yourself first and making 'me-time'. On the contrary, I
think that putting others first often makes you
happier because you get such a massive
emotional payback. You can see that others
need and value you – perhaps more than you
value yourself. This is particularly important as an antidote to unhappiness if your shopping problems stem from
undervaluing yourself or feeling empty or unwanted, as many
do. I am not suggesting you martyr yourself or turn into a doormat for rude or abusing people. You have to find a balance.

Try to be active rather than expecting other people to do things
for you. I get wild when people excuse vandals by saying,
'There's nothing around here for them to do.' There is always
something to do, but you have to find it within yourself or in others.

Practical ways to make yourself happier today

'There's no one so poor that they can't tidy their own back yard.' American saying.

None of the following suggestions has anything to do with going on a spending spree. If you find yourself overspending as a result, pull back!

Set yourself a challenge. Overcome something that you thought was stronger than yourself. Run a race, climb a hill, answer all the questions in a quiz, do a crossword, start a help group.

Try something you didn't think was 'you'. Go to an art gallery, a dog show, learn how to dry-stone-wall, cook dinner from food you already have or have picked or found.

Ask a stranger, 'How are things going for you?' (If necessary, explain I set you this exercise!) You will be amazed and fascinated by the extraordinary window into someone else's life you will get.

Think about the future rather than dwelling on past wrongs. That's not to say that you should forget or devalue what happened, but learn from it and resolve not to let 'them' get you down and see you on the floor. Make plans – for today, next week, next year.

Learn a new skill. Write a play or book, learn to drive or dive, learn an instrument.

Fix something that's been irritating you. Or throw it away.

Find something – either that you thought you had lost or search for something rare and strange like a bird or a four-leaf clover.

Get yourself in order. Tidy yourself, your room and your life. That includes making your peace with someone you have fallen out with or if you can't bring yourself to do this, ask someone, even a higher spiritual power if you believe in one, for help. Because you get back what you give out.

Enjoy natural sights and sounds – walk in the country, even look closely at a flower as you wait for a bus, listen to the different birdsong in the morning.

Go and help at your child's school or a hospital or club for a while.

Volunteer to do something you would not normally do.

See or talk to a friend face to face. NOT a miserable, demanding or draining person.

Have a laugh.

Have pets. If not your own, visit someone else's and learn about them.

Do someone a good turn or a small service or favour without expecting rewards.

Listen to music.

Go to the library and look at the 'large book' section where all the lovely glossy picture books are kept.

Breathe fresh air.

Sit in a beautiful building, a church or temple and think of the glories of the past.

Admire a view. If there's no view, look at a leaf or a flower and admire the intricacy of the way it grows – its network of ever-more tiny veins.

Think of all the people who did heroic and self-sacrificing things because they believed in freedom, free speech, and creating a better world for people they didn't even know. Try to live up to them.

Helpful websites

www.43things.com lists other peoples' happy-making things.
www.mindpub.com has some interesting reflections by Dr Vijai P. Sharma.

For more ideas and inspiration try:
www.en.wikipedia.org/wiki/hobbies
www.ufindus.com (type in your town and it will find specialist interest local groups)
www.stationinformation.com

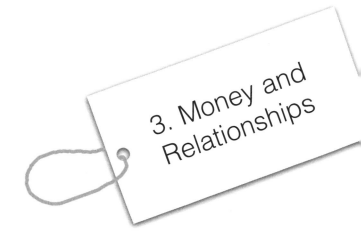

3. Money and Relationships

Money and Relationships, Including How To Say 'No'

Money is as important as love and sex in relationships, and causes just as much passion, happiness, chaos and misery. Money means power and control over others. It also means security. It can be a gesture of thanks or of deep caring. It is not the root of all evil, nor something to feel guilty about having. It is neutral, like chocolate.*

Here, we will try to get to the root of what money means to you and those around you, and how you, and those closest to you, use money in your everyday emotional dealings. The aim is to help you to learn, rebalance your relationships if necessary and pinpoint any self-destructive attitudes that cause you to overspend.

---

* Chocolate is a positive force for good.

What is important in a potential partner?

59 percent say personality
56 percent say humour
55 percent say honesty
29 percent say looks
26 percent say intelligence
7 percent say family
7 percent say religious beliefs
...and only 5 percent say money!

Only 16 percent of people think that money is not important in relationships. 15 percent of adults admit extreme wealth makes someone more attractive. Nine percent say it makes someone LESS attractive. (Source: Survey, Prudential)

As I have said, money and deception go hand in hand.

11 percent of men admit to spending over £800 on one occasion to impress a woman. An 'average' man is willing to spend £453 on a single night to impress a woman. Women would spend an average of £176.

We bring our past experience of money to bear at turning points in life, like when we form a partnership, because at that point, we form a new economic unit with another person which affects the rest of our life. We tend to repeat the past, or react against it. If we are single, this can also happen with our choice of career.

People often subconsciously choose a partner who balances their own traits, by having a contrasting attitude: for example, one will worry and the other will be more relaxed. With money, one of you may be tight and the other extravagant. One partner can frequently be secretive. Women often have 'secret' bank or savings accounts that they keep from their husbands as a gesture of defiance against control. A partner can run up debt secretly, even forging the other person's signature on a re-mortgage or loan application.

Different attitudes to money within a marriage may not emerge or cause problems until a life-changing event occurs, like having a baby, becoming ill or losing one's job.

Christine Northam is a counsellor for relationship guidance charity *Relate* and finds that couples conceal the problems caused by money, initially. 'Couples might say, "He's always working and never has time for me." It's actually about money. He sees career success in terms of how much money he can bring home.'

Her solution is to draw a 'family map' or genogram. I suggest that you try this in order to understand yourself and your relationships better. You may have preoccupations, or even personal demons, that are to do with your past. It may help you to solve your specific spending problems.

A genogram is a potted family history in a diagram like a family tree – though if you don't feel like spending ages drawing it up, just write the lot down in notes.

Concentrate on the factors that formed your attitudes to money and spending. What your family and those close to you were like, can explain and clarify why YOU do some irrational things with your money.

Each partner should write down answers to these questions. If you are single, just write out your own answers or include anyone significant, like an ex-partner, if they are still affecting your economic or emotional life.

Making a family map

Your Father

What is his family background?
What was his job when you were growing up?
What is his job now?
What did he earn when you were growing up?
What does he earn now?
Does he get perks?
Is or was he ambitious?
What was his attitude to money when you were growing up?
Did you like or dislike certain things about this?

Your Father's parents

What was their family background?
Was their standard of living lower than your father's when you were growing up?
What are or were their job(s) and earnings?
What were their attitudes to money? Were they frugal or extravagant?
Did you like or dislike certain things about this?

Your Mother

What is her family background?
What was her job and earnings when you were growing up?
What is her job now?
What does she earn now?
Does she get any perks?
Is or was she ambitious for your father?
Is or was she ambitious for you?
What was your mother's attitude to money?
Even if she stayed at home, did she support your father's attitude?
Did she push your father to work harder, for instance?
Did you like or dislike certain things about this?
In your childhood family home
Who took responsibility for money?
What did you notice about the way they handled money?
Did you like or dislike certain things about this?

Your Mother's parents

What was their family background?
Was their standard of living lower than your mother's when you were growing up?
Do you think they were richer, poorer or 'about the same' as your father's parents?
What are or were their job(s) and earnings?
What were their attitudes to money? Were they frugal or extravagant?
Did you like or dislike certain things about this?

Your Grandparents

Was there friction or social or financial competition which affected your parents? Did your parents react against them or try to emulate them?

Your wider circle of relations

Is there anything here in that could affect your attitude to money? For instance, were your family immigrants who felt they had to work harder to be accepted? Or if one relation is richer than the rest, did you overhear comments – positive or negative – about this? Did it form your attitudes to money?

Your Brothers and Sisters

What are their earnings and attitudes to money?

Any other relevant people in your childhood?

What about their attitudes to money or effect they had on you? Did you like or dislike certain things about this?

Any events or crises in your childhood that affected your attitudes to money and security?

For instance, your home being repossessed, your parents divorcing, a sudden traumatic change in circumstances? 'When I was fourteen, my parents lost a lot of money. I was taken away from plush boarding school and sent to a local comprehensive. I hated it. I decided I would never let myself be pushed around like that again, so I worked hard and got to Oxford University.' *Trish, computer executive*

Yourself

What is your job, and what are your current earnings and perks? Are these better or worse than in the past?
What do you think is your attitude to spending? Is it extravagant, over-controlling, indulgent, carefree, careful or anything else you can name?
Does your partner agree with your assessment? If not, what do you think they would call it?
Did you like or dislike certain things about your attitude?
Do you have any regrets about certain spending?
Are you pleased with anything you have used your money to do?

Your partner

What is his or her job, and their current earnings and perks? Are these better or worse than in the past?
What do you think is his or her attitude to spending? Is it extravagant, over-controlling, indulgent, carefree, careful or anything else you can name?

Do you think your partner would agree with this assessment? If not, what do you think they would call it?
Did you like or dislike certain things about your partner's attitude?
Do you have any regrets about certain spending?
Are you pleased with anything your partner has done with money?

Conclusions

You may see that in your career and your spending, you have either reacted against or tried to please your parents or even your grandparents or another important adult, at some formative time in the past. We sometimes repeat the past or want to change it by replaying it and putting it 'right' in our own lives.

If your parents were poor or strict, or controlling, perhaps you are determined to give your child 'everything', and hang the financial consequences. Or if your father was a gambler, and your childhood consisted of a series of moonlight flits, you may have an iron determination never to inflict this on your family – or be a gambler too or marry a gambler.

HELPFUL HINT **If you think you can stand it, go on into the future. Look at your own children and grandchildren and see how what you do now, may affect their attitudes to money and spending...**

JANE'S TRUE CONFESSION. It was my son's fifth birthday. From nowhere, it seemed, the idea popped into my head of buying him an expensive yellow and red trike. I knew we couldn't afford it but I asked my husband and he agreed. I knew it was too extravagant, but remembered a similar bike I had owned as a child. Another bit of me also said, everyone will admire my good judgement in buying such a beautiful classic bike. Before buying it, I asked my son if he would like one. 'No. I like the bike you bought from the car boot sale,' he said. I had 'saved' a stupid sum of money and overcome some inner drive to repeat the past....

There's nothing wrong with wanting to 'better' yourself by becoming more prosperous or secure or having nicer things. It's one of the great motivations of life. But you may be trying to use money to buy your parents' idea of a better social position, perhaps a golf club membership, or a smarter car, when that is not 'you' and you might use that money better elsewhere.

You may have chosen a wife whose approach to money mirrors her or your mother's. In which case you know how things will end up as you have the older woman's example or warning in front of you! (Or father.)

Use your family history, and your partner's, as a tool to make a balanced assessment – or warning light – to check where you are emotionally, regarding money.

Consider past mistakes – other people's or your own.

Think whether you have 'donkey' events – that's my name for traumas which take the load of guilt or whatever emotion, for any mistake you make. Your mother beating you in the past does not entitle you to blame her for buying a new handbag twenty years later, to give a crude example.

Think whether, perhaps like your father, you use money to impress or to make up for your absences or poor behaviour. (Grand gestures can rack up grand debt.)

Let things mull over for a few days. Ask your mentor if you want to. Discuss it quiotly with your partner and pool insights. Don't let this discussion dissolve into

HELPFUL HINT **Go back and ask the people involved. Elderly people can have remarkably clear views of mistakes they – or others – made and if they are not embittered, will make honest, if scathing, judgements.**

acrimonious accusations or explorations of old wounds. Try to write down positive points for improvement. I want to see four resolutions – two each. These are changes of emotional attitude which will positively help you resolve your financial problems.

When you finish this book, I expect that you will still be mulling over your conclusions about your family past and finances. You can change your mind about your conclusions. That's OK.

> **JANE'S GOLDEN HINT.** *Lots of people are adults but they are not grown-up. You only really grow up when you realise that you have no need to damage yourself to please your parents or to do what they say. You can make your own judgements.*

Here are some typical problem case-studies, revolving around money, which I have encountered among people I've tried to help with their spending problems. You may find yourself here, and if so, please use my experience to help yourself.

Are you living in a fairytale marraige?

CASE STUDY 1: THE PRINCESS PROBLEM

In relationships, many spending problems stem from the fact that the woman has become her partner's princess. (This also counts for dads and daughters.)

The man loves to lavish money on her every whim – the more luxurious, the better. That makes him feel bigger: a powerful provider. She won't rein him in because being a pampered pet feels so good. But the downside of this is that the man shoulders the debt alone – and it becomes a heavy burden to shoulder.

Instead of a co-dependent, equal partnership, they have

constructed a Victorian marriage where the man is the parent-provider and the woman, the child-taker. That can only lead to long-term problems.

Beth and Nick met on a blind date and soon sealed their romance with a £3,000 engagement ring which Beth chose. A month later, she lost the ring when she took it off to wash her hands in the ladies at a restaurant.

The insurance company offered to replace the ring, but only if Beth and Nick bought a new one at their designated jewellers, whose rings Beth did not like. So she flew to Hong Kong, saying that they could get 'better value' there. Her excited phone call, Nick confessed, caught him by surprise when he was concentrating on something else. The effect was like a toddler pulling a parent's sleeve in a shop and getting sweets to shut up. 'She wanted the best diamond in the shop, which cost £7,000, and the jeweller said it was a brilliant investment and bla, bla, bla …When I said, 'Sure, buy it if it makes you feel good,' I felt fantastic when I heard the exhilaration in her voice as she thanked me. The couple refused to disclose to me how much extra it had cost to set the stone in a ring, and how little the insurance company had given towards it.

There was one problem. Nick's income was £25,000 a year and Beth's, £10,000. He had spent nearly a third of their income on two rings, the one Beth lost and the new one.

I discovered that Nick and Beth had never discussed money. First, tackling Beth, in front of Nick, I pointed out how unfair she was to him in asking for extravagant 'proofs of love' like a ring. 'Have you ever considered that he does not want to deny you anything?' I asked. I suspected Nick was having sleepless nights thinking how to make up the financial shortfall, though he was too proud to admit it.

There were practical considerations. 'After you marry, your engagement ring is not going to be important,' I told Beth. 'The wedding ring is the one you wear every day. And it is a bad idea to go round flashing a huge diamond ring, unless you want to be mugged. Also, by the time you add in the cost of your trip to Hong Kong, you have not got better 'value for money'.

Beth had never thought of any of this. She was genuinely sorry. After I left, the couple had an explosive argument about money. Nick wept that he thought Beth only liked him as long as he lavished gifts on her. That gave Beth a chance to change the balance of the relationship from fairytale to reality by assuring him that she loved him for himself and not for a diamond ring. She could take the pressure off him and also build up his self-image, removing her love away from being conditional on money.

They agreed to reallocate her earnings away from beauty treatments and clothes for herself, and share everyday expenses. They also agreed that he would be more honest about whether they could afford luxuries.

 JANE'S TIPS. *If only Beth had thought of the kitty as their money, not his money.*

An adult thinks: 'I lost the ring: I'll make it up to him'.

Men love being presented with solutions, not problems, and by sorting matters out herself, Beth could have gained Nick's respect as a suitable life partner who would share problems.

Unfortunately Nick had spoilt her. He let her get away with her pampered-pet status. But, like the cute dinosaur in Jurassic Park who can turn into a hellhound and slash you, people who are squashy and sweet have another tougher side.

With would-be princesses (or princes), it does no harm to let them stew in their own juice, rather than to rush in and rescue them from their own dippiness. Once you rescue someone, you are stuck and must always rescue them. Eventually you will resent this. On delving further, I discovered yet another twist in this diamond ring tale. Beth confessed to me that at Heathrow, she lost her air ticket and used Nick's credit card to buy a new full-price seat to Hong Kong, there and then.

My sneaky brain wonders if subconsciously, Beth dumped her first ring, because she wanted one bigger and better. Nick could have stopped this entire huge waste of money by showing her the bank statements, giving limits and placing the responsibility for sorting the problem out, onto her.

Don't travel: do research. Beth could have talked to American jewellers on the internet. I would prefer her to save the travel money and go to Hatton Garden in London where jewellers buy their stock, find a ring there or have one made, bargain over the price, then make a deal with her insurers.

Don't agree to expensive purchases quickly when you are thinking of other things. Never give in to sales pressure to decide then and there. That always means the purchase is overpriced.

Buy a 'like for like' insurance policy, which replaces items with similar ones, rather than a policy with restrictions you don't want.

CASE STUDY 2: THE REVENGE SHOPPER
Davina knew her marriage was going sour, but she was scared. She wanted the house with the pool and the car, and life outside her world of school runs and sports classes would be cold and

Are you living in a revenge tragedy?

uncomfortable. She didn't want to discuss what she knew with her husband, Ed.

Things came to a head when she realised that while he had been away on a sales conference, he had slept with his secretary. The hotel had sent a follow-up letter thanking them for their custom and hoping they would stay again addressed to Mr and Mrs Tucker, and she opened it. At first, she thought he had booked a nice surprise for her – until she read further and realised that this referred to a stay in the recent past.

She went out and spent all his money. Later, she described feeling that the credit cards were as sharp as knives and every time she put them in a machine, she fantasised that she was pushing a knife into him.

She bought things she always wanted. All the gifts she felt he 'owed' her, trying to fill the gap in her heart by loading it up with things. She spent £36,000 before Ed discovered that he had no credit limit left. He had been trying to buy her a 'yesterday, today, tomorrow' diamond and platinum pendant for her birthday.

I asked Davina and Ed to go out of their home, away from the children and sit facing each other. Ed explained that he hadn't slept with his secretary or shared a room with her. In fact, the girl had hoped he would and had deliberately booked a room, but when he arrived and found out, he had insisted she had a separate room. The hotel had made a careless mistake in sending the letter, based on their original booking notes rather than the real, revised, bookings. His company accountant would not have tolerated adultery on expenses and he later showed Davina the receipts for both rooms to prove it.

I phoned the hotel and told them what a dreadful mistake they had made. Mortified at causing so much heartache, they offered Davina and Ed a free weekend. Just what they needed.

> **JANE'S TIPS.** *You are using money as a weapon, externalising all the anguish and emotion of feeling a failure. Nothing you buy in hatred will have any charm, so your gifts to yourself are self-defeating. The meaning of a 'present' is that someone else is 'present' inside the gift, and if you hate that person, why remind yourself of them? You are damaging both your present and your future. If you split up, you will need all the money you can get to start again.*

All the money in the world will never make you feel better, because the depressing or humiliating situation which triggered your spending spree remains. You will end up even more unhappy because you have no money.

Be extremely specific if you want a change in the other person's behaviour. In the case of Davina, screaming, 'I don't want you cheating on me with that woman', she was being very specific!

Be gradual and try to hold out a carrot nor a stiok. Not 'Don't ever play golf again' but 'I should like you not to spend all weekend playing golf, so I have booked us dinner at a restaurant on Saturday.'

Don't bottle it up or the stress will come out later in some physical form, according to whichever areas of your body are weakest, e.g. throat infection, stomach pains. Seek some help, either from a professional counsellor or life coach, a priest, friends and family, or a service like *Relate* (*www.relate.org.uk*, 01788 573241 for head office).

There is a variation to revenge shopping. It's consolation prize shopping. When your husband buys you a red sports car or the necklace you pointed out to him on a magazine cover, perhaps you and he know he's been cheating – but you don't want to discuss it.

Are you egging each other on?

CASE STUDY 3: THE SEE-SAW COUPLE

Alan and Michelle had stand-up rows about her desire for an expensive pedigree cat. That particular breed, Maine Coons, were scarce, but a breeder who was a friend had offered to reserve one of a forthcoming litter for Michelle.

Alan disagreed. He felt they were saving for a deposit on a house and Michelle was putting the cart before the horse. Or the cat before the house. Michelle reluctantly agreed to put off her desire for the cat for another year.

Then Alan was offered the opportunity to buy a unique and expensive motorbike. He felt it was a once-in-a-lifetime chance and wanted to take the savings to buy it.

Suddenly his attitude to saving for a new house changed. Michelle found herself on the end of speeches about how hard she worked and how he felt that, after all, she should have the cat. She deserved it.

Then he sent her an email announcing that he had bought the bike. He said that he had been having a tough time and felt that he needed a more reliable, faster motorbike. They would have to put off their hopes of buying a house for a year or two.

> **JANE'S TIPS.** *If you are dithering about whether to buy something, and a partner or friend tells you that you deserve it, think: what does the other person want from you when they say this? I don't suggest having a stand-up row with them, but THEY aren't entirely picking up the bill. Think for a second rather than accepting 'you deserve it' as permission to get into debt. It may be that if your partner or friend inveigles you into buying something silly for yourself, you can't then criticise when THEY want to do something equally daft.*

The skill in countering a 'you deserve it' or 'I deserve it' game – that's what it is – is to say, 'Why is that? I'm not clear about what I have done to deserve a manicure.' Then start negotiating. That's why for every motorbike my husband buys, I can have another pet …

There is a variation to this. 'Your stuff is extravagant; mine is necessary.' This is a form of selfish and controlling behaviour. There is no easy answer to the person who plays this card except to write their purchases down and compare them with yours at the end of a month. Even then, they will probably go into a tizz.

CASE STUDY 4: THE GIRL CAN'T HELP IT

Rosita spent £200 on a new pair of jeans. Well, it was Friday, as she explained to darling Johnny over a drink that night. She shrugged so prettily, her whole body language said: 'What's a girl to do? She confessed, she was feckless, reckless … but so lovable that she knew she would be forgiven, even if Johnny had to work overtime to pay the gas bill, now she wore it on her backside instead.

Are you playing a dangerous game?

Rosita was asking Johnny to show that he loves her right to bankruptcy. She aspires to be a high-maintenance woman, a trophy wife. But Johnny didn't want a trophy: he was a plasterer, not a lawyer earning thousands.

I explained to Johnny that he had to stop indulging Rosita and paying her credit card bills. He had to show her that he loved her in other ways – and she had to stop behaving badly, deliberately breaking agreements about money.

As part of his explanation, I suggested he showed her a doormat. 'This is a doormat. This is me. Don't confuse the two,' he told her. For a time this worked – but Rosita slipped back into her old high-spending, irresponsible ways. She even persuaded Johnny to sell his computer to pay for her plastic surgery. Unfortunately, this relationship went on until Rosita, inevitably perhaps, found a richer man. He was a lawyer.

I came across a sad variation of this game, played this time by the man in a marriage. He gave up his job saying he wanted to write 'the great novel'. His wife, a librarian, said she would support him. 'Instead of staying at home and writing, he has spent all our money,' she wept to me, 'going out to expensive restaurants by himself. Now he knows all the waiters, and they know we are bust.' The couple divorced.

Changing your relationships

How to say 'no' to those you love

'Saying that you can't afford something or don't

have much money is like an admission of failure to many people,' says Christine Northam of *Relate*. 'It links into insecurities about the past. People are judgmental and if another person admits they don't have much money, it frightens them by reminding them of their own precarious position. If many people come from less well-off backgrounds, losing money or having less of it leads them to think, "Where do I really belong?"

'If you have sold your children the myth that you are a happy and successful family, and that this is demonstrated by your material goods, you worry that they will lose respect.'

Here are some suggestions.

Tell them the truth. Don't lie, don't get over-emotional. Control your tone of voice. 'This has happened. We can't go skiing.'

Don't say a direct 'no'. Try giving them the responsibility of making a choice. 'You can either have an engagement ring, or we have a car. I'm happy either way. You choose.'

Make it a serious occasion. Turn off the TV and sit opposite each other. Have physical bills to hand. Explain, repeatedly if necessary, the financial situation 'and that is why you cannot have skating shoes/an iPod/a remote control plane'. Teenagers may need it repeated several times a day.

Try a little by little approach. 'I love you but I can't afford it now. Can you think of something else that's a little cheaper and we can go out together and get it?'

Don't go back on your refusal. If you refuse to buy one thing and then buy something else later, 'to make up for the disappointment', you have confused the other person and they won't believe you next time.

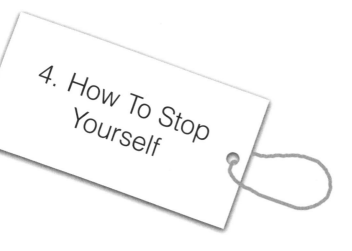

4. How To Stop Yourself

How to stop yourself buying
what you think you can't stop buying

Men and women can have similar addictive impulses to buy more and more of one item. But they focus on different areas of the body. For women, it's shoes (which instant psychology would say means sexual power) and men, tools (sex again, surprise, surprise).

Let's take a closer look under the bed and in the shed, where you keep those unworn shoes and discarded tools but no girly magazines ...

Some women cannot pass a shoe shop without buying something. They suffer from – or rejoice in – SSA, the official name for 'shoe shopping addiction'.

It is considered particularly feminine, an easily forgiven peccadillo. Saying 'I couldn't help buying them. I'm just addicted to shoes', is playing your joker, your get-out-of-jail free card, pleading your weakness with a little girly smile, a defiant 'proof' that women can go out of control and spend money like children, without being told off by their partners for blowing the budget.

It's as if shoes were a medical necessity, or a 'grudge purchase' (necessary but basic) like sanitary towels or deodorant. But women get away with it, because shoes have a status outside the normal rules of shopping: intimate, sexual and personal.

Actresses and people like that boast about their shoe 'addiction', but they can afford it and you can't. Magazines love talking about expensive shoes that *everyone* is wearing, but take this with a big pinch of salt – it may mean that one of the writer's friends owns a pair or the press release had a nice picture. They get advertising from shoe companies, remember.

Boasting about 'shoe addiction' is nothing to be proud of. It demeans women into a childlike, defiant and selfish state, allowing men to feel secretly superior and in control. Real addicts are sad, stuck, out of control people who damage themselves and those who love and care for them. Do you want to be like that?

Might you mean 'I am the slave of my slightest whim to the point where I spend silly money on an item I use to walk along a dirty pavement'? Personally – and this has NO basis in psychology that I can find but I don't care, I believe it – I consider that the more shoes a woman buys, the more sex-starved she is. Not so flattering, eh?!

The simple solution is, tell your partner to give you more sex! Even if you don't agree with me, try it. You will have less time to buy shoes.

The average woman spends £31,680 on shoes in her lifetime. (Source: Prudential)

Nearly a fifth of women have five pairs of shoes they have never worn. (Source: Vogue)

'My sister buys at least a pair of shoes a week. She wears them once and throws them under the bed.'
Keith, Canterbury

Are you addicted to shoes?

Do you consider that shoes marked down from £600 to £300 are a bargain?	Yes/No
Do you get physically giddy, short of breath or rushes of warm, excited feelings when you enter a shoe shop?	Yes/No
Have you ever hidden shoes from your friends or family?	Yes/No
Do you talk to your shoes as if they were pets or people?	Yes/No
Have you ever heard shoes calling to you from a shop?	Yes/No

Results measured in yesses
Yes – You are saving money now. You need to get back down to earth.
Yes yes – Oh dear.
Yes yes yes – Oh very dear – too dear for you to afford.
Yes yes yes yes – Oh my dear, you must try to get out more. Preferably wearing sensible shoes and walking in some nice fresh air. Not fashionable? Well Madonna, apparently, is turning into an English country lady and if Hush Puppies and loafers are good enough for sex icons…
Yes yes yes yes yes…you are lying. Shoes do not speak. Only chocolate calls to its devotees from shop windows. This is because the experience of eating chocolate is near heaven.

Here's why you do it. Research reveals that shoes fulfil all sorts of psychological needs. Pick yours:

The warmth of new leather makes you feel comforted, like a baby.

The smell of new shoes makes you feel richer.

You want to emphasise and even reward your feet for staying the same size, no matter how much you eat.

The sound of your heels clicking on the floor makes you feel more powerful.

Buckles and laces signify enslavement and restriction, plus offering men the provocative and flirtatious fantasy of releasing all that taut flesh. Kicking off your shoes signifies shedding your last sexual inhibitions.

Now understand and conquer your shoe addiction

HELPFUL HINT **High heels make you look taller, but ironically, only if you are already tall enough not to need to wear them. Short people look ridiculous in high heels. Don't buy them to compensate for your shortcomings.**

High or built-up shoes make you feel superior or dominant. High-heeled shoes are considered dangerous but attractive: symbols of love, sex and aggression. * **

FUNNY MONEY. *I once worked with a woman who became terrifying on the days when she wore tall, shiny black leather boots. 'Watch out for Harriet today,' we would warn each other. 'She's wearing her bossy boots.'*

* Not to me, as a woman in stilettos once stood on my foot in the middle of theatre. My toe went black and nearly fell off.
** They also throw the female body into a sexually provocative position because to walk in them requires you to adjust your balance, tilting your pelvis, a change which doctors and osteopaths have said is not good for women's health and posture, especially in pregnancy.

Trainers

Feet become 'addicted' to the kind of shoe you habitually wear and adjust their muscles to match. Some experts say that if you like to run or jog, cushioned and built-up shoes (like some expensive trainers) are less good for feet than cheap basic thinner-soled plimsolls or sneakers. They claim that the padding forces you to adopt exaggerated postures, can cause more injuries and uses up more of your energy. Also, the cost of a fashion or running trainer, includes squiddly design 'features' which you don't need, plus the massive cost of marketing the darn thing. Both for your health and your pocket, consider going barefoot whenever you can. When you swap the shape of your shoe, your feet and legs may ache for a while as your muscles adapt. If in doubt, seek advice from a doctor or chiropodist.

How to stop yourself overspending on shoes

Think of the freedom of paying off your credit card debts this month. Buying shoes will make a huge dent in your budget. How many times will you wear them? And once your friends have seen them and marvelled at your amazing radiance in said shoes, you'll probably be bored with them. Your debts will remain long after your shoes are gone under your bed with all the other shoes.

HELPFUL HINT **Don't wear the same shoes every day. Wear them on alternate days. Resting your shoes allows them to recover from stress, sweat and stretching, and each pair will last longer than if you took two pairs of shoes and wore pair a) all the time and then pair b) all the time.**

I want you to pay off your credit cards, not look good once on a Saturday night. Have you ever considered that clubs and pubs are dark places and no one looks at your feet when they can look down your cleavage more comfortably?

Before you walk into a shoe shop, think of all the smelly feet that have squashed themselves into the shoes, and discarded them. You don't honestly think you're being sold virgin shoes, do you?

'When I have to treat women who buy too many shoes, I tell them, 'Consider how many shoes you've already got. Think: "I've only got two feet. I'm not a centipede."'
Francis Lillie, cognitive behavioural therapist.

At home, get all your shoes out and put them in a line.

Are your shoes all the same or similar? If you have more than two pairs of black court shoes, etc., do not buy any more. You really can't afford to be silly at this point. We are saving money, remember?

Take the ones you never wear and give them to your nearest charity shop or shoe recycling bin.

HELPFUL HINT **If you walk past a shoe shop, rather than going in, reward yourself with a small treat like a magazine, glass of wine or bar of chocolate. Not a fashion magazine.**

Then photograph your shoes and stick these images on the outside of their shoeboxes. This shows you what shoes you already possess, at a glance. So you won't buy look-alike pairs again.

If you think you can't live without a huge number of shoes, ask a friend to take away all but two pairs for a month. I have done this to someone and although she kicked and screamed, after three weeks, she was cured of trainer addiction.

Never buy more than one pair of shoes at a time.

If you think shoes are an extension of your personality, you must be a real heel.

Don't bother to buy shoes if you are going clubbing. Everyone will be standing up and no one will look at your feet. The only times your shoes really count, are at job interviews, court appearances and certain TV shows where they squeeze your feet into red stilettos from a Chelsea charity shop, which you kick off in favour of your slippers when off-camera.

These days, it is not true that you need shoes to match each outfit, nor handbags to match your shoes. One or two good handbags are quite enough. Next, you'll tell me that you need a little Audrey Hepburn hat to match your outfit, too!

Don't go near shoe shops at sale time.

Don't go into a shoe shop to buy shoes for your children or slippers for your auntie and then 'sideways shop' i.e. add 'one for me, one for them'. Just as food stolen from someone else's plate counts when you diet, shoes bought as 'extras' for yourself DO count!

These stain-proofing sprays that they sell you in shoe shops are good, but buy one and know where you put it at home and don't buy one each time you buy shoes. One of these sprays lasts about ten years.

Don't buy coloured fashion shoes each season. Buy a few pairs of classic shoes that work well with everything. You can always mess around with coloured tights or socks, which are a lot cheaper.

Don't buy white shoes unless they are bridal, plimsolls or trainers. They are considered vulgar and on the practical side, they get scuffed as soon as you look at them.

If you must buy fashion shoes, browse charity shops first. Many people have shoes they have worn only once, briefly, usually at weddings.

Repair and wear. Don't wear down the soles and then use this as an excuse to buy new shoes. Shoe repairs are very cheap and your shoes will seem like new ones.

Don't buy. Dye. Give shoes a new lease of life with shoe dye. Also try customising shoes with bows, buckles, badges etc.

There is no law of nature that says you need a new pair of boots each winter.

Substitute cheap for expensive. If you feel the need to splurge on winter boots, buy cheap decorated wellies from supermarkets or chain stores.

Never economise on children's shoes. This is one area to go for quality. Their feet are soft, and fashion shoes and heels that are too narrow can ruin them. Always get their feet properly measured for width at a good shop like Clark's or Start-Rite. You can still economise by buying in the sales.

Don't buy babies rigid leather shoes for this reason. These are expensive and tiny feet don't need shoes until they walk, and then these need to be fitted carefully.

JANE'S TRUE CONFESSION. My personal preference is for cheap flip-flops which I customise with matching nail varnish. These save money on buying and laundering tights and socks.

Guys, did you think you would get away without being ticked off? I know your guilty secret. You have too many tools!

Men like to think their spending is rational and their choices are made on functionality – that they buy something because it does exactly what it says on the tin. But in fact, men are bigger fritterers than women are.

**During Spring 2005, men spent an average of £324
on self-indulgent treats for themselves against
women's £176.** (Source: Morgan Stanley Consumer Bank)

Has life – or the wife – knocked you back? Never mind. Once you get into that glittery tool shop, the feel good chemicals flow to your brain and a feeling of excitement takes over and dulls your rational thinking. The shop assistants seem like little gods, all-knowing. You don't stop to think that if they really knew how to wield these tools so well, they would be doing it, not selling them.

Are you a tool addict?

'I'm obsessed with tools. Every weekend, I get up early to go to car boot sales and auto jumbles, looking for new tools I haven't got. I comb all the magazines for the newest features and functions and surf the web at night searching for obscure all-powerful devices. I tell myself I need them for various home improvements, but by the time these wonder-tools arrive at my home, I often don't unpack them. I'm too busy searching for the next big tool.'

Matt, Cambridge

The problem with having too many tools

The cost.

The shed you have to have, to go with it. (Don't bother to pretend it is an ironic statement – we all know it's an escape hatch.)

Once you don't get the job done, the tool is an embarrassing reminder of your failure. That is why many tools are never even unpacked.

'I bought a toolbox at auction and it contained a beautiful grease gun still in the box.' *Tony, Glasgow*

In time, the tools meld into a kind of crunchy heap on the garage or shed floor. Then when you want a tool, you can't find it and have to buy another one.

I make no apology for what I'm going to say now, nor is there psychological research that I can find to back up my thoughts on this but I know they are right. *Having too many tools makes you look as if you think you haven't got big enough private parts.*

Take it from me. Having a big hammer drill will not make you more of a man!

> 'I used to share a shed with someone called Smelly Tony. He was always buying tools and parts. The more stuff he had, the harder he found it to find the things he needed to do a job. One day I found that he had lost his temper while looking for a tool and kicked some expensive equipment round the floor, which added to the things he needed to fix rather than reducing them. If he had fewer tools, he would not have lost his temper and broken his stuff.' *Ian, Barrow-in-Furness*

First understand why you buy tools.

They are your instant biography. A stranger not knowing you would think that you knew how to use these tools. So they give you an air of confidence which is especially important if you feel low.

Do you want to conquer your tool addiction?

You equate tools with power. You get a real buzz from contemplating what they can do – shedding sparks, hammer drilling, making a lot of noise and thunder. Of course they represent the penis too.

They give you a fantasy about all those jobs you will get done. In your head, buying a tool equals having the job done, dusted and finished.

The tools enable you to win the respect of your peers. You are the hero with all the equipment anyone would want. It doesn't matter that the equipment you use the most is a glass at the pub.

The solution to tool addiction

Have a tool audit. Spend a day picking up and unpacking all the tools lying around.

Clean them and put them in order.

If necessary, make a plan of your tool storage area or an alphabetical list of where your tools are. Put all the cables and power leads with each tool and put all instructions in a file or box. Put paint tins in order and throw away nearly empty tins and congealed brushes.

Have more sex. You will have less time to drone on about tools. There is a strong chance that you already have the next tool you are intent on buying.

Make a list of your projects.

Time for a dose of realism. How many of these projects have you had on a back burner for more than a year? Write the answer here, if you dare!

And how many for more than three years? *Hmm, I thought so.*

Decide which you will never finish and sell the tools you bought to do them with. NB You are allowed to sell tools to friends, or at car boot sales, or using a postcard in the window of a sweetshop or the local DIY shed, but NOT to buy any more there.

Concentrate on one project at a time and finish it.

Only start the next when you have finished the last. Alright, NEARLY finished the last…

Get up early. Don't lie in bed dreaming that you are in that shed! This gives you time to watch the match later. (Note to my husband: I hope you are reading this.)

> **HELPFUL HINT** You may think this is an awful idea, but actually you will find it incredibly liberating – no more worry or guilt.

Pay attention to your comforts. Be warm enough. Have a radio, but don't spend more time organising your entertainment than the work. Get a workbench and stop grovelling about on the floor, which will lead to injuries. Organise a tea-train of people willing to take you regular refreshment in your shed or garage while you are working.

Agree your work time with people you live with. Ensure their goodwill by cleaning up after yourself.

If you really need a push, get people to sponsor you.

Don't buy things advertised as 'good projects' like pianolas and half-finished expensive kit cars. If they were *really* good projects, the seller would have completed them first.

Steer clear of expensive hobbies. Go for useful ones instead. Women really like men who can build bookshelves that don't fall on them when they are breastfeeding the new baby (personal experience here) and they particularly like men who can save money by doing the plumbing.

When buying equipment, be realistic. Buy good quality, but

don't buy tools to do a job until you have ensured you don't already have them, and reached the moment when you really need the item.

There are three things you can have:
- **A pile of tools.**
- **A collection of unfinished or not even started projects.**
- **And a set of finished projects.**

Only the third will get you real respect. None of the others are a sign that you are a success; more like a continuous failure.

HELPFUL HINT

These days you are not allowed to do your own electrical wiring and a good thing too.

Don't visit a tool shop this weekend. You are saving money, mister!

Don't try to get round my stricture by buying tools on the internet, at a car boot sale or even at a garage shop. There is a Fleet Street phrase, 'a story too good to check', used to justify the most outrageous wastes of money on hoax stories like Hitler's Diaries. Think of this when buying second-hand tools. They *may* be thirty years old, the result of a garage clearance by a grieving widow. But many second-hand tools are not too good or their owners would not sell them. If in doubt, remember the prices of new tools are falling due to an influx of Chinese-made equipment.

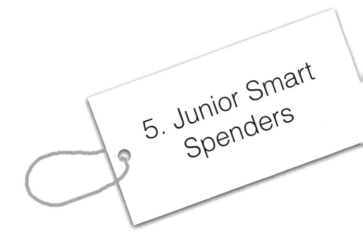

5. Junior Smart Spenders

How to create junior smart spenders

' If a stranger knocked on your door and said he wanted
to come in and talk to your children, you'd tell him to
go away. But that is precisely what is happening to
children when they watch television advertisements.
It's a huge challenge for parents. There are all these
strangers out there who want to get at your children
in order to get at you.' *Frank Furedi, Professor of
Sociology, University of Kent*

**Parents spend around £715 a year on toys, according to a
survey by Egg. That's per child. I hate to think how much
parents spend on their own toys.**

One survey concluded that children ask for a product for up to fifty times – and 70 percent of parents give in. I think this is not because we are indulgent, but because like a fox watching a henhouse, the child has all day to ask obsessively and wait for our weakest moment, when we are too tired to say no again. We can only recognise this and guard against it.

Children are extremely suggestible, as we know. Teach your children to be critical of what they see and hear. That something available to buy is not always the truth, or desirable, just because it is on TV or in the newspapers. Let your children hear you discussing adverts. The best journalists always ask one question about those they interview: 'What's their game?' I mean, what does the person with a message WANT you to think and why will it benefit or profit them?' If you can teach your children to look under the surface of the glossy advertising sell, they are on the right track. Remember to point out that commercial TV, newspapers and magazines make immense sums from advertisers and publishing pages of 'new stuff to buy each month' is another form of advertising.

'One of the things that I find works well with Alice and Harry is to watch the kids' TV adverts together and dismiss the claims loudly, saying things like, "They always look better on telly than they really are", and "It can't really do that"

'It is also worth buying one of these advertised toys to "cure them". Kids learn very fast and only have to be disappointed once by toys that don't live up to the dream to realise that other overblown ads are a similar ruse. They soon come back to trusty old favourites like Lego, Knex, footballs etc. that work every time and do just as they promise on the packaging! Now when we are in a toy shop, the kids can see that they are just

> bits of plastic and nowhere near as good as the
> adverts make out.... they even tell me that something is
> rubbish and that they don't want it.' *Ruth, Kent*

Encourage your children, too, to resist pressure from other children to conform 'because everyone else does or has it'. This takes guts, but you do it by example. I may be a fat old bat but I am not a walking billboard. I wear a dress, not a designer. Nor would I ever wear anything with a label on the outside. My eldest son, when 16, has absorbed these values by silent osmosis. I bought him a school bag with a certain international sports logo on it, as it was the largest and cheapest I could find. He refused to be seen with it. Why did I expect anything else?!

It is hard, but if kids say that their friends don't want to know them if they don't have certain named products, tell them to get new friends not new things.

Otherwise, there will never be an end to the tunnel of consumerism you enter – and the children you buy these things for will not appreciate your sacrifices to give them the latest trainers or bling. They think it's their 'right'.

> 'The message children are being given by advertising
> is that their status is inexorably linked with what they
> buy and what they wear. It causes a huge amount of
> conflict and misery. Working parents who feel guilty
> about not spending time with their children, compensate
> by buying them what they want. The whole of our
> society is predicated on buying. There is a huge
> amount of guilt involved.' *Greg Philo, Professor of
> Communication at Glasgow University*

We must not abdicate responsibility for our children's consumerist behaviour. The solution to the problem lies with us. 'Parents can restrict television viewing to half-an-hour a day or refuse to buy certain foods if they want. Parents need to get back in control and set some boundaries. You don't have to give children television in their bedrooms,' Greg adds.

Age compression. Children aspire to be more grown-up than they are. Products and advertising originally aimed at older children are re-marketed to younger children who have seen their older siblings with the item and want the same. This means that inappropriate things like thongs or saucy tee-shirts are sold to girls as young as seven.

Merchandising. My three children have all liked, at various ages, Thomas the Tank Engine, Fireman Sam, Dr Who, Spiderman and Noddy. That means shelling out extra money for the breakfast cereal, socks, pants, trainers, bag, bedside lamp … a hundred everyday things with the favourite character on. Merchandising is not all bad. If this is the way to get a child to brush their teeth, it's not so terrible. But it becomes very expensive, especially if the child thinks it is his 'right' to have the Spiderman socks.

HELPFUL HINT
Don't encourage this by kitting out a bedroom in a theme. You will have to do it all again when the child moves on to the next obsession.

Dual marketing. Children receive one image of a company and their parents, another. Mothers are comforted by fast food companies who tell them that they sell salads and carrot sticks; children order burgers and chips. Make your own versions at home and if necessary, slam them in a box with a free toy.

'**Trans-toying**'. Everyday objects are turned into toys – sticking plasters made to look like tattoos and scratch and sniff jeans or socks. Again, I don't think this is so terrible, unless you are indulging a child's every casual whim and overspending as a result. But child development experts worry that if every item becomes a toy, there is little space for pleasure derived from ordinary things, like the taste of good food rather than food that is liked because it looks like dinosaurs or smiling faces.

It may be worth looking at the magazine *Adbusters* (£40 for six issues, *www.secureadbusters.org*.) or signing up to a Jambusters group, of which there are many around Britain. Another site to discuss with teenagers is *www.buynothingchristmas.org*.

HELPFUL HINT

Buy Nothing Day, on one of the busiest Christmas shopping days last November, was the most visible tips of the antiprenenurial movement, an anti-big business worldwide pressure group with interesting alternative ideas we can all embrace, and no doubt will be embracing when the current bling and chav cultures lose their charms for trendsetters. Older children, teens – and everyone – can opt out of being advertising billboards for brands by inking out the brand names on their clothes and kit using a black spot. Or a rather hefty £65 buys a pair of unbranded 'vegetarian' shoes – making me wonder when a brand is not a brand ... etc.

How much
pocket money
should you
pay?

According to national government statistics, the average paid per week is £13. Girls cost slightly more than boys.

Ages 7-9	£7.00	Boys	£6.80	Girls	£7.20
Ages 10-12	£11.30	Boys	£10.80	Girls	£11.70
Ages 13 –15	£20.40	Boys	£19.30	Girls	£21.50

I suggest paying basic pocket money and top-up sums for special jobs. But don't encourage children to demand payment for things they should do as a matter of course as part of living in a family, like walking the dog, clearing the table, washing up dishes and tidying their rooms. Top-up money is for extra jobs like cleaning the car or mowing the lawn.

> *Encourage an entrepreneurial instinct. One of my sons wanted a toy but was told he had to wait for his birthday. 'How much is in my savings?' he asked. I told him that there was not enough. He looked dejected but soon cheered up. 'But I've got teeth!' he said, thinking of how much the Tooth Fairy would leave him.*

I never give my children pocket money unless they ask for it, teaching them a vital lesson for life: If you don't ask, you don't get. I write pocket money in a book which they keep, rather than giving them the sum in cash which they invariably lose. If they want it, I make them ask me for it again and explain why they want it, then we discuss it. It means they have to think how to 'sell' me the idea of making that purchase, rather than buying indiscriminately. The cash book allows them to keep a record of their spending.

I keep money one step back from them because children seem to go through a stage of wanting to buy anything at all, up to the limit of the money they have in their hands, just for the experience of immediate possession. I have seen a child (not mine, fortunately) have a tantrum because they were not allowed to buy slippers they would never wear and the wrong size, but the 'right' price i.e. all their spending money.

Discuss priorities with children. 'We can have this, or that, but not both.' Let young children buy things for themselves in shops. They get used to making decisions and understanding that they can have one thing but not both. Supervise and choose a quiet moment or the assistants get tetchy.

HELPFUL HINT

If your income is around £30,000 a year, your 16–19 year-old who does 12 hours of study at school or a college – even for GCSE retakes – can claim Education Maintenance Allowance (EMA), worth up to £30 a week plus a bonus of up to £500 in two years, and still have a part-time job without affecting your other benefits. For details, try *www.ema.dfes.gov.uk* or call free on 080 810 16219.

Explain that the hole in the wall does not give you any sum of money you want. Most children think it is magical.

'During an outing at a shop, I get this little diversion out of the way earlier on by visiting the shop with an allocated budget of say £3, or bypassing it in favour of an ice cream.' *Maria, Bridlington*

Exciteditis

I have mentioned elsewhere the phenomenon of children being overdosed on fun and buying things, but I'll remind you of it so it doesn't take you by surprise. I have noticed that if you take a child out for a day, say in an amusement park, you will spend a fortune, but should be prepared for temper tantrums by the time you get to the shop at the end – from the children, not yourself, though that would be understandable. After many years of this, I concluded that because the experience is essentially meaningless and there is not much thought-provoking to take away, children take out their frustration on wanting rubbish from the shop as they feel empty and they think there must be something that will appease that feeling. By this stage, there is nothing you can buy them that will please them. So buy them nothing.

HELPFUL HINT

If a child has a tantrum at me in a shop, I have a tantrum back. 'Yes, it's awful isn't it? I just WON'T buy it for you,' I wail. That stops them as they find it embarrassing to be in the shop with you and may resort to dragging you out or offering you a treat like chocolate to shut up.

Another good anti-tantrum technique is to say, 'If you don't stop I will tell the man.' This can be any man who looks decent and has a sense of humour. If he tells them to stop, they assume he must be in authority. I once took my son into a police station and asked the receptionist to tell him to stop crying for sweets.

A good game for very youngest children is *Up Jenkins* or *Tip It*, in which you hold a coin behind your back and make them guess which hand you are holding it in, and they do the same to you. The cry to reveal the money is 'up Jenkins' or 'Tip it'. This gets them used to handling money and the names of coins.

Games to help children under-stand money

I used an old-fashioned number frame with beads to try to teach my four-year-old how to add up money. I thought I was doing well, explaining that one and one pennies equals two, two and two equals four and so on. After a while he asked me, 'But when do all the eagles come into the shop?'

HELPFUL HINT **Wash hands after-wards. Money is filthy.**

When they are a little older, teach them to recognise different coins and notes by putting money of the same value but in different denominations on a table – say a line consisting of a 10p coin, two 5p coins, five 2p coins and ten 1p coins. Then mix the coins up and encourage them to put them in the right lines again. They take time to understand that one small coin, like a 5p, is 'worth' five pennies – and I agree, it's not logical.

Playing shops at home with real money and real things is an excellent way to explain the idea of paying or saving money. Eventually they under-stand that once money is spent, you don't have it again. In my experience, the concept of giving and getting change is hard for youngsters to grasp, but essential or they tend to get ripped off in shops at first.

Games to show that once the money's gone, it's gone

It is hard for children (and many adults) to grasp that we cannot spend *all* our money on fun, but have living expenses. If you tried explaining that Mum earns £6.50 an hour, they think she 'only' had to work six hours to buy them a remote controlled Dalek at £39. You can tackle this by demonstrating how your money is spent, using this game.

The balloon game

Buy an economy-size bag of balloons and blow loads up.

On each one, write sums of money like £10, £50, £5, whatever – high and low amounts. All the balloons in the room should add up to your earnings that week or month.

Have a list of your bills and call each one out, then let the children find balloons to that value and pop them. Popping the balloons shows them that once that money is gone, it's gone. You can't have it back and play – or pay – with it again.

If there are any balloons left over, you can talk about what to do with them, saving or spending.

Spending diary

If you prefer drawing or sticking, devise a spending diary using block graphs, showing how you spend and save day by day. Get them to colour the blocks in.

Day 1	4 hours @ £6.50 = £26	Living costs = £25	Savings fund for Dalek = £1
Day 2	5 hours @ £6.50 = £32.50	Living costs = £20	Dalek = 50p
Day 3	3 hours @ £6.50 = £19.50	Living costs = £8 plus new tyre for car at £75	Dalek = £0

Incomings/outgoings/going-outings chart

Make a chart using sticky symbols and a piece of card, the kind you peel stickers off from, or use tape. Each sticker represents say £10. As you tell the children your bills, they can gradually remove the income stickers and stick them into the other columns.

Incomings	Outgoings	Going-outings
Mum gets twenty stickers = £200.	Make several columns depending how elaborate you want to be – house costs; food costs; car costs; others.	Spare stickers can cover 'luxuries' like toys and entertainment. This is the column where THEY get to decide. If you want a takeaway, you will have spent your 'spare' stickers and you can't have a Dalek.

You can hold small investments for your children in a simple trust called a 'bare trust' without any expensive legal hoo-hah merely by placing their initials after your name on savings or shares documents. If you think this may be queried, fill out a 'declaration of trust' form which any savings organisation should provide, or add a note to your application form stating that the child is the beneficial owner of the investment.

Savings

Children can start having their own building society savings accounts from the age of seven.

Children have personal tax allowances – the amount they can earn before they pay tax – identical to adults (currently £4,745). But if you the parent pay money into their savings and it earns over £100 in a year, it is treated as your income, not the child's, and you pay tax on it. If both parents put money in, it can earn £200 before you pay tax. Most unfair.

The solution is that other people, like grand- or godparents, can set up a bare trust for your child in the same simple, child's initials-after-their-name, way. Then the child's own annual personal tax allowance (£4,745) and capital gains tax exemption can both be claimed before tax is paid on the interest earned.

However, the person who generously set up your child's savings must try to live for seven years more, or the child may have to pay inheritance tax on the gift. (This actually happened to my eldest son with my mother, who sadly died a few months short of seven years after giving him a lump sum to pay his school fees. I reflected that he would have been better off if she had given him this money year by year.)

Before a bank or building society will waive tax on the interest paid to a child's account, you generally need to fill out form R85, which they should be able to give you. That's unless the savings account is specially for children, in which case this tax form stuff should be all done for you.

JANE'S GOLDEN TIP
Large sums? Seek legal advice.

Trusts normally end when a child reaches 18. But trust law is complex and there are ways of keeping money back from the untrustworthy (pun intended) for longer. With the help of a trust specialist, you can place all sorts of savings inside trusts so that trust fund babes can limit their tax bills in later life. Trust funds to pay private school fees can use a child's tax allowance to stretch the money available.

JANE'S GOLDEN TIP
If you borrow your child's money, do pay interest on it!
You are teaching them fair p(l)ay.

National Savings offer Children's Bonus Bonds in £25 units but uncles and aunties must know the child's saving number before buying, so it's easiest for them to give you the money to buy on their behalf. *www.nsandi.com*, 0845 964 5000.

Individual Savings Accounts (ISAs) are open to teens over 16 and are ways of getting interest without paying tax on it. You can invest £7000 per tax year: £3000 in cash, £3000 in stocks and shares and £1000 in an insurance ISA. Ask an independent financial advisor, found via IFAP, *www.ifap.org.uk,* 0117 971 1177, or IFAS, *www.aifa.net,* 020 7628 1287.

Friendly Societies take a regular sum and repay the money, usually after ten years or more, tax-free in addition to your ISA tax-free allowance. The rates don't knock my socks off, I have to say. *www.friendlysocieties.co.uk*, 020 7216 7436.

Children born on or after 1September 2002 receive at least £250 from the state Child Trust Fund, and a further gift on each birthday up till the age of seven. The child can't touch the money until their 18th birthday, but relations and friends can add up to £1,200 a year. An extra £250 is paid to children from families on incomes of £13,500 or less who are eligible for the full Child Tax Credit.

HELPFUL HINT

Financial Discounts Direct does not offer advice about choosing an ISA but once you know what you want to buy, may offer discounts you could not get by buying direct. 0500 498 477, *www.financial-discounts.co.uk*

Research suggests that many parents have not placed their child's gift in a savings account yet. For details of special savings accounts for this money, go to *www.childtrustfund.gov.uk*, 0845 302 1470.

HELPFUL HINT

It is worth investing in insurance in case your children have disabling accidents, which will help pay care fees for their lives. It should cost a few pounds. Many private schools offer this, or check with an insurance broker.

Children, money and divorce

Money is power and divorce is the great forum for power fights. A typical problem (there are others, of course) is the father not paying enough child maintenance to the mother, then shelling out eye-watering sums for toys and clothes when seeing the children, to buy their favour. Such people remind me of African dictators who steal their people's financial aid, then drive around throwing money out of their limo windows so they are considered generous.

So try to get the maintenance payments right to begin with. Include an agreement with your ex about treats and shopping, discuss large gifts with the other parent before bestowing them.

A present is literally this – a way to be 'present' in someone else's life, although you are not physically there. An ex may be giving gifts out of guilt. The most important thing is that the child knows there is no room for manipulation about money and material things, or the sky is the limit.

Bribery creates unhappy children and especially, girls who may seek to marry sugar daddy partners and have the princess personality I discuss elsewhere in this book.

Bribery doesn't make children love you. It makes them despise you. If you continue to use money to exert power over them, as they grow up, they will want the money but they won't want to be controlled by you.

If your ex doesn't believe or appreciate this, show them what I've written here.

The parent support charity Parentline Plus made the point to me that it's important not to get into a competition with your ex about giving the biggest gifts.

> 'Remember all the things you do give to your children. Don't see your ex's behaviour as an attack on you. It's more about their feelings about the children and them-selves as parent than about you. If they have more money – ask if the two of you could work out a way of communicating about what the kids would benefit from and need. After all, there is no point in having lots of expensive toys if what they really need is a new pair of shoes or school uniform.'

Parentline Plus has a free helpline, 0808 800 2222, *www.parentlineplus.org.uk*.

If you have trouble with your ex and money, mediation may be cheaper than going through a solicitor. For more information, try *www.divorce.co.uk*.

6. Don't Let Them Get to You!

Be wise to the dark arts of marketing

To me you are each precious souls whose money I am trying to help you save. But to those in the marketing trade, you are mere 'punters', put on earth merely to be separated from your money.

The boring meetings I have sat in during my years in advertising, listening to marketing people think up ways of making you spend more! They make it sound as if they were waging war. You are a 'target'. Impromptu research interviews with you in the street are 'intercepts'.

I want to introduce you to some of their ruses, so that you won't be taken in and spend more than you should.

Creating a need in you. As one top adperson remarked, 'Advertising makes people feel that they are losers if they don't buy the thing we want to promote.' This is so tacky that I don't think I need to say more.

'You'll wonder how you ever managed without it' says the advertising blurb. If only people did wonder – and then manage without it – life would be easier and cheaper. You can probably dispense with buying anything 'disposable' as it is a marketing person's way of getting you to buy the same thing again and again.

> **SHOP HORROR STORY.** *'I started buying wetwipes to clean the kitchen floor – until I realised I was starting to use them for every little thing. Soon I was spending twenty pounds a month extra just on things that went straight into the bin. I went back to mopping spills with detergent and paper towels or washable rags.' Sandra, Bolton*

Viral marketing. A sneaky way of getting you to advertise their products at your expense. Marketing whizzkids boast that it can be virtually free to the advertisers. You receive a cute, funny or weird little message or film clip on your phone or computer, so you email it to your pals. Voila. The advertising is done, and you paid the message costs.

'I received an email from a friend telling a 'ghost story' supposedly that happened to someone whilst filming on a car advertisement , and attaching so-called 'unseen film' of the incident. I emailed her back, saying that she had been 'had' but she wouldn't believe me.'
Paul, Middlesex

Tweaking or relaunching the product. When 'they' can't think of anything else to do, they smarten up a product's packaging. Its new look gives you the illusion of the item being more upmarket and therefore 'better value' without adding anything – apart from to the price.

The power of colour. When I worked in an advertising agency, I recall one particularly awful discussion between the client and the art director. They went on for forty minutes about whether to change a bath oil label from lilac to darker lilac. I commented that I couldn't see that it mattered: surely Mrs Consumer would not notice such a minute difference. I was treated as if I had said something ridiculous. Which I had – because colour can give you 'buy me' messages that are hard to resist. Bright colours work on your brain at primitive levels to excite your hunting, sexual or aggressive instincts. Why do you think sexy underwear is red? Why does research claim that if you want to succeed in sport, you should wear red? As I said, 'they' get into your head! Beware!

Size matters. Another ruse to make more money is to make the product smaller than it used to be, and therefore cheaper to manufacture, or to make the applicator opening larger, so you use more each time, for instance with cream. The price is the same, but if you find you get through more of it than you used to, think about changing to a cheaper product.

Selling you a lifestyle. Sunny picnics, angelic children with flowers in their hair and pretty china … don't you just want to be there, to escape into some of those advertising or catalogue pictures? To be that person, wearing those clothes, using those things, on that lovely Caribbean beach? I confess: I have created lifestyle pictures for all sorts of occasions, including Christmas. It is great fun, imagining every possible accessory and choosing the most chic or interesting to prop a table or whatever. It takes hours. *But it is all a dream. It is art. It is theatre.* Very powerful it is too – that is why luxury hotels are delighted to welcome the photographer, models and stylists to their beach bungalows in Hawaii or whatever, at reduced prices or free. This stuff sells.

An advertising spread can cost £100,000 in a magazine – and who pays? *You*, of course. Readers rip pictures out and buy every single thing in them.

The power of an image

An editorial picture, created to go with a feature, is free, so no wonder the shops are delighted to bike over anything the stylist wants for nothing. Stylists have to think of something new each time, so they 'call in' anything and everything you can imagine from shops, encouraging eagle-eyed consumers to shell out on glitter to cover a tablecloth (that idea only came in a few years ago, from nowhere), place cards, wineglass charms and all the other stuff that will end up clogging up the vacuum cleaner. Then you will need a new vacuum cleaner, and so the merry marketing dance goes on.

> **ANTIDOTE.** Imagine you are there on the shoot. Turn away from the camera and face it. Behind it, you are sure to see exhausted-looking people, sweating with concentration, and piles of junk that has been moved just to make the picture look beautiful. *Life ain't like picture books.*

Tempted to spend money on things in a catalogue with beautiful photos? You are best off chucking the whole thing in the bin, unopened. But if your fickle fingers have found a way into the envelope and you happen to have flicked through, find a pencil and mark the things you would like to buy immediately. Don't make the order immediately – go and call a friend, have a cuppa, whatever, but leave the catalogue closed.

Catalogue power

When you return, look again if you like, but don't buy and close the catalogue so you can't see it. In due course, you will receive a second mailing offering more money off. It will happen! When you realise that they haven't sold so many of that desirable bed spread or whatever, it may lose its attraction. If it doesn't, you could go for it and spend the money. Or, with any luck, you will have gone off your original choices and a new lifestyle catalogue will replace this one, in your fantasies. You will have saved money but had the pleasure of window-shopping.

Advertising Weasels

I am not about to discuss people who advertise weasels for sales. A weasel is a get-out, a form of words that you believe means one thing, and in fact twists away from meaning anything much, like a weasel down a hole when you try and pin it down.

'Nothing works better than' and *'there is no better product than'*. It does not mean it is 'the best'. It means it is first equal to its rivals. 'Just as good as' doesn't have the same ring, though! Choose the cheapest.

'It's better.' Than what? That is never stated.

'Premium'. The word means 'price' in Latin and 'pricey' in marketing speak. The product labelled this may be the most expensive, but is not necessarily the best quality nor what you need. Having it does not tell the world that you are richer or superior. Just that you have spent more.

'Exclusive.' Translates as 'expensive.' I don't think they'll be checking your family tree in Debrett's before taking your money.

'New.' 'Free.' The most powerful words in the language according to adman David Ogilvy. Don't assume they mean anything is improved.

'Can'. Does not mean *'will'*.

'Helps towards the symptoms of ...'. It's not going to cure your cold, and probably will take away your aches and pains like cheaper aspirin.

'When we say value, we mean cheap.' I saw this line in a poster advertising a tailor at a bleak station one day and it really cheered me up. The epitome of northern straight-talking, it undermined the faff talked about 'value' by so many adverts.

REMEMBER, all these beautiful pictures are a fantasy backdrop to sell you something that isn't real. You will still be Mrs Smith of Surbiton.* The £250 French bedquilt does not arrive with a free backdrop of a French chateau or whatever. It comes in a box dumped on your porch by a man with a van.

Value, like glamour, is hard to define – as ad people know, which is why they use this tarnished word so much. For instance, DVDs have been around a few years now but retain an aura of being up-to-date and with more expensive technology than videos. The latest blockbuster can cost £20 on DVDs – but the disk costs as little as 42p to manufacture, according to an analysis by Merrill Lynch. Is that value?

There are other phrases which amused me when I was an advertising copywriter. I learned from working on holiday brochures that you never 'drink' in a bar – you 'relax'. You don't 'stretch your legs' in hotel grounds: you 'stroll'. This is a killer – you never have a 'chance' to buy something; you have an 'opportunity', which implies you have been waiting for this all your life.

These words are carefully chosen to give a more expensive, exclusive impression and make you feel good about spending money. A really useful weasel to an ad writer was the meaningless phrase pointed out to me by my former colleague, direct mail writer Peter Clark: 'up to any number' as in 'you can have up to any number of chances to make a complete idiot of yourself by buying this product.'

A special word on the names of things you buy. A clever product name means money on a price-tag. It implies 'aspirational' things to a potential buyer: with this name, their dreams will come true and at a stroke, they will be thinner, younger, more

---

* Terms and conditions apply. You won't be Mrs Smith of Surbiton if your name is Albert Dunstall of Blackburn or whatever.

stylish, of a higher social class or whatever. I confess, when I worked in advertising, I invented some names supposed to imply that the special new formula in face cream was rocket science.

You won't be taken in any more, will you?

Prices

How do you think these are decided? By finding the least amount they can charge us, through the process of adding together the manufacturing costs, transport, shop, marketing and advertising, then some for the shareholders? Perhaps that is the case in some spheres.

Don't assume a high price means something is 'worth more' or has better quality ingredients in it. In fact, bath oils etc. can contain the tiniest fraction of so-called 'active' ingredients, for whose therapeutic values you pay handsomely. You can get the same effect from hot water relaxing your muscles and a bit of baby oil.

There are **'swagger' products** that are just highly priced so that your friends know you can afford them or to convey an air of exclusivity. Stella Artois, the beer, is 'reassuringly expensive' in Britain but I am told its 'selling platform' is quite different elsewhere.

HELPFUL HINT

I keep all nice boxes, ribbons, cord from carrier bags, tissue paper and bubblewrap etc. and re-use it for gifts. Buying special gift boxes can cost a fortune.

I have been in research groups for beauty products where prices have been decided by asking women how much they will pay for a particular cream, taking this information back to the office and adding another 30 percent for luck 'because people always underestimate how much they will pay, hoping for a bargain'. Very scientific.

Smart packaging has a lot to do with how much you and I may pay for a product because we PERCEIVE it to be worth more. Ironically, we are paying more for the packaging that tells us this, and so we go round in circles. This 'value added' moulded plastic and gold-foiled card is the stuff we throw away at home.

They sell you the feel-good illusion of security. Once you enter a shop, you are escaping your everyday worries – and the more expensive the shop, the deeper the carpet, the more cushioned you feel.

How shops get you to spend more

That blast of warm air at the door is there is make you relax and feel cared-for and secure, with people to look after you. This is a type of instant care in the community, that makes you feel big about yourself – and no wonder it's addictive, because it's free and totally undemanding. Perfect if you feel low.

If you blow your budget, you will feel lower and more insecure than ever. It won't only be a feeling – it will be a reality.

> **ANTIDOTE.** Who do you think is paying for the carpet? *You are!* So many people think that large companies have a sort of secret slush fund from which they pay their overheads and it is not all added to the prices. Imagine – would you still feel good if as you walked into the store, someone held out a bowl to charge you £1 for the carpets and 40p for the air conditioning that day?

They sell you a perfect life in Shopland. Rows of beds are beautifully made up, like chorus girls in a cabaret. Here are cushions, comforters and every luxury known to a tired woman, with no mess. Tables are beautifully arranged with spotless china and gleaming glass, with special halogen lighting to bring out the zing in glass – it's a trick of the trade that this makes things more sparkly. Suddenly it seems 'normal' to buy a linen tablecloth for £200.

ANTIDOTE. Peek or sneak behind the scenes to the shabby stockroom where all those attractively laid-out, so unique goods come in bashed-up boxes by the ton. Even behind the till is pretty grubby.

They sell you a perfect you. It is not unknown for mirrors in changing rooms to reflect you in a way that makes you slimmer or taller, and lighting adjusted to make your skin look 'warmer' and more suntanned.

ANTIDOTE. Walk into natural light and find a mirror on the shop floor, having first got permission from the assistant in charge. Personally I prefer the movie-star technique of having the harshest lighting in changing rooms, so that if you survive that, your purchase must be bullet-proof in the outside world.

They sell you the security of being one of the gang. Psychologists tells us that we humans don't like empty places. We sit down in the crowded restaurant, rather than the empty one, even though we can see the serving-staff are rushed off their feet and we'll have a longer wait to be served. You enter a crowded shop.

The spending brakes come off your brain when you see everyone around you with exciting carrier bags. You deserve convenience and luxury; everyone else has it so why can't you? And here, helpfully, is a storecard offer to help you get it today... *You are being groomed to spend money!*

This is the name given to how shops present stuff to make you spend more without realising. Watch out for:

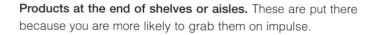

Price tags that end in 99p. That missing penny makes you think it's a pound cheaper.

Products at the end of shelves or aisles. These are put there because you are more likely to grab them on impulse.

Items at eye-level on the shelf. Psychologically, you are more likely to buy products in your sight-line. This is where you find the shop's most profitable items – perhaps the most expensive.

Repeated special offers, in a dump-bin around the shop.

'I see three pairs of scissors for £1 as I walk into a store and ignore it. Halfway round, I see the same offer. By the time I get to the till, I buy them. They must be a good bargain, despite the fact that I have three pairs at home already.' *Di Hallstrom, London*

Anything piled by the till. You will either buy it from boredom as you wait, or if you grab it as you are paying for something else, you won't have time to think straight.

Special offers. There is nothing quite like the feeling of winning one over on 'them': getting a bargain. But don't assume anything in a dump bin or on tatty-looking shelves of the shop is actually cheaper. It might be put there to clear it quickly by giving the illusion of a special offer.

JANE'S GOLDEN RULE
Look on the top and bottom shelves for bargains, not on the middle shelf.

Shops can sell you more by controlling your every movement. Most shops only invest in 'up' escalators, making it easier for you to go in and buy, not carry your purchases away. And in department stores, you have to walk round to the next 'up' escalator, tempt you to wander off and buy something before you get there.

Shops with layouts as twisty as Hampton Court maze don't make money, psychologists tell me. We like to see what's ahead rather than go round corners. Swedish furnishing giant IKEA is known for 'guiding' shoppers round the store as if they were visiting a stately home, with few alternative routes. This way, they ensure that you admire their products from the most attractive direction and are more likely to pick up a picnic hamper and a packet of pegs on impulse as you go round.

HELPFUL HINT

When you are attracted to a store by special prices on certain goods, watch out for price-hikes on other things to make up for the bargains. When a shopkeeper sells you something at cost price, use your commonsense. 'Why should they sell me this so cheaply?' is the obvious question.

They sell you five minutes of friendship. Nice shop assistants are such a change from our families. They agree with everything you say, no matter how stupid, and they treat you like royalty.

TRUE CONFESSION. *When feeling low and tired, I went into a shop to buy two guest-beds, and came out with three plus a wardrobe and a mirror, because I was blown away by the obsequious French salesman with come-to-bed eyes. After a down-to-earth conversation with my husband, on the subject of the bill, I had to cancel most of the order the next day and believe me, that salesman was neither obsequious nor sexy by the end of our conversation.*

Shops sell you a party atmosphere. Music is the food of spending. Professional party organiser Peregrine Armstrong-Jones once told me that music is the easiest way to 'furnish' an empty space. It alters your mood magically. Jazz makes you relax and lose your inhibitions about spending; rock may make you excited and defiant ... So you have shot your credit cards to the limit? Never mind. Live for today.

Music is a very powerful selling tool. In restaurants, they play fast music at lunchtime to make you eat faster, so they get rid of you and can seat more customers. In the evening, slow music makes you linger and then order dessert, cheese, cognac, coffee, chocolates...

> **Researchers played slow and fast music to shoppers in a department store. Slow music encouraged shoppers to browse, taking 19 seconds more to cover the distance between two points, than when fast music played. Customers spent more when slower music played.** (Source: Milliman)

A supermarket played French and German music in front of a display of wine. When shoppers heard the French music, they bought bottles of French wine; with German music, the German wine sold twice as much as French.

Smells that sell. We are told to sell our houses using the smell of newly-baked bread and coffee. Shops use synthetic smells, pumped out near the doors, to make you hungry and thirsty – and a hungry person buys 20 percent more food. There are more subtle selling smells, like 'new car scent', for instance. Did you think plastic, metal and carpet naturally smell as good? Tests prove that people stay longer in a shop with pleasant smells.

> **ANTIDOTE.** This is the ideal opportunity to use up that horrible overpowering perfume or aftershave which Aunty Doris bought you last Xmas. Or dab Vick vapour rub or equivalent under your nose.

How a salesman hooks you

Smooth-talking salesmen are called 'liners' in the trade. The classic salesman's technique is to become your 'friend'. In fact, they want to find out how much money you have to spend. If you prove reluctant to buy, they can become more aggressive, trying to play on your pride by taunting you with lines like 'You can't afford this; that's why you don't want to buy.'

I am rather grateful when shop assistants are rude. It puts you off buying things.

> **TRUE CONFESSION.** *I went into a smart underwear shop, planning to buy an expensive 'body' that a friend told me would take off half a stone in weight. When I said it didn't do anything for me, this assistant snapped, 'It can't perform miracles.' End of sale!*

Beware of being sold to at home. Inviting a salesperson in puts them in the position of quasi-guest. You want to make them comfortable – by signing up for a sale.

> **ANTIDOTE.** When you buy something, remember you don't need to sell yourself! Sales staff are there to sell you something, not for you to impress. I know millionaires who eat in greasy spoons.

One of the quickest ways to save money is to stop buying brands.

The power of brands

From Marmite to Mercedes, brands are the shopper's equivalent of football teams, religion or an extended family that they feel part of, and loyal towards, without question. If this is you, stop it at once! I would hope, by now, you had more sense.

Brands tend to be expensive not necessarily because they are 'better' but because they need more development, advertising and packaging. Something you see on the telly is not necessarily better. It has had money thrown at it. You will be paying for that in the price. Brands will also argue that you pay more for their higher manufacturing standards as they have a reputation to uphold.

Once a brand is stuck in your head with the tenacity of chewing gum on the sole of your shoe, the manufacturers can increase the price of a £5 tee-shirt to £50.

Some people fall in love with brands so much so that they even name their children after them, as in Chanel, Armani and Chevrolet. Marketing Professor Mark Ritson from the London Business School has strong words of warning:

'People are not brands. Brands are things we buy, use and discard. When we apply the concepts of branding to people or to ourselves, we lose something very important.

Try a cheaper brand. Or buy your preferred expensive brand once in every three times, so you buy cheaper tea-bags twice and your expensive ones the third time. Or only buy your preferred brand when it's on special offer.

We are supposed to love our families, not our cars; be loyal to our partners, not a supermarket.'

If you want to be a smart shopper, get wise to hidden messages in the way brands are presented, in packaging and advertising. Marketing people spend ages compiling lists of the 'personality' of a brand: young and trendy, old and classic, fun, etc. Particularly pernicious to me are brands that are supposed to embody mother-love. The way they hook you into buying various items, often unnecessary and overpriced, is to persuade you that by buying x or y washing powder or food or even medicine, you love your children more than someone who buys a cheaper, unbranded or 'generic' item.

Let's shine the light of sense onto this idea. Of course you love your children. You don't need to prove it by buying anything.

SHOP HORROR STORY. *In her book, Born to Buy, American academic Juliet Schor asserts that babies recognise logos at 18 months and by the time they are two, ask for 25 branded items a day. They know 200 brands by the time they go to primary school.*

Once you are hooked on a brand, marketing people say you have 'bought the proposition' – I would translate that as 'fallen for the bait hook, line and sinker'. Then they concentrate on 'extending the brand', i.e. selling you more of the same for more money.

JANE'S GOLDEN RULE
Quality is important. Brand name is not.
Stop trying to impress people by wearing certain
branded clothes or driving particular marques of car.
Be impressive in who you are and how you behave.

Where your money goes
You buy a product for £117.50. Here's how it goes:

£79 goes to manufacturers and distributors
£10 are wages
£6 are rent
£5 are shops profit
£17.50 is VAT

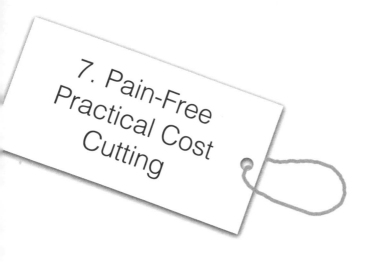

7. Pain-Free Practical Cost Cutting

How to maximize the money that you have and minimize the money that your owe.

You could owe a few pounds. Or a fortune. You may want my advice on how to jog along steadily, or to save up for something big like a house deposit. Whatever you need, here are all the options available to you in a Pick and Mix format.

Don't go back to bed with your head under the duvet, moaning softly. You won't need to do everything here!

HELPFUL HINT

Don't keep the odd bill or two a secret, as many people do. You are only cheating yourself as you will still have to pay.

Include money borrowed from friends and family members. Taking them for granted can cause family fallings-out – and if nothing else, you want nice presents and a free lunch next Christmas!

Make a list of what you owe

To those who would rather drink Baby Bio than make this list. Please put the bottle down. If you poison yourself, your pot plants will have no one to feed them and how could you be so cruel?

Now listen! *Which is worse, nameless fear or the fear you know?* Fear of the unknown is why you don't sleep at nights. You will feel more powerful once you have made this list, because you are taking control.

It's only money. The sun will still shine and small things like your children's smiles will delight you. And with the help I offer you, things will improve. I promise.

The first thing to do is get all your nuts and bolts of life tightened! You would be amazed how many every day bills are wrong. People pay them because they think they are 'official' and who are they to argue? You are my responsibility and I have your best interests at heart. So set time aside and do it.

Check whether your bills are correct

Two years ago, I set myself the task of reviewing the family's basic bills, carefully reading (and understanding) the phone and utility bills. As a result of querying items, I managed to 'claw back', as they call it, several hundred pounds. Last year when we moved home, I saved even more by querying estimated bills from utilities. My bet is, just by reviewing the various 'payment plans' you are on, you will save yourself hundreds of pounds which you may be pouring away in a year, and gaining nothing in exchange.

Companies reduce their prices – they have to remain competitive – but when they introduce new offers they don't tell existing customers. *You have to ask in order to be changed onto these newer and often cheaper options.*

It's boring but effective and at least it means you can save substantial sums without tightening your belt or making sacrifices.

For instance, is your electricity measured on some old payment plan like Economy 7, which is great if you want to run all your appliances in the middle of the night, but not so hot for general all-day consumption? If you have an 'estimated' gas or electricity reading, is it too high? In which case, you have overpaid. Do you have all your friends and family phone discounts for the phone, or do they need updating? Are you on the right phone tariff? Do you have the cheapest phone supplier? *Don't let these things slide – they are costing you money!*

Go through your bank details for direct debit payments. Are there any that you have *forgotten to cancel*, which firms are still collecting, without providing any goods or services in return? I once found one that was two years out of date.

Are there direct debits that you should set up, for instance, linked to credit cards you forget to pay? For instance, MBNA credit card did not answer the phone for long and so often that I forgot to set up a direct debit payment to them. The result was a £25 late payment fine and they switched my 0 percent rate to a substantial interest payment saying that one missed payment negated the 0 percent deal.

Now check direct debits for *poor value*. Payment protection insurance on credit cards or borrowings including a mortgage is one thing to look at. The Citizens' Advice Bureau has made a super-complaint to the Office of Fair Trading about this insurance, as the charges can be hefty but only 4 percent of customers feel the need to claim, of which a quarter are turned down. (DTI figures).

A survey (September 2005) for the Portman Building Society showed that 40 percent of those taking out a direct debit magazine subscription regretted it as 'bad value'; 35 percent felt the same about their gym membership, 21 percent for their life insurance, followed by internet connections, club memberships, car purchase loans and timeshare or holiday clubs.

Cancelling a magazine subscription can typically save £30 a year; gym membership, £600; life insurance, £90; internet connection, £216; club membership, £800.

> **SHOP HORROR STORY.** *A girlfriend who worked in a prestigious store told me how a customer bought an expensive saddle on his store account, but the credit slip became torn so that his name and account details were illegible. 'Don't worry. We won't lose out,' said the department manager. He added the cost of the saddle – several thousand pounds – to every single account bill that month. Few customers queried it because they didn't read their statements properly. The store made a mint.*

Thirteen percent of people who check, find a mistake. People think that banks' computers are never wrong, but they can overcharge on everything from ordinary accounts to loans and overdrafts.

Check your bank statements

If you suspect a mistake and want professional help, either ask your bank to check, which is free, or pay an accountant, or for larger sums, try John Moran of Bank Calc Associates Ltd, *www.bankcalc.co.uk*, 01372 479799, who for a foo of around £350 plus 25 percent of the sum recovered, will do the spadework for you. If he finds no error, he returns the fee. *He says he has never had to return a fee.*

SHOP HORROR STORY. *'My husband spent six months reading someone else's bank statements, sent to us by mistake. This other man's outgoings bore no relation to ours, but my husband budgeted accordingly. He had not read the name at the bottom of the page.'* Diana, Chippenham

You may also be entitled to refunds on things like insurance if you have prepaid then stopped the policy half way through the year, but you have to keep a close check and hassle. For instance, when my mother died, the TV licensing people – renowned for this – kept sending her bills, then rude letters refusing to believe that she was dead. After the umpteenth time, I spoke to someone there who saw sense and informed me that I should have claimed a large refund on her estate's behalf.

Don't lie in bed letting it all go round your head. Get the back of an envelope – don't waste good money on notepads! – and jot it down. In the morning things will look better. Get up – medical research shows we feel more in control when we're standing rather than lying down.

Don't bottle up the stress. If you become depressed, nothing will get paid and things will never improve. Talk to someone. If not a friend or member of your family, try a professional from one of the debt counselling charities listed here. They have heard it all before and aim to get you out of trouble. No one is going to tell you off. What is done, is done.

If you can't stand opening your letters because of the bills, get someone else to do it. When my father died, we thought he had no money. I steeled myself to open a pile of old letters and found they contained several cheques.

FUNNY MONEY. *The actor Jack Lemmon is said to have found Rita Hayworth tearing up a pile of unopened letters. 'But there might be cheques in there!' he remonstrated. 'Yes,' replied Rita. 'But there are also bills. I find they cancel each other out.'*

Find a time when even teenagers can make it, and allow over an hour. Turn off the TV and phones. Have this book to hand and work through this list. Put everyone in the picture of how serious the problem is and ask them to give up one thing. Try not to argue.

Hold a family meeting so everyone knows it's important

Don't waste time in recriminations. We are now problem-solving. Just plod on. Tell everyone in advance that if anyone storms off, a decision will be made and enforced by the remaining members about how the stormer-outer can cut down their spending – for instance, all surplus DVDs and games will be sold – so if they prefer to have control, they had better stay. Ask everyone to think what they can give up and what other people in the group can give up. If they don't want it to be personal they can write suggestions down and put it in a hat to be read out by the chairman of the meeting.

Work out whether this is a one-off situation or a long-term problem. An unexpected dental or vet bill, or a sudden demand for money for a school holiday can strain a budget that's already on a knife-edge. Debt advisors say that one of the biggest causes of running up debts is your overtime suddenly drying up, so if this has happened, read my section on making extra money or make a cunning plan.

Think big

You may decide to make sweeping changes to your life to improve your financial situation. It can be easier and more effective to do one big thing, and save a lot at a stroke, than to do loads of little things.

'When our third child turned four, we realised that our school fees bill for them all would be well over £20,000 a year. So we moved ten miles to an area where the state schools are better. Suddenly, we were free of those bills and extras that mount up over a term. Now fruit, milk and music lessons, are free. Even uniform is cheaper.' *Michael, Kingston, Surrey*

Jane's Golden Hint
If you have set your heart on a particular school, move to a house outside the gates. Or become the caretaker and live in a little house just inside the gates. State school waiting lists don't give priority to your children according to how long you have waited, but by considerations like siblings in the school and how close you live – so you can wait for a year and still find your place taken by someone who moved in yesterday. Also don't believe estate agents who say a particular house is in a school's catchment area. Phone the school and check, then check again before exchanging contracts on your new home. Some catchment areas change annually depending on the number of applications and siblings.

'My husband has given up work to stay at home and look after the children. Childcare was costing us £500 per month and his petrol bill commuting to work was £70 per week. He was earning £20,000 as an export manager. Financially, we're around £150 per month worse off now, but he's a lot less stressed and as a family we're happier than we've ever been.'
Cassie, Midlothian

'I decided not to run a big car and got a Smart Car instead. I haven't missed the car and the savings are tremendous.' *Headmistress, Sussex*

Now we have dealt with the basics, let's see if we can make your existing income magically expand. Check whether you're making the most of your income here.

FUNNY MONEY. *'Cheque enclosed.' Attributed to Dorothy Parker, on being asked what the most beautiful words in the language were.*

Are you owed money? It always astonishes me how few companies know that you can claim huge sums in interest from them, if they don't pay up in time. Under the Late Payment of Commercial Debts (Interest) Act 1998, if you are self-employed and have money overdue from a business, after 30 days of non-payment, you can charge a substantial one-off penalty sum (which varies with how much is owed) plus interest on the debt at 8 percent above the Bank of England interest rate in the January or June closest to your invoice date, making at the time of writing, 12.75 percent. The business that owes you money is not allowed to dictate its payment terms to you without your prior agreement, so it can't say: 'Not paying you for a year is our standard business practice so take it or leave it.' A gentle reminder of the legal position may work wonders.

HELPFUL HINT Send regular updates with the penalties and interest sums added. If the people who owe you money want to negotiate, you can offer to reduce the interest. For more information and a calculator, see *www.late-payment-law.co.uk*.

JANE'S GOLDEN TIP. *Join a union. If you have any trouble like not being paid, their free legal advice, personal support and extras like insurance cover are more than worth the subscription, which is tax-deductible if you are self-employed.*

If the debt is personal, you can take someone to court at the Small Claims Court. I have done this successfully, though it was stressful and time-consuming, not least for the three good friends who took time off work to support me and give evidence. I was awarded a good rate of interest on what I was owed and my court costs of around £230, and was 'lucky' enough to be paid by my opponent, a store which had not delivered the goods I paid for. (See below.)

HELPFUL HINT Don't pay someone else to handle your case. It is easy and straightforward and you will just waste money. You don't usually need a lawyer.

You can start proceedings over the internet at *www.moneyclaim.gov.uk* but if you can't resolve your case before going to court, check with your local court on the cost of court fees on top of the initial payment. If you win, it may be hard to get your money if the other person is an experienced dodger or just plain hard-up.

JANE'S GOLDEN TIP. *Be prepared for your opponent to allege that you behaved so appallingly, that you don't deserve to be paid. This is my experience and that of every single person I know who has been to court.*

MY GOLDEN RULE OF LIFE.
*People who behave badly will go on to
behave worse. Only in stories do they reform.*

I am told that the Inland Revenue aims to get only three out of
four tax calculations right. Check your bill before paying. If
you are an employee, rather than self-employed, Instant
Tax Refund's software can help you reduce tax and claim
obscure allowances, backdated for up to six years, as long as
you have worked from home at least one day a week, with no
complicated forms to complete. If successful, the company
claims it can help you save an average of £400. The software
package costs £29.95 from 0800 064 0270 or *www.instant-
taxrefund.co.uk*

Can you claim Tax Credits? Is your tax code right? Don't
assume the tax people are always right. For more information,
try *www.taxcredits.inlandrevenue.gov.uk*. Ask the Inland
Revenue, 0845 300 3900 (UK); 0845 603 2000 (Northern
Ireland). Or contact an accountant.

Refunds Direct, 0800 107 7188, *www.refundsdirect.co.uk*, has a
one-minute questionnaire you can fill out and submit online to
discover whether they can help you make savings.

The website *www.msn.co.uk* has a useful tax calculator.

Is everyone in your house contributing to bills? I have
helped families simply by telling them to charge their
grown-up children some rent and living expenses.

'The way you're living in your grandmother's flat rent-free is like
climbing on her back and asking her to carry you" I told one

young lady who at 22 was old enough to know better. She was upset at the time, but a week later, the message had sunk in and she thanked me for pointing this out. She started paying rent, and said she felt better because of it. Her grandmother could then afford a few little extras which was great as before then, she sat in the local launderette to keep warm.

Under the **Inland Revenue's Rent-a-Room scheme**, if you have a door between you and a lodger, even if that is your teenager and/or the door is locked all the time, you can charge £4,250 in rent tax-free each year, split between couples if the house is jointly owned. This also applies, apparently, if you rent out your home for a couple of weeks a year while you are not there. You have to declare this income on your tax return.

HELPFUL HINT

If you have family members who want to go to college, seek extra funding through scholarships offered by colleges and by outside businesses and organisations. For instance, the Army offers financial help to people who pledge to join them afterwards. There are also engineering scholarships and advertising scholarships. Try *www.scholarship-search.org.uk* for more information.

Insurance. If you owe money because you are sick or have lost your job, check with your credit card companies in case you are covered by Payment Protection Insurance. Check your insurance policies in case there is any help lurking in the small print.

Unlocking part of your pension. If you are over fifty, you may be able to get hold of part of your pension fund as a tax-free lump sum. Check with your pension provider. Or you could do things with the equity you hold in your house. See my lumps and bumps of life section, p.263.

Benefits. £4.5 billion goes unclaimed every year, because people don't know they're entitled to it. Don't be shy. Any household earning up to £58,000 per year or £66,000 if you have a child under one, is entitled to children's tax credits – and if you are borderline, claim pension contributions and charitable donations off that income to get the money.

Rebates. Are you sick or disabled? Or if you have a low income, perhaps you can claim a rebate on your rent and council tax.

There are some benefits for everyone, whatever your income or savings. I have lost count of the number of people I have told to claim an **Attendance Allowance**, a small non-means-tested (so you don't have to state your income and savings) sum to pay for carers if you are over 65 and in need of personal care. The Citizens' Advice Bureau may even send someone to help you fill in the form, if you ask, though that means waiting and meanwhile losing money.

> **JANE'S GOLDEN TIP.** *Fill in any official application form as fully as you can. Leave no space blank, even if you write not applicable or put a line through it. Otherwise you face delays.*

Then there is the **Nursery Education Grant** which you have to ask a nursery to claim for you. That covers up to two and a half hours a day of free nursery care for pre-school children. For information, ask the Maternity Alliance, 0207 490 7638, *www.maternityalliance.org.uk*.

The Community Legal Service Direct, *www.clsdirect.org.uk*, 0845 345 4345, gives clear advice on all benefits available. Or contact your Council's Welfare Rights Office or a local (free)

Lawcentre, listed in your phone directory or via *www.law centres.co.uk* or the Law Centres Federation, 020 7387 8570. A second website, *www.lawcentres.org*, has useful links to other specialised helplines to advise on benefits for specific groups like the disabled. Finally, you can contact *www.adviceguide.org.uk*, the website of the Citizens' Advice Bureau, whose local branch will be listed in your library.

British Gas Warm-a-life is a scheme offering benefit checks and free energy-saving tips to people living in privately owned or privately rented houses who receive income-related benefits **(not just British Gas customers)** 0845 605 2535.

If you are over sixty, check what you are entitled to by contacting Age Concern's information line: 0800 00 99 66, *www.agecon-cern.org.uk*. Or try Help the Aged's Seniorline: 0808 800 6565 (0808 808 7575 Northern Ireland) and The Pension Service, *www.thepensionservice.gov.uk*, 0845 60 60 265.

Charity funds and grants. Contact your workplace or industry union, even if you are not a member. Some have hardship funds and can pay to support people who have suddenly fallen on hard times.

There are also substantial charity funds to help people, some set up centuries ago by benevolent old buffers and under-used because no one knows about them. Consider your present or former work, and also family connections with specific types of work. If you have ever worked in the theatre – even selling ice-creams – or on newspapers, for instance, or as a travelling salesperson, you may be able to get crisis payments. You can also get funding towards private education and even free places or bursaries – contributions towards bills – at various top schools and universities reserved for specific individuals like 'the daughters of clergymen in the West Riding of Yorkshire' (I'm not making this up!). You need to do some research. Contact your local reference library for The

Charities Digest 2005 (ed Claudia Rios), published by Waterlow Professional Publishing, 020 7490 0049, *www.thanet-press.co.uk*.

FUNNY MONEY *Holidaying in rural Ireland, we visited an eccentric castle where we were invited to see their 'sculpture park'. Lord Whathisname's daughter drove us to a huge, well-lit and air- conditioned barn in a deserted field, where a European sculptor had erected some stones. We gathered that this important plank of the household income was supported lavishly by an EEC grant. You never know what you can get, until you try. The Pilgrim Trust, for example, makes grants averaging £25,000 for projects that give a new use to obsolete buildings of historical interest. 020 7222 4723, www.thepilgrimtrust.org.uk.*

Take on a second job. Gain extra income from occasional work or make the best use of what you already have, without setting up a business or working full-time. See my chapter on ways of making extra money without getting a regular job.

Sell something. See page 118.

Remember forgotten savings. Go through old files and check whether policies are worth anything, or if old building society accounts are dead or just dormant. By doing this, at a time of crisis, I discovered a life policy worth over £2000 that saved my bacon at one stage. The Unclaimed Assets Register can help you track down old savings policies. 0870 241 1713, *www.uar.co.uk*.

Here's how to make your existing income go further.

Ruthlessly renegotiate your mortgage

It is said that we waste up to £1,200 each year because we don't switch to better deals. If you pay a standard variable rate, I suggest making it a

Restructure your financial arrangements

priority to find something lower. Saving even one percent of a £90,000 mortgage over 25 years can net you £22,500, according to *www.debtfreeday.com*.

The bean-counters among us get very worked up about making sure mortgages are the first things to be paid off, but I have to say, I don't think this strategy is right for everyone.

I actually don't think that paying off your mortgage quickly is a social or financial necessity, if it makes you live uncomfortably. I have done it once and it didn't make me feel I had achieved a great life goal, though my husband disagrees.

Here's my view and it's controversial. Life can be short and uncertain. Make sure you buy a saleable house that you enjoy living in, in as good an area as you can. Don't deceive yourself on this and don't tell yourself your house is worth a lot more than it is. (I confess, I've done this before now.) IF you plan on selling your family home and can bear to down-size when the family move out, and If house prices in your area go on rising, I hope you could pay off your mortgage from the profits of its sale.

By flogging yourself now to pay off that mortgage extra fast, you are just giving yourself a needlessly hard time. Going without family holidays, for example, to pay off the mortgage a month or two earlier is all very well until you realise that your family has now grown up and gone, leaving you sitting in a paid-for pile of nice bricks but wishing you'd done more with the kids when they were younger. I am not advocating spending all your money on luxury hols but simply achieving a balance.

If you pay off your mortgage before you die, your children may end up paying inheritance tax on the value of the house. But if you don't and the rest of your mortgage is subtracted from the house value after your death, that may push the value of your estate underneath the inheritance tax threshold.

The websites *www.landsearch.net* or *www.ourproperty.co.uk* will tell you how much houses really sold for, rather than estate agents' headline prices.

FUNNY MONEY. *Research from First Direct threw up the bizarre finding that 37 percent of those in the East Midlands would rather have cosmetic surgery than use the money to clear their mortgage. However 32 percent of all those questioned in the U.K. had no idea how to save money on their mortgage.*

Renegotiating your mortgage can actually be fun – well, a little. Because don't you love to extract the max from financial institutions?

> 'I took up one of those bank advertising claims to give me £100 if they couldn't offer me a better mortgage deal. The paperwork took forever, and they did offer a slightly better rate. But the hidden charges were so high that it didn't make any sense to switch, so they didn't have to give me the £100, they had taken up my time and got my address for future selling.'
> *Don, Uxbridge*

Before starting to renegotiate your mortgage, check what rate you are paying, and whether it will change shortly – if you are about to come out of a special deal, for instance.

Check that your mortgage provider won't charge you a penalty to leave them. But even if they do, it may be worth paying it for a better deal. Also, check a potential new lenders' arrangement charges, plus legal and valuation costs which can make the cost several thousand pounds higher. That means that a saving of £25 a month on a slightly better interest rate won't be worth moving for.

So many silly spenders just ask the nearest bank or building society and assume these are all the same. If you can't be bothered to do the rounds, research from analyst Moneyfacts (2005) named the five cheapest mortgage providers, at standard rates and omitting special deals, as Egg, HSBC, First Direct, Intelligent Finance and the Nationwide Building Society. The Mortgage Business was the most expensive provider named in the survey, which said that for value, Barclays, Lloyds TSB, the Royal Bank of Scotland and the Halifax ranked beneath mutually owned building societies and direct lenders.

To find better deals, you can use internet sites like *www.thisis-money.co.uk* or check the best mortgage' columns in the money pages of the Saturday papers, but personally I prefer using an independent mortgage broker. They often have more muscle to wrestle the best deals from mortgage providers and justify their fees which should be stated transparently to you. *These are not the same as independent financial advisers, who often then use mortgage brokers as part of their team.*

For example, brokers London & Country Mortgages claim to have 'exclusive deals not available elsewhere'. 0800 298 3948, *www.lcplc.co.uk*.

Building societies like Nationwide and Cheltenham & Gloucester are known for not charging fees, but may offer higher interest rates. At time of writing Abbey was offering a no-fees mortgage and also offering to pay your costs.

To compare offers, ask for the total cost of the mortgage over two years, including repayments, fees and your exit penalties from your present mortgage provider. You can use a mortgage calculator like *www.msn.co.uk* on any money site to work out your payments. Personally, I should make the provider sweat for your business by making them do the maths for you. (Money websites also have calculators for stamp duty, endowment policies and virtually every other financial product you own.)

> **JANE'S GOLDEN TIP.** *When you call your mortgage provider and announce that you intend to switch, add enough detail to convince them that you are serious. They will almost certainly put you through to a special branch of customer services with orders to offer you their best secret/cheap 'discounted rate' deals to stay.*

They won't show all their cards at once. They may start by matching the deal you have found. This is the point at which you play mortgage providers off against each other in a bid to get them to add extra freebies like flexible terms, payment holidays, waived fees, survey fees and legal fees if any. *Don't agree to any deal without going back to the other side to see if they can better the offer.*

Why does it happen? These days, staff at financial institutions are under tremendous pressure to sell their products to customers. I have heard of senior managers with thirty years' experience being told off for not reaching marketing departments' dreamed-up targets. One financial friend of mine left because he could no longer offer clients a normal service, he said.

Invent a 'her indoors' or equivalent who you 'have to' consult before agreeing to any offer. When trying to decide whether to take an offer or not, buy time by acting helpless. ' I really don't know what to say about your kind offer of a reduced interest rate/free fitted kitchen/crate of wine/woolly hat with your logo on it. I'll have to ask my husband/friend/the other mortgage company/accountant/penfriend in Kiev/pet Siamese/Oracle and come back to you.' Keeping companies waiting before you take up an offer tends to extract the last possible ounce of lowered interest rates from them as further inducements to you.

Also check offset mortgages which combine your mortgage with your savings and current account, and perhaps your loan and credit card balances. When your salary is paid into it, it reduces your mortgage and interest, if only for a few days. Offset mortgages can save money long term, but tend to charge higher interest rates.

HELPFUL HINT **If you are locked into an annual mortgage deal and you repay a large sum into it, phone the mortgage provider and ask for the date when the interest is calculated. Repay in time to meet that date and no sooner. Meanwhile put that sum into an interest-paying ISA account. The money may simply sit there doing nothing, otherwise.**

Look out for new Euro mortgages. By taking advantage of exchange rates, they could save you money. Coming soon, apparently.

Check whether your mortgage interest is calculated daily. Daily interest calculations save you thousands.

Consider tracker mortgages which automatically vary interest according to Bank of England base rate. If this falls, the rates adjust immediately. I have heard people complain that with ordinary mortgages, it takes several months for rates to adjust in line with interest rate changes.

If you want to pay debts off, put mortgages with cashback on your 'to check out' list. These give you an upfront sum. That doesn't mean it is free, though. There is no such thing as a free lunch.

You can also consider interest-only mortgages. These give you a reduced payment. But they do nothing to pay back the original house loan. At the end of that time, you have to repay the original price of the house, either through savings you have prepared – or simply sell the house. This assumes that house prices go up and you will make a profit, though it may not be large enough to buy you another house or see you through retirement. Consider but treat with great caution.

Putting credit card debt onto your mortgage gives you an interest rate that is much lower than credit card charges, although you will be paying it off for years and it is ultimately more expensive than a short sharp repayment straight back to the card companies. Keep putting debt onto your mortgage and you could lose your home.

HELPFUL HINT

Don't assume that you will receive Aunty Mavis's priceless silver spoons in her will to help you out. Don't ever rely on legacies until you see a cheque.

'I avoided paying a redemption charge on my mortgage by cancelling my direct debit a few months before the mortgage was due to end and sending a cheque for the rest of the money. My lender contacted me asking me to pay a redemption fee, but I said I was not interested in paying it! After a while, they wrote off the redemption fee and returned my house deeds.'

David, Leeds*

* I do not endorse not paying justified bills, but thought this was an interesting story. Others avoid fully repaying their mortgage by say a token of £1 in order to get the mortgage company to continue storing their deeds safely rather than paying a solicitor or bank much more for the same service.

Look again at your home and buildings insurance

Don't automatically buy it through your mortgage provider and don't assume you have to have contents and buildings insured with the same company. I always think it pays to go to an independent insurance broker. They will want your business and will do all that boring phoning around to get you a better deal. A broker need not live near you as you will probably never meet. Find one via BIBA, the British Insurance Brokers' Association, 0870 905 1790, *www.biba.org.uk.* There are also website that will do all the legwork, so you only have to fill in one online form to receive quotes from many of the biggest insurance houses. *www.confused.com* is very efficient.

> **JANE'S GOLDEN TIP.** *If your house is worth more than £350,000 (at rebuilding cost), and/or your contents over £50,000, a high net worth insurance company may prove a better deal. They work on the principle that better-off people look after their things more carefully, i.e. have burglar alarms, house sitters etc., and are not such a poor general risk. These high net work insurers tend to offer more benefits, like new for old cover rather than marking down the value of items for depreciation, home business cover, cover for outbuildings, free fire checks, and a more personal service. High net worth insurers are listed on the website www.householdinsurancenow.co.uk and include Chubb, Axa, Hiscox, and Norwich Union's Tapestry Policy. It is worth getting quotes from all, or saving time and trouble by getting a broker to do it.*

Things you can do to lower your insurance bill, without changing insurer. Check whether you are in a Neighbourhood Watch area (or start one yourself if you are not, via the Police). Install mortice door and window locks – check which are specified first, with your insurer. Also check with your insurer before installing a serviced alarm. An approved brand should reduce your premiums.

It takes about six weeks and doesn't involve relaying pipes or cables to switch gas, electricity, water, TV and phone providers. You can save hundreds. The comparison service Simply Switch, *www.simplyswitch.co.uk,* 0800 781 1212 claims that you can cut your phone bill by up to 70 percent by switching phone suppliers, for instance.

Renegotiate your basic utility bills

Before starting assemble your latest bills. Ask suppliers if they charge different rates at different times of the day and whether there are any penalties for ending a fixed contract, or deals for supplying both gas and electricity.

OFGEM, *www.ofgem.gov.uk*, 020 7901 7295 has a full list of licensed energy suppliers. Consumer watchdog Energywatch, *www.energywatch.org.uk*, 0845 906 0708, also has useful information. Some comparison services don't carry all the options because they take commission payments from energy suppliers to be listed. It is worth getting feedback from a few comparison services before settling on one. Personally I have found it easier to grab the numbers of the recommended new suppliers from the internet sites and phone direct, rather than to go through the internet forms.

www.energyhelpline.com, 0800 074 0745, may offer you £10 cashback to make a switch. *www.switchand-give.com* offers a donation to charity for a switch. Other services include *www.uswitch.com*, 0845 601 2856, *www.loot.com* (telephone details for your local office listed on the website and in the magazine), *www.switchwithwhich.co.uk*, 0845 307 4000 and *www.cheapest-utility.co.uk*, 07002 316746.

HELPFUL HINT Once you have changed suppliers, you can add the cherry on to the icing on the cake by adding additional discounts for paying via the internet, direct debit etc., not to mention bonuses such as Nectar points.

Not a lot of people know that two companies specialise in providing cheaper power to homes with large bills. They are Scottish Power, *www.ScottishPower.co.uk*, 0845 027 8791 and Telecom Plus, *www.telecomplus.co.uk*, 020 8955 5555.

If you have a low income, you probably pay more for your fuel because you can't take up discount offers for direct debits. Check the rates offered by EquiGas and EquiPower, non-profit-making companies offering gas and electricity to all customers at one rate. *www.ebico.co.uk*, 0845 456 0170.

> **JANE'S GOLDEN TIP.** *If anyone messes up the transfer of power, extract extra credit from them, normally in £20 chunks for the inconvenience.*

Saving money on broadband connections

Costs have decreased to as little as £9.99 per month, at time of writing. But many broadband providers lock you into a year's contract, so don't waste your time shopping around until you are free of any existing contracts. Use a comparison service like *www.net-search.uk* or *www.buy3cows.com* to find a better deal. Here are the questions to ask:

1. Is there an extra set-up fee?
2. Do they provide an engineer to come and get you started, or do they simply send the kit and instructions in a box? Getting started, especially if you are not IT-literate and have an Apple Mac, can be tricky in my opinion. Treat telesales-people's assurances with sceptism – you'll never find them again to wring their necks when it goes wrong.
3. Would you be on a time-limit or a maximum download limit which might drive a coach-and-horses through your plans to download music or upload photographs? (1GB equals 205

music tracks or 10,500 web pages per month).

4. What is the speed of connection? 1 Mb is around twice as fast as the cheaper 512kb service, though the latter is adequate for browsing rather than downloading music or film clips.

The switch to a new broadband provider should take about 20 minutes. But if you work from home and rely on broadband to do your job, be wary of changing. I have received consumer complaints, hoping I would help, that the old broadband service stays 'camped' on your phone line, stopping the new one from taking over – and some people have ended up paying for both. Use only Internet Service Providers (ISPs) who have signed up to the Ofcom code of practice, and who give you a migration authorisation code (MAC) within five days of your request to transfer.

Switching to a cable broadband can be even more problematic as you need the new line installed before switching your phone line and again you can end up paying for both. If you encounter problems try the Internet Service Providers' Association, *www.ispa.org.uk*, 0870 0500 710.

Phoning using your broad-band. Save money on phone line rental and call costs by connecting a modem to your PC and phoning for nothing via your broad-band connection. You can use the computer at the same time. The snag is, calls inward to you cost more, BT tells me 5p a minute as opposed to the usual 3p ioh.

HELPFUL HINT

You no longer have to pay BT for your phone line rental – the factor that pushed up the price of switching phone providers. OneTel guarantees lower rentals than BT Together. 0800 957 0178, *www.onetel.co.uk*.

Here are the main options:

FreeView. This has nothing really to do with free satellite channels and gives you access to digital terrestrial TV – around 30 channels including BBC3 and 4, ITV2, CBeebies and UKTV History. To get this, you buy a decoder box for around £40 and pay nothing more or buy a new TV with the service built in. *www.freeview.co.uk* will tell you whether you are in the right area to receive the service. 08708 80 99 80.

Top Up TV enables you to see some programmes using a paid-for decoder plus a card at around £8 a month. Channels include UKtv Gold, Food and Style, British Euro Sports, Cartoon Network, Discovery Channel and others. *www.topuptv.com*, 0712 712 712.

Free To Air (also known as FTA, Free-To-Air, In The Clear). Basically all BBC channels are free, but you need a digital receiver. You can buy a new one from any high street electrical store but I found much cheaper second-hand receivers on eBay.

FreeSat. Sky Digital's name for a one-off £20 card enabling you to view ITV, Channel 4 and Channel 5 through its Sky Digibox. Does away with monthly fees and provides access to over 120 digital TV channels and 80 digital radio channels. *www.freesatfromsky.com*, 0870 240 5651.

Consumers' Association magazine *Which?* claimed in a survey (July 2005) that customers of the big five banks (HSBC, Lloyds TSB, RBS-NatWest, Barclays and Halifax-Bank of Scotland) pay an average of £400 a year on unnecessary charges. These charges are racked up by selling products that customers don't really need, and charging ridiculous sums for small services. Cancelling a

HELPFUL HINT

You may find that when you call to change your bank, you are offered much better deals to stay so don't be too hasty – let them woo you.

cheque costs £50 among the big five, but £30 for Cahoot, an internet bank.

The *Which?* survey put the smaller banks higher in terms of customer satisfaction. Smile topped the list, followed by First Direct, Intelligent Finance, the Co-operative Bank and Nationwide.

There is no point in having savings if they earn you less interest than you pay on credit card debts. Are you getting the best interest rates, and making the most of your tax-free allowance by putting them in an ISA? You can get wraparound' ISAs that allow you to put your own mix of investments inside them. Seek independent financial advice by finding a paid-by-the-hour advisor at IFAP, *www.ifap.org.uk*, 0117 971 1177, or IFAS, *www.aifa.net*, 020 7628 1287.

Check your savings

Independent Financial Advisors

All independent financial advisers, including brokers (known as inter-mediaries) have to tell you how they operate. They will be either totally independent, taking either a fee upfront from you (plus VAT), or a commission from anything you buy from their recommendation. Or they will be 'whole of market' which means they only take commissions. If they are 'multi-tie', that means they are tied into a number of insurance companies or investment groups. If they are 'tied' that means they only offer the products of one financial company – rather limited.

All IFAs have to product a document called 'key facts about our services' and the costs of their services at a meeting or within five days of a phone enquiry.

Try to get a better deal from your pension payments

This can be done painlessly by swapping your broker to one who doesn't take commission, or so much commission, allowing more to go into your pension pot. So if the commission offered by a pension investment company to the adviser were 3 percent, either you pay the adviser a fee upfront and take that commission for your pension fund, giving you 103 percent of your investment; or the adviser may split the commission, giving you 101.5 percent and keeping 1.5 percent instead of the full 3 percent. There are lots of variations on this. To read the regulations, go to *www.hmrc.gov.uk/pensionschemes/pso64.pdf*

'What we've seen in the last few years,' says award-winning independent financial intermediary Yvonne Ridley of *Pearson James PLC*, 'is pension providers giving people 100 percent allocation into their pension plans, no bid/offer spread and no penalties for withdrawal, and they pay us commission. In some cases, it is therefore cheaper for the client for us to take the commission (as there is no VAT to pay as there would be on a fee). It could, of course, be argued that we would choose a company that paid more commission than another, but in reality this doesn't happen as we have to produce a suitability letter explaining why that particular pension plan is more suitable than the others available, including the fund choices in accordance with the individual's risk profile.'

HELPFUL HINT

Hargreaves Lansdowne is a large firm whose Pension Discount Service number is 0117 900 9000,*www.hargreaves lansdowne.co.uk*. They claim to offer the best range of initial savings of any UK broker and also offer a Vantage Service which shares renewal commission with you annually – check for details.

So now you know.

I am astonished by how some families allow their teenagers to live rather privileged lives, with their phone bills paid, for instance, while the parents scrimp to save money. If you have the same problem, deal with it as a family by explaining the debt, repeatedly if necessary. Show them bills they have run up and ask them to pay or contribute. Set up a bank or savings account for each teenager and paying into it a budget which has to cover everything, from travel to going out. Help them to budget by making lists.

Making older teenagers responsible for their own spending

Talk to them about what is smart spending. I have never forgotten my mother giving me my first monthly allowance as a teenager – £5 – a princely sum supposed to pay for everything. I blew it on a long white wool skirt, which stained after a day. I couldn't afford the dry cleaning bill, so washed it and it turned to felt. As a result I had no skirt and nothing left to pay my travel costs to school and had to walk for a month, which taught me a lesson.

See if you can get a better rate of interest elsewhere. You may well find that you are offered a better rate with a payment holiday of up to four months. *Which?* Magazine reported that Barclays charged £1,319 for a £5,000 loan over three years, but its Barclaycard subsidiary only charged £542. See my section on pawnbrokers below, too.

Check car deals, like car loans

Credit Unions are alternatives to conventional savings and lending financial institutions, which have been around for decades. Groups of people – they could be members of a village, pub or club – save and borrow together in a legally regulated

Join a credit union

organisation. Rates may be better than banks, and there are no arrangement or early repayment fees. All loans are automatically insured at no extra cost. Check *www.abcul.org.uk* for your nearest union.

Getting better interest rates

One of the most farcical facts of finance is that rich people get lower interest rates than poorer people, who are seen as a credit risk. I should have thought that making people with less money pay more to borrow it increases the risk that they won't pay it back.

However, you can do certain things to improve the rates you are offered and get higher credit limits. I don't advocate the latter if you are thinking of going on a little spree! (You can turn down automatic credit limit increases, by the way.)

When you apply for credit, the lender will check your credit rating with agencies like Callcredit, Equifax and Experian and give you a score called a Credit Rating. The higher this rating, the lower your interest rate.

You are entitled by law to see a copy of your Credit Rating. It normally costs £2 to apply. If it's wrong, you can ask the holding company to change it. Notorious mistakes in the past include confusing you with others who used to live at your address.

Others you are 'financially connected with' may be taken into account too. Your lender should allow you to choose whether to include 'financial associates' in your application. If you have lived with someone who defaulted in the past, check to see that it is now noted that you are not connected.

The credit check companies don't always hold all information on which credit cards you have. Some credit card companies only log information on people who are in arrears for three months or longer.

The signs that give you a top-score credit rating

You have other active loan or credit card accounts. I find this hard to understand, but credit grantors prefer 'active' accounts which you are still paying off, to accounts that you have settled. I found this when I moved home and decided to buy an anti-snoring adjustable bed for my husband as a surprise. I had trouble getting credit to buy it in instalments, as I had no loans, so no credit check company had a record of me!

You can pay things off over time. Credit grantors prefer to see that you have a credit history – accounts maintained for at least three years.

You have not delayed payments or defaulted. They call this 'having derogatory items in your payment history'.

You have lived in your home for six years. They check the Electoral Roll for this.

You don't have a lot of recent credit searches. If you make over two credit card applications in six months this may well be frowned on as showing that you are overstretched. Other incidental searches, such as for opening a new bank account, don't count.

You have no county court judgements.

You can get a free copy of '*Credit Explained*', a Government-funded booklet explaining your rights to information held about you, which affects your credit rating. Call 08453 091 091 or go to *www.information-commissioner.gov.uk*

Jack bought a scooter on a loan agreement and after a time, decided that the payments were costing more than the scooter's value. He planned to save money by defaulting, and asked the loan company to take the machine back. He only stopped this at the last minute when he realised the hidden cost of saving those few hundred pounds. Making a loss of a few pounds on a machine which after all, he could still ride, was nothing compared to the dent he would make in his credit rating by defaulting.

Sell a second car

Or stop using it until you can afford it again. Park it off road so that you can reclaim part of your road tax and save on insurance. Or get a motorcycle or bicycle.

HELPFUL HINT

Cash Convertors, 01920 485696, *www.cash converters.co.uk*, **offers a 28-day 'buy and buy back' service and will also lend small sums to keep you afloat till pay-day. I found more explanatory notes on specific city sites, like** *www.cashconverters norwich.co.uk*, **than the main website.**

Pawn something

If you need up to £5,000 for up to six months and have ID and any-thing from a ring to a computer or car to put down as security, a pawnbroker can be better than a bank loan because the process is fast and there are no early repayment penalties. If you don't repay your loan after six months, the pawnbroker warns you and then sells your item, giving you the balance if the item fetched more than your loan. You pay interest on your loan at rates higher than credit cards, but they don't charge interest on the interest as credit card companies do. Pawnbrokers are regulated under the Consumer Credit Act so must behave legally. Avoid those who charge a setting-up fee.

The National Pawnbrokers Association can give you local members and sort out grievances. 020 7242 1114, *www.npa.com*.

These are the ones they advertise on TV, explaining that you lump together all your repayments and get one lower interest rate. Debt counsellors don't like them because they say the interest rates are usually higher than those charged by banks and building societies. Also, they often come with 'built-in payment protection insurance' with terms which may not cover you if you are ill or made redundant. They tend to be secured on your house, which means if you don't repay them, you lose your house.

Consolidation loans

HELPFUL HINT **Don't *please* let yourself be hurried into taking out loans on the phone. Anyone who refuses to send written details or offers you an inducement to sign up on the phone, can't be offering the best deal.**

I don't see why you shouldn't ask for written terms from these loan people, as long as you make a sensible decision eventually. But I have my own objections to the way their ads suggest borrowing yet more money than you owe, to go on holiday for instance. I beg you not to do that. Particularly telling, to me, is the customer in one ad who referred to his loan application as a 'claim' as if he was applying for insurance or social security to which he was entitled.

Rate card tart is considered an unpleasant name but personally I am fond of apple tart so I just think 'yummy' when I hear it. Shop around for the best 0 percent offers and use the money to repay a credit card charging interest. Transfer balances to a new card just

Transfer your credit card balance

You occasionally see newspaper adverts offering 18-month interest-free offers but you have to phone quickly to get these offers and quote a code given in the adverts. Some companies will extend the 0% interest rate if you ask nicely.

before the six or nine month interest-free period ends.

NB: Don't leave it quite to the last possible day to repay, as I did recently. I had not taken account of a bank holiday as not being a working day and suddenly realised that I needed five full days for my payback cheque to clear. The card's own phone-in service line initially said it would accept a debit card transfer over the phone, then declined it saying it 'exceeded our house limits' (in other words they deliberately at their end, not the bank's, limit the sum you can transfer by phone, to catch you out). Eventually I managed to transfer the money in tranches over the internet from my bank, but the whole process took several sweaty hours.

The problem with credit card tarting is, the day of reckoning will come sooner or later. You are putting it off. But if you need to put it off, fine, as long as you have a plan in place and are not just dreaming that Father Christmas will descend and pay it off.

JANE'S GOLDEN TIP
If you play the 0 percent game, you must apply for a new card as soon as you see a new deal advertised and at least six weeks ahead of the date you need a new card, to get it in time.

It is possible to make a few hundred pounds on 0 percent balances in order to pay off something else. Check whether the card will put money into your current account. Put it straight into a tax-free ISA savings account. You will make interest on the money. But you have to note the payback date carefully in your diary and repay ten days before that date, or they will charge you interest in full on the whole time. See the detailed credit card shuffle' on www.moneysavingexpert.com for the latest ideas but do not attempt if unless you are extremely organised and disciplined.

Before transferring a credit card balance, look out for hidden charges, typically two percent of the sum capped to £50, just to switch balances. Some companies transfer for free. Phone and ask – don't just transfer and bury your head in the sand, later complaining that you didn't realise.

A 0 percent interest deal gives you time to repay something else. It is NOT a holiday from repaying debts. If you don't make a plan, your debt will increase.

Go through your budget and make cuts

See the whole of this book.

Getting your payment priorities right

First, always pay your mortgage and utility bills (gas, water, electricity etc), car insurance, road tax and council tax – anything that could result in you losing your home or being taken to court and fined.

Then check which credit card or loan has the highest rate of interest. Pay that first.

Subsidise that payment by asking for a payment holiday from non-essentials like odd little insurance policies you might have, or even your pension. Some pensions have built-in flexibility for you to do this.

* For everyday spending, only use credit cards that give you money back on the sums you spend – see my separate section on credit cards, p.172.

8. Selling Your Stuff

So many would-be Smart Spenders have a rusty old car or other vehicle lurking somewhere. You can't sell it because 'the dog likes to sit in it' or you delude yourself that you are about to do it up and make a fortune.

Do yourself a favour. Just sell it. www.autorola.co.uk, 0870 351 3288, will give you a free valuation and list your car. You pay commission of between £100 and £225 only if it is sold.

Also sell that second freezer. (Yes, I *have* been to your house, down the chimney like a sort of Anti-Santa, looking for things to take away rather than gifts to leave. You were asleep and I didn't wake you.)

You need the money and the space, so it is worth admitting that you will never again wear a floppy hat and a feather boa, nor finish the million-piece jigsaw. You have also moved on from certain hobbies so you might as well sell the trampoline and its matching set of fluffy handcuffs. (We won't ask ...)

When selecting stuff to sell, the iron test is, have you used or worn this for a year? Does it bring you any joy? If you can't or won't make a Sell Pile, get a friend to make a pile of suggested throw outs. Go through these. Other people don't know what is of sentimental value.

> *The Smiths had just negotiated a £100,000 loan for a loft conversion when I met them. I pointed out that the main item they intended to store in the extension was a lot of out-dated computer equipment. They had paid for this, and now they were paying again to store it. When they threw away most of it, they created so much space that they didn't need the conversion.*

You soon learn the hard way that things that cost loads in a glossy store change hands for a few pounds in the open air. Here's how to do it.

Car booting

- Start saving all your carrier bags immediately as you will need loads on the day.
- Pinpoint the right sale. Check the local paper. A few weeks before you plan your sale, tour some sites for the ones that attract most customers.
- Ask some sellers if they have covered their pitch fees – around £12 – and if the market is good.
- Check which positions are busiest and ask those sellers what time they arrived to secure their sites. If you can't be bothered, go for a site near a refreshment van but not on top of it, or queues will stop your customers seeing you.
- Compare prices of things you hope to sell.
- Think how to display your stuff. Can you beg or borrow from local churches or scouts, a wallpaper table, clothes rail and lockable cabinet if you have decent jewellery?

'I bought the cheapest clothes rail from Argos and thought I was really clever. At the car boot sale, it collapsed when I hung anything heavier than a few shirts on it.' *Eddie, Kendal*

JANE'S GOLDEN TIP
Save money on tables by laying things out on the ground on a large plastic groundsheet, the kind of thing you can buy to cover furniture when you are painting. If you have one, take a plastic gazebo or even umbrellas against rain. Old clothes-horses are great for displaying curtains, tablecloths and bed linens.

The week before the sale

HELPFUL HINT *www.carboot calendar.com,* 01981 251 633, lists all major car boots, markets, fairs, flea markets, county shows, steam rallies, auctions, etc. but it costs £8.99 online per year or £14 for an annual magazine subscription. Or you can buy the magazine at £1.50 from big car boot sales.

If you don't have much stuff, club together with friends to halve your overheads. You need a fair amount of stuff to sell to make a car boot worthwhile.

Don't leave getting your stuff together till the night before. Wipe, dust or mend anything you plan to sell or people will haggle the price down over a small mark which you could have sponged off at home.

'I wish I had written price tags before I arrived at the sale, and researched prices on the internet, especially for old records, books and china. We had dealers searching for jewellery, old Blue Peter or Rupert Bear annuals, old bibles and Smurf toys!' *Juliet, Norwich.*

JANE'S GOLDEN TIP
It doesn't matter if your price tags state high prices. People will haggle anyway at a car boot sale and feel they have got a good bargain – yet you know you would have gone lower. Write reduced prices on the tags when the first rush has gone.

Don't sell Granny's belongings which could have fetched more in an antique and collector's fair at £25 for a table and a calmer atmosphere. Load your car the night before so you are ready for an early start. Park it somewhere safe.

Take lots of wrapping for fragile things and aprons with pockets on the front or a tin with a lid for money, plus 'float' – lots of pound coins, silver and a few fivers. Note how much you started with so you know how much profit you made at the end.

Prepare flasks and food, as you will be tied to your pitch for hours.

On the day

Go to the loo just before setting out. Wear layers of clothing to cope with weather changes. Arrive as early as you can. When the gates open, you may be swamped and if you are still setting up, some people 'help' by pulling things out of your car and tearing bags apart.

Do not be cowed by these pushy buyers. They are usually dealers, whatever their scruffy appearance, and are expert hagglers and they will put your things – and a few more you haven't noticed – into their bags while offering you silly money. A common con is to gather an armful of things and offer a few pounds – concealing hidden riches in the middle before you realise. Or to bargain down a price for one thing, then a second – and offer

HELPFUL HINT **Don't accept £20 notes. Car boot sales are a prime way of disseminating forgeries and they are incredibly difficult to detect. Ask the buyer to change the note elsewhere and come back to you.**

an even lower price for the two things combined as if doing you a favour!

Around 10am the casual shoppers arrive and will buy your things for a better price.

Keep your 'shopfront' looking nice. As you sell things, fill the gaps as people will walk around a few times.

FUNNY MONEY. *Put the naffest and worst-taste things at the front and charge most for them. I got the highest prices on my stand once for a disgustingly ugly wooden gong and a broken china well without a bucket. It's amazing what people will buy.*

'Don't spread your stall out too far. A beautiful patchwork quilt draped over our car, parked right next to us, was whipped and we had two adults and two kids milling about.' *Barbara, Enfield*

If you don't want to take anything home, offer your dregs to another stall-holder who does it regularly.

Charges involve a fee for listing (from 15p) and a percentage of the selling price, plus more for photographs and having your item listed in two different categories. For a guide, check *www.eBay.co.uk* and go to 'help'. To pay the minimum, start simply.

Register first using a credit card. Use 'search' to scan the site for similar items to the one you're selling, then 'advanced search' to eliminate the dross and find the price bracket of your item. It may be that there is no market for it on eBay. Inside 'search' you will find an icon which emails you so you can track bidding on similar items.

Follow the accepted postage and packing charges, or weigh your item, wrapped, at the post office. You may make extra money here: sellers of postcards costing a few pence add £1.50 p&p for instance.

In almost every case, you need up to six photos of your object, taken using a digital camera, loaded onto your computer, and around 150k in size.

Write a headline, subhead and some description, giving an honest account of any damage. Spell words correctly or buyers won't find you. Avoid pointless puff like 'amazing bargain'. Put in as many keywords as possible that will bring potential buyers in: 'antique blue and white Furnival china cup' will attract collectors of blue and white china, antiques, cups and Furnival china.

HELPFUL HINT **Look out for eBay's cheap deals for sellers, usually on Thursdays. Time your auction to end on or after Sunday night, when lots of people are bidding.**

Don't fill your ad with hostile warnings like 'no refunds' – you need to be human and nice or it will count against you when the buyer fills out a feedback form. Over 5 percent negative feedback and many won't trade with you again.

You can sell an item for a price using 'buy it now' but you stand to make most money from putting something up for a ten-day auction. You need to be around during this time as potential buyers may email questions and you need to answer these, e.g. 'how badly cracked is it?'. If you are polite to a buyer at the boginning, you will build up a loyal customer base.

When the auction closes, an email tells you who your successful bidder is and you receive your money into your credit card through PayPal, eBay's payment system. Yippee – less credit card to pay off this month! The convention is that you send the item within five days unless you warn of some delay such as going on holiday.

Escrow is eBay's system used to avoid both buyers and sellers being ripped off when buying or selling paying large sums. It holds the buyer's money until the buyer receives the goods and reports that they are happy with them.

Beware a scam in which unsuccessful bidders are emailed offering them the opportunity to buy the item outside the eBay network. They send the money and never receive the goods.

'If you see the price of something you want to sell is not moving, some sellers invent an alternative identity for themselves. They then gently edge the bidding price upwards by putting in a series of small bids until they just cross the other bidder's maximum in the hope that they will butt up their bid one more time. At which time the fictitious buyer withdraws. It isn't quite moral and the danger is, you'll end up selling things to your-self, but it may bring the price up.' *Anonymous seller*

Advertising your things

For one or two items you could try any of the following to advertise your stuff:

- **Free postcards on the noticeboards near the tills in supermarkets and big DIY stores like Homebase**
- **Postcards in sweetshop windows**
- **School and church magazines**

- Loot, *www.loot.com*, 08700 43 43 43 and *www.exchangeandmart.co.uk*, 0800 680 680
- A specialist club or collectors' magazine, if the items are of specialist interest. Find these by keying in words like 'antique fans' or 'Jaguar' etc into a search engine like Google. Phone the club magazine editor and ask advice first.

> 'I was pleased to buy a secondhand rowing machine for £25 from a man who lived nearby, from a postcard in the local sweet shop. He had to give it up for the sake of his health!' *Chris, Epsom*

At the lower end of the auction market are local auctioneers who specialise in the rather sad remains of house clearances – boxes of china, board games, tatty sofas. You are not likely to make much on a treasure through them. Do some research. Phone around a few auction houses. Some offer specialist sales and you may be better to wait for those. Register or make an appointment with them in advance, or take your item and queue for a free valuation. (They may visit you for larger pieces of furniture if they are local.) To get the best price, tell the valuer everything you know about your object, no matter how insignificant – they are like a murder detective, trying to put details into place! Try to get several opinions.

If you sell, the valuer should recommend the minimum 'reserve' price so that you don't give your treasure away for a song. You will also be charged a price to put the item in the sale catalogue plus up to 15 percent commission on the price your treasure sells for, other costs like handling and insurance, and VAT on everything. If the item doesn't sell, you may still have to pay something.

Selling books

Your easiest option may be to take them to a second-hand book dealer for instant cash.

If you have paperbacks to sell, *www.green-metropolis.com* charges nothing to you to put your books up for sale, at a standard price of £3.75 per book to buyers. If a book of yours sells, you receive £3. Some of the proceeds go to the charity Woodland Trust.

You may get the best price for a book in perfect or near-perfect condition on *www.amazon.co.uk*. Have it ready to go before advertising. My teenager has sold his A level textbooks in this way and comments that it is much easier than eBay.

Always wrap a book in bubblewrap to post.

DVDs and electronic games

You can sell DVDs, videos sometimes, and games for cash or credits (a more generous deal) to exchange for other movies at Blockbuster, *www.blockbuster.co.uk* for your local store. Also try Choices, *www.choicesvideo.co.uk,* 0870 24 22 800. Aficionados of this activity tell me that you are likely to get slightly better prices at local independent stores.

Selling your clothes

Dress agencies. (See page 230.) You take your clean things along to be valued, then once they are sold receive a percentage of the selling price.

HELPFUL HINT

If you have found a forgotten Da Vinci in granny's attic, check *www.bbc.co.uk/antiques* for buying and selling hints, and an online price search service.

If like me, you bought a few snazzy things BC (before children) – I mean interesting clothes like Quant or Katherine Hamnett – you may be best selling them at auction. Kerry Taylor organises vintage clothes auctions and gives free opinions. 020 8676 4600, *www.kerrytaylorauctions.com*

Good quality curtains can fetch surprisingly high prices. Don't clean them before offering them for sale: if accepted for sale, the shop will clean them and deduct it from your profit. Try Yellow Pages under 'curtain agencies', or Curtain Exchange, which only takes interlined curtains (stiffer than lines). *www.thecurtainexchange.net.*

Selling your curtains

Branch phone numbers:
Bath – 01225 422078;
Newport Pagnell – 01908 218 118;
Essex – 01376 561199
Cirencester – 01285 643303
Dulwich – 020 8670 5570
Fulham – 020 7731 8316
Norfolk – 01263 712 724
Somerset – 01823 681281
Bury St Edmunds – 01284 760059
Dublin – (353) 01230 4343

HELPFUL HINT **Before carrying your curtains to an agency, check for fading in hidden places which makes them unsellable**

JANES TRUE CONFESSION: The curtains left behind by the sellers for us in our new home looked like a shameless hussy's frilly Victorian pantaloons. They weren't interlined – that's an extra stiffening between the curtain and ordinary lining – and they were patterned – making them harder to sell – I didn't hold out much hope of selling them. But I was awestruck when a curtain agency sold them within three weeks and sent a cheque for £500. The buyer left the frilly tie-backs and extras behind too and didn't want the wooden mounts I offered for free.

9. Making Extra Money

Making extra money without getting a regular job

Forget ads in the newspaper saying that you can earn vast sums as a writer or proof-reader. These are selling you courses – and any writer or proof-reader will tell you, it's not *that* easy or lucrative, or everyone would do it.

The following are suggestions for ways of making money, even if you have no qualifications, skills nor time. The ideas here range from jobs that take a few hours to occasional work that you can fit in at weekends, around the school run, or even take a toddler to.

As a member of a focus group for market research, you spend a few hours discussing anything from beds to baked beans with others. Don't expect more than the occasional job, and a pittance – tales of £100 a session are wildly exaggerated – but you get somewhere to sit out of the cold, saving on home heating, and refreshments, saving on food. You can also earn extra if you use your home for the market research group. Saros (see below) pays you something for suggesting other people suitable for focus groups. The British Market Research Association, *www.bmra.org.uk*, lists all market research companies – see Selectline on the website then call around for work. Also try National Opinion Polls, *www.nop.co.uk*, 020 7890 9000, *www.sarosresearch.com*, 0870 240 7923; *www.criteria.co.uk*, 020 7431 4366 and *www.biotrax.co.uk*, 0161 736 7312.

www.gozingsurveys.com offers you £25 for completing online surveys. Others to try include American Consumer Opinion, *www.acop.com* and Global Test Market, *www.globaltestmarket.com*. Both will send money in pounds sterling. GTM has developed its own worldwide point scheme MarketPoints, (once you have 1000 points they send a local currency cheque) and Vouch4Me www.netfreestuff.co.uk which sends vouchers for filling in its initial questionnaire, for example a free weekend away voucher plus you are entered into prize draws to win bigger prizes each time you complete another survey. Also check out *www.ipoints.co.uk*.

If you feel able to hold a checklist and interview people on the street, you can earn around £8 an hour, though budget for woolly vests and gloves when standing in the cold for hours. *www.flow-interactive.com*, 020 7288 0884.

Mystery shopping

Just promise me you won't *buy* anything while you are acting as a spy, reporting on the tidiness, staff behaviour, or what-have-you at clubs, shops, restaurants or pubs. You can earn anything from £7 per visit to £100 a day. Try it.

www.cinecheck.com, 0800 5870520, who specialise in cinemas;

www.fieldfacts.com, 020 7908 6600;

www.ukims.co.uk, 0870 701 0866;

www.mysteryshopagency.com, 020 8325 8974; and

www.retaileyes.co.uk, 01908 328 000.

Competing

If you have the time try your luck at *www.loquax.co.uk*, registration is free at this portal that lists all the major competitions and updates the list daily. As does *www.Win4Now.co.uk* and *www.instantwin4now.co.uk*

Gardening

The slickly-named 'Women Returners to Amenity Gardening Scheme' places learners in private gardens for 15 hours a week, paying £58.80. For information, call the Women's Farm and Garden Association, 01285 658339.

Exploiting your car

www.ad-wraps.co.uk (020 7534 5490) provide you with a free car if you are deemed the right kind of ambassador for certain brands. Or they may pay between £66 and £200 per month to wrap your car in an all-over ad, which they point out protects against body damage. Ask if you're suitable.

Scaring people

If you have a ghost, *www.frightnights.co.uk* may pay to rent the place for parties. 0114 251 3232.

Giving Lifts

If giving lifts to schoolchildren with your own children. You can legally claim up to 40p per mile for car-sharing passengers. Try *www.school-run.org* for information.

Renting a room

You can do this, even to your teenager, and need not pay tax on the first £4250 of rent. For details see p.128.

Renting your home as a film or TV location

It can be unique or quite ordinary-looking – one lady rents out her late husband's garage, as he left it immaculately stacked with bottles and tins and it has atmosphere. Daily fees are from £400 to £10,000, It helps to have parking for film equipment lorries (the size of very large removal vans) and good access and transport links.

Don't pay anyone money to put your house up as a location. There are plenty of free agencies and most councils have a 'film officer' to keep a list of properties. Also try: *www.locations-uk.co.uk* and *www.oic.co.uk*, 020 7419 1949.

Also *www.ukfilmcouncil.org.uk*, 020 7861 7861 and your appropriate regional screen agency: Derbyshire, Leicestershire, Lincolnshire, Northamptonshire, Nottinghamshire, Rutland: EM-Media, 0115 934 9090, *www.em-media.org.uk*; Greater London: Film London, 020 7387 8787, *www.filmlondon.org.uk*; Cumbria, Durham, Teeside, Tyne & Wear, Northumberland: Northern Film and Media, 0191 269 9212, *www.northernmedia.org*; Cheshire, Greater Manchester, Lancashire, Merseyside: North West Vision, 0151 708 2967, *www.northwestvision.co.uk*; Bedfordshire, Essex, Cambridgeshire, Hertfordshire, Norfolk, Suffolk. Screen East,

01923 495051, *www.screeneast.co.uk*; Berkshire, Buckinghamshire, City of Oxford, Hampshire, Isle of Wight, Kent, Surrey, Sussex, Channel Islands: Screen South, 01753 656412 *www.screensouth.org*; Berkshire, Buckinghamshire, City of Oxford, Hampshire, Isle of Wight, Kent, Surrey, Sussex, Channel Islands: Screen West Midlands 0121 766 1470, *www.screenwm.co.uk*; Yorkshire, Humberside: Screen Yorkshire, 011 3294 4410, *www.screenyorkshire.co.uk*; Cornwall, Devon, Dorset, Gloucestershire, Somerset, Wiltshire: South West Screen, 0117 952 9977, *www.swscreen.co.uk*; Northern Ireland Film & Television Commission, 028 90 233 444, *www.niftc.co.uk*. Scottish Screen, 014 1302 1700/1723/1724, *www.scottishscreen.com*; Wales Screen Commission, 0800 849 8848, *www.walesscreencommission.co.uk*

Renting your land, spare barn, workshop or garage

If you can keep your grass growing and have at least an acre of spare land, with fencing and shelter, you can rent it out as grazing for a horse for at least £10 a week. The British Horse Society will help, 08701 20 22 44, *www.bhs.org.uk*.

You can rent out your spare barn, workshop or garage if it has natural light. *www.property.org.uk* carries ads from artists and craftspeople seeking places to work, to rent. You should search the "properties wanted" section.

Lying down naked for arts sake

Few of us possess the face and body of fashion models – though if you want to get into that, haunt Top Shop at London's Oxford Circus every Saturday where scouts are looking, or the BBC Clothes Show at the International Exhibition Centre in Birmingham, where the big model agencies all have pitched sites which you can approach. However, people of all ages and shapes are in demand as artists' models at your local College of Art or College of Further Education. You just have to be able to sit or lie still and you get up to £11 per hour nude and £8 clothed.

If you can travel to a studio early in the morning, you can earn from £64.50 to £200 a day as a film extra. You don't need film star looks – in fact, the more ordinary you are the better, as you will be asked to stand at a bus stop or walk the dog – but you must not giggle or shout 'Hello Mum' when the camera rolls. Expect lots of waiting. Try *www.castingcollective.co.uk*, 020 8962 0099 or *www.rayknightcasting.co.uk* , 020 7722 4111.

Acting naturally

To donate sperm, you must be under forty and fit. Payments for sperm are rapidly dying out as they are deemed unethical and a recent report recommended paying reasonable expenses and loss of earnings only, defeating your object. Some places may still pay, however, up to £25 a time; check your nearest university's Medicine Faculty notice board or find a fertility clinic or sperm bank through The Human Fertilisation and Embryology Authority, 020 7291 8200, *www.hfea.gov.uk*, or *www.mannotincluded.com*.

Giving of yourself

Laboratories will pay about £60 for 600 ml of your blood and £5 for your travel costs. This is not the same as donating your blood free at a local donation clinic or mobile van for which you get a free biscuit and a cup of tea. To find your closest session call 0845 7 711 711 or enter your postcode at *www.blood.co.uk.* Alternatively see BBC2 Ceefax p. 465.

Giving blood

You need not be in perfect health, and can be any age, depending what the test requires, to test anything from drugs to face cream to contact lenses for between £80 and £200. The downside is, there might be unpleasant side-effects but if there are, the tests stop. You must judge whether to go ahead for yourself. There are also psychological tests – things like memory games – for which it is worth asking at your nearest university Psychology faculty. Try *www.biotrax.co.uk*, 0161 736 7312, for details of trials all over the UK. For £20 you can buy their fuller directory of medical testing centres and surveys going on. Also try *www.gpgp.net*, *www.hotrecruit.com* (search "crazy jobs" for relevent info) and the Common Cold Centre, Cardiff, *www.cardiff.ac.uk/biosi/associates/cold/hctrial/html*, 02920 874099 (or search their website for Common Cold trials). Clinical Neuroscience Research, Dartford, Kent, 01322 286862 *www.psychmed.org.uk*. Manchester's School of Psychiatry and Behavioural Sciences, *www.medicine.man.ac.uk* (keywords = research+volunteer), 0161 306 6000. Each survey has its own contact numbers also check your local university's medical faculties.

Becoming a football club steward and help out a club by watching the crowd during match days. This pays between £20 and £40 for four hours. Contact your local club's safety officer.

This is the crème de la crème of occasional jobs. There are 30,000 part-time paid jobs on government advisory boards which fall vacant regularly. For a relatively handsome sum, if you have experience of a certain trade or they like the cut of your jib, you could spend a few days a year sitting on committees running hospitals, trade boards or even wine-testing for the Government Hospitality Advisory Committee! Try the office for the Commissioner for Public Appointments, www.ocpa.gov.uk or telephone 020 7276 2626, or email *public.appointments.unit@cabinet-office.gov.uk*.

When selling stuff to friends and neighbours. Trust your intuition. You may have to make a substantial outlay to buy the stock, and the glossy predictions of huge sales may not come true. However, here are some of the main companies.

- Virgin Vie – cosmetics and jewellery
  www.virgincosmetics.com. 0845 300 8022. Pay £25 and £140 for registration fees, either one-off payments or in instalments.
- Formative Fun – educational toys
  www.formativefun.com. 0845 890 0609. You earn 25 percent of value of any sales you make at parties or direct; 10 percent if your customer places their order online or by mail order. £25 outlay for 60 catalogues and stationery plus a day's training.
- Kleeneze – cleaning products, wine, telecoms
  www.kleeneze-team.co.uk. 08703 336688. Kleeneze can be found on *www.kleeneze.net*, 0870 3336688. 21 percent commission plus possible bonuses on all orders you receive through door-dropping catalogues. Start up costs from £75 for registration and catalogues.
- Avon – cosmetics, bathing, jewellery, and a few clothes
  www.avonuk.com. Rather secretive, so I pretended to want to join and received an email telling me that there

is a joining subscription of £15 deducted from your first two orders, then you have to sell a minimum of £68 of goods, to receive 24 percent commission, with 30 percent commission for orders over £128.

> JANE'S GOLDEN TIP. *I have been an Avon lady in an attempt to make ends meet and made a loss. This seems most profitable if you live on a large housing estate full of bored and moneyed women or if you work in a large office.*

- The Gift Experience – soft toys, novelties, photo albums, candles, jewellery etc *www.tnjp.co.uk*. 01691 624672. Send £90 for initial £180-worth stock, which can be deducted from your commission as you go along. Earn 20 percent on all sales plus monthly bonus scheme.

Tax matters

Naturally you should pay tax on your earnings, even if they are cash.

Money you can claim off your tax bill, in connection with your extra earnings, includes:

- Travel – bus, train, planes, bicycle, whatever, and part of your car running costs and petrol, also parking charges.
- Part of your phone bill. Some of your coucil tax, insurance and utility bills.
- Research materials (books, papers, magazines you might buy).
- Equipment and any special protective clothing.

Treat collecting receipts as a savings game. When you fill out a tax return, these are taken away from your earnings and you are taxed on the remainder, so the more receipts you collect, the better. See my section on tax for more details, p 127. For a comprehensive and inspirational guide to all sorts of other work, from casual to starting a business, see *A Bit on the Side: 500 ways to boost your income* by Jasmine Birtles, published by Piatkus, £10.99, or free from the library.

For an awful warning about which jobs not to take, including a very funny account of what it's like to be a sex-line call answerer, see *The Idler Book of Crap Jobs*, edited by Dan Kieran, published by Transworld, £9.99, or free from the library.

HELPFUL HINT

Keep a record of what you are paid and – this is totally vital – your expenses, keeping all your receipts in a shoe-box and a running total in a book to save time. Keep these receipts for up to seven years (depending on what type of business you are running) as this is how long the Inland Revenue can demand to look back, if you are unfortunate enough to be 'investigated' for potential tax back-payments. Visit *www.hmrc.gov.uk*, call the tax hotline on 0800 77 88 87 or pick up or download leaflet SABK4, a guide to record keeping.

10. Credit Cards

Credit cards are magic money. Invisible, almost miraculous access to anything you want, from the Bank of Fairyland. But Fairyland also contains trolls, and they can eat you.

To survive and save money, some people have an 'all or nothing' approach. They put all their credit cards away from temptation and just pay cash.

Despite their tendency to fuel our 'want it now and darn the consequences' culture, credit cards are also jolly convenient tools and unless you have a shopping-addictive personality, you should have a few.

Credit card convenience

They are safer than carrying wads of cash around.

They may offer you 'purchase protection' insurance if the thing you buy through them breaks within a few months.

They are useful to book hotel rooms in advance, by quoting the card number as a deposit.

They can offer you discounts on things like holidays if you book through them.

Some offer extras like automatic travel insurance.

Credit cards can also be useful if you have a dispute with a shop about something you have bought with a credit card, or if a supplier goes bust, as the credit card company can be liable to repay your money. Because of this, credit card companies have departments aiming to resolve consumer problems by negotiating with the shop. I have to add, on the two occasions I have asked a credit card to refund money denied to me by a shop, they have suggested that I take the shop to court first.

HELPFUL HINT **Before going away, get your credit card company to send you a copy of the insurance policy and all the contact details or it will be pretty useless. Check whether the insurance is activated when you pay for all of your holiday or only some of it, through the card.**

However, this convenience comes at a hefty price, with most interest rates way higher than the Bank of England base rate. However, some credit card companies do offer long-term low interest rates. You can find the best deals on internet money websites or in the money sections of weekend newspapers, in tiny tables on the back page.*

You can find a list of best credit card and loan deals and instant calculators to help you work out how long your loans will take to repay at various interest rates, at *www.best-prices-uk.co.uk* and *www.thisismoney.co.uk.*

The 'fire and ice' trick

I picture my credit cards as books of matches. They will burn me if I play with fire. If you feel in danger of doing this, freeze your assets, literally. Get a long tin, like a sardine can, which can't be put in the microwave. Wrap your cards in plastic, add water and place in the freezer. If you want to use them, you will have to defrost them and that gives you time to reconsider.

Repaying the minimum each month will barely dent your debt. Some cards have reduced the smallest monthly payment to 2 percent. At this repayment rate, if you owe the £2,100 average balance at 14.9 percent APR, it would take 27 years and five months to clear and if you are paying 'purchase protection' as well, you will still have the debt.

Don't let the trolls catch you

'At the moment, credit card companies make less than 60 percent of their profits on interest. The other 40 percent comes from penalties levied on people who are either inefficient or in difficulty.'
*Malcolm Hurlston, Co-founder, Credit Card
Counselling Service*

* At the time of writing, the cheapest I found was the Co-operative Bank's Clear Visa at 8.9 percent. Barclaycard's Combinations charged 9.9 percent and three times a year, clears the balance into a linked loan at 6.9 percent.

SHOP HORROR STORY. *As you get older, you stop lusting after people and lust after things instead. This is my excuse for falling desperately in lust with a complete set of old Liberty bedroom antique furniture – as I said earlier, this kind of thing is my weak spot. Not having the money to buy it, I phoned a large bank's credit card call-centre to ask what the repayments would be on the sum I wanted to borrow. Their staggering reply was, 'We have no way to tell you.' Calls to their press office for clarification were not returned. 'Yes, but you will be quick to tell me on the bill,' I thought grimly as I abandoned the idea of buying the furniture.*

Check the card's standard interest-free payment time. It may be shorter than you assume. I'm not talking about 0 percent payment deals on cards – we'll get onto them – but the ordinary time between making the purchase and getting the bill. It used to be a standard 56 days, but an increasing number of cards now give you 45 or 46 days. If you don't pay in time, they slam on interest charges backdated to the day you bought the item.

If you have used a 0 percent balance transfer offer to transfer money over from a higher interest card, put the card away and don't use it for purchases unless it includes a 0 percent deal on these too. Cards tend to use your payment to repay the 0 percent balance offer first, racking up interest against your purchases.

Don't incur late payment charges or you tend to get a £20 'fine'.

One nasty little habit that credit card companies can adopt is to be slow at answering the phone, if you want to set up a direct debit, hoping presumably that you will give up

HELPFUL HINT Set up a direct debit minimum monthly payment, or write payment dates in your diary.

and then forget. If you do set up a direct debit, they are extremely slow to action it, enabling them to charge you a late payment fine for the first repayment.

Don't exceed your credit limit – another £20 fine. You can phone the card and check your balance instantly, so don't bury your head in the sand when out shopping. You can also ask for your credit limit to be increased, even for a few months, though I don't recommend it.

Never write credit card cheques. You are usually charged a two percent 'handling charge' and interest, even if you repay the money in full on time.

Never withdraw cash on your credit card for the same reason. Don't use any old credit card to get cash abroad. Most 'load' – or 'charge' as we Smart Spenders call it – a typical 2.75 percent on your money. *Nationwide and Lombard Direct credit cards were the only ones I could find with no loading*.

HELPFUL HINT

Some cards have a maximum annual cash-back, of which I think Alliance and Leicester's Credit Card, offering £75 a year, is the most measly.*

Don't set up regular payments using your credit card rather than your bank account. If you want to cancel the deal, the company you pay have to do it not you – and if they prove slow to cancel, you pick up the bill.

If your card offers points or 'cashback', use it for all your purchases but pay the bill back in full

* At the time of writing, American Express Blue offers cardholders 2 percent back on purchases for the first three months, then 0.5 percent for the first £2,000 spent each year, and 1 percent after that with no maximum limit – but you get nothing if you spend less than a thousand pounds and if you spend less than £500 in a year, you face a £15 annual fee. Other cards to check are Abbey Cashback, Leeds & Holbeck Mastercard, More Than Cashback Mastercard, Smile, Morgan Stanley Platinum, Mint, Nationwide Cash Reward, Capital One Circle Rebate, Create Card (Lloyds TSB), Egg Blue and Scottish Widows Cashback Mastercard.

every month or you will stockpile debt. You receive the cash-back payment paid annually, not monthly, so don't rely on it.

> *'Before Christmas 2004, I and my husband took out an Egg card specifically to get the rebate on our Christmas shopping. We both used the cards exclusively, and were still several thousand pounds short of our limit when Egg simply decided to decline our cards each time we used them at the till. We could not get through on the internet to find out why. By this time, of course, our Christmas shopping had finished – and mysteriously, when we stopped spending so much, our cards were restored to working order.' Aretha, Folkestone*

M&S's & MORE card and John Lewis's Partnership card, both ordinary credit cards, give a point per pound spent in their stores or per £2 elsewhere, with a hundred points giving you £1 voucher to spend in their stores.

Air Miles are currently offered by NatWest and the Royal Bank of Scotland credit cards, one per £20 spent on the card. I have had two family holidays to Italy using Air Miles collected in this way, but usually after several years and after using credit cards for major purchases like computers.

Don't use credit cards to impress others. Do you really care if a waiter fawns all over you because he hopes for a big tip? Does the fleeting admiration of a complete stranger in a shop or club really make you feel better about yourself? Even if you do have more money (or rather, credit) than others, it is dangerous to advertise the fact by flashing cards around.

IKEA charges 70p per transaction to anyone using a credit card in their stores.

Storecards are often the last hope of those who have shot through their credit card limits and are *still* trying to commit financial suicide by continuing to shop. Nearly half the people who take out credit in shops hadn't planned to do so when they left home.

> **JANE'S GOLDEN TIP.** *The only use for a storecard is if you have your eye on a big purchase in the sale, like a piece of furniture, and the storecard is offering a percentage off everything you buy on the day you get the card. Take the card, hit them for the sale price minus your discount, then cut the card up and pay the money off quickly.*

11. The Secrets of Savvy Shopping

First, get the right mindset. When we venture to the shops, we are not princes and princesses with infinite time and money. We are busy and important people, with more pressing things to do than to shop all day. Shopping is not our *raison d'être* but a way of getting hold of life's necessities.

The last time I went shopping in a department store was two years ago. I can't say I feel culturally or socially deprived. I suffer less from 'analysis paralysis', the panic we feel when faced with too many choices in a shop. What's analysis paralysis? For instance, toothpaste. Large, small, pump, sensitive, bicarbonate of soda, anti-cavity, minty, stripey, for teeth over 40. If you can't decide, give up and go home.

I suspect that the idea that shopping makes you feel good was invented by some evil marketing genius, to sell us the idea of spending our precious time fighting our way through the Car Parks of Infinity to the Malls of Money-Wasting.

Research reveals that rather than feeling happier, around one in four of us gets worked up into a state of fury when shopping. When you consider that the average person spends a total of three days of the year queueing, you realise why.

Shopping is not healthy. A BBC documentary called *Shopology* monitored the blood pressure of a man shopping in Oxford Street, and found that it rose to dangerous levels.

Jane's aversion therapy for shoppers

Next time you are tempted to go shopping, read this. In fact, cut this out and keep it with you. Think of:

People with honking coughs who breathe germs over you.

People in front of you at the till, who only fumble for their wallets when the assistant asks for payment.

Families who hold hands and amble along the width of the pavement so you can't get past.

Having to climb stairs to the next floor to buy baby things, because that's where shops put the children's section – perfect when you have no one to help with the buggy.

Shop assistants who know nothing about the products and care less.

Merciless till assistants who load all your things on the fast-moving conveyor belt . As you struggle to open a carrier bag that some-one seems to have superglued up, your eggs and bread are crushed under a bottle of bleach.

The irritation of taking things back after Christmas and discovering that they have now been marked down, so you are only entitled to a refund at the sale price. (This is true, unfortunately.)

Have I said enough?!

SHOP HORROR 1.

JANE: [in small curtain-maker's shop]: Can I look at your discount fabric remnants?

ASSISTANT: We don't sell anything like that.

JANE: So why is there a sign painted in huge golden letters on your window that says 'Come in and see our large selection of bargain curtain remnants'?

ASSISTANT: I've worked here for twenty years and I have never seen that sign.

JANE: Have a look.

ASSISTANT: (Steps out of the door and returns). Yes, you're right.

JANE: Bye.

ASSISTANT (urgently): Wait! It says we have remnants so we MUST have them. I'll ask the boss. (She disappears into a back room and returns). No, we've never had them.

The skills that can save you thousands

How to cut your shopping costs

THE GOLDEN RULES

Never use shopping as a habitual pastime or entertainment *unless you are extremely strong-willed and leave your credit cards behind. (You aren't and you won't – who are you kidding?!)*

Dump the idea that it is OK to go shopping in discount or factory shops. *People think they are frightfully clever to go there, but I think only an idiot pays full price for most things these days. Discount places are not the natural home of any disciplined money-saver.*

If you go shopping, you don't have to buy anything. *'Just looking' is your mantra. If you go out shopping and return empty-handed, congratulations. It means that you are a discriminating shopper, not a pushover, not a punter, and not easy meat for marketing experts to manipulate.*

'I went to buy a handbag/drill bit/pair of medium-size rubber gloves but there was nothing to suit me in the shops,' *is the war cry of smart shoppers.*

Returning empty-handed actually shows that you are fully in control of your money as a shopper rather than frittering ... and you know how we hate fritterers!

You can waste money on cheap things as easily as on designer chic. *Never get into the habit of thinking, 'I'll buy this, even if I don't like it/need it. It's only a few pounds.' If you get on a bus and you can't pay the fare – even if you are one penny short – you don't ride. Do supermarkets let you have things if you don't give them all the money? So that money you wasted would have been handy. Think how much more handy it would be to pay off those credit cards.*

Finally, don't let other people put you off.
Your abstemiousness may make them feel uncomfortable about that little pair of earrings they bought at lunchtime, so they act the agent provacateur, like the person who offers you chocolates when you're dieting. If anyone around you at home or work dares to make any critical comment about you coming back empty-handed but full-pursed, it is none of their darn business. Tell them I say they are sillies.

JANE'S MOST GLEAMING GOLDEN RULE.
Don't go shopping unless you really have to.

The real key to money-saving is to treat shopping as the last resort. The process of saving money begins much earlier.

If you ask these reasonably frequently, it will soon become second nature to stop and think about purchases before spending. I hope I will save you a huge sum, not just in the next month but for ever.

The vital questions to ask before you buy anything

1. Do you need it that much? Doing nothing IS an option! Look deep into my eyes on the front of the book cover. You are getting sleepy. OK, I may not be that boring, but the feeling of wanting something normally goes away in a few hours, days or weeks. After all, you have managed without a flat screen TV for all these years and if you get it now, a newer, better model will come onto the market later. *Remember, you don't have to keep up with the Joneses.*

2. Being too lazy or busy to shop is good. Offer to look after someone's toddler or dog for the day. It is hard to shop with either.

3. Do you have the money in your account? If you don't have the money, don't buy it.

'But Jane, it's a money-saving item!' People forget their budgets if they are told something will save them money, especially if it is a large and exciting purchase. They fast forward in their heads, as if they already have those savings in their wallets. But if you don't have much money at the moment, don't bother to buy anything that takes years to recoup its costs.

For instance, you could spend thousands on a condensing boiler, but it will take years to save that cost in lower energy bills. Less pricey, but more prosaic sums will reap bigger savings benefits. £50 spent on a new insulated jacket for your water tank and another £50 on lagging your pipes will save enough energy to pay you back after around a year. Insulated curtain linings and draught excluders should pay for themselves after two years.

4. Is there a way to fulfil the need without buying something?
Can you make it? If you need to acquire a new skill, enrol at a local adult education class. You will find lists in your library or by typing in your local authority name, or that of the area where you work or go to school or college, into your internet search engine.

Do you have something similar that you can adapt?

Can you borrow it? From friends or from a hire shop?

You have to be very quick to claim anything. **When collecting anything from a stranger, take a friend and tell people where you are going and what time you are due home.**

Can you get it free? *www.freecycle.com* is a free message board on which anyone can offer anything they have, free. Buyer collects. Start by going to the main web page, which is American, then work backwards to the page for your home town, e.g. freecycle-brighton, freecyclehull (visitors need to register before typing in required location.

To stop yourself being overwhelmed with messages, fill in the profile indicating what you are interested in and press 'digest' to get your emails in a batch.

www.freebies.com, *www.freebieholics.co.uk*, and *www.freeukstuff.net*. For many of these freebies you have to fill out a questionnaire. If your friends are happy for you to pass on their details, you can also get freebies from *www.referralfrebies.co.uk*.

Useful websites for those who prefer the zero-cost option

Also check *www.britishfreebies.co.uk*; *www.bigmoneyleague.co.uk*, *www.greasypalm.co.uk*, *www.luckysurf.co.uk*. I particularly like *www.top50freebies.co.uk* which offers cash back from fifty companies and extra freebies like a cinema ticket voucher when you sign up.

Cold drinks cost around £2 when you are out. Carrying bottles of water is becoming a norm. Take a flask or refill a bottle at home with tap water. Asking for tap water in a café or pub is free and I find waitresses understand. A surprising number of shops offer free drinks in hot weather. Large furniture stores, estate agents and car showrooms are all good. The latter are also good for hot coffee, soup and tea. Starbucks offers free muffin tasters.

Rather than buy, can you barter something in exchange? LETS is the national bartering system. Most areas have bartering schemes. You think of a skill you can swop, such as babysitting, plumbing, gardening, anything. A friend of mine makes a wonderful chocolate cake and offers this. This skill is allocated a value in points and in return, you choose a skill valued in points from anyone in the local directory. *www.letslinkuk.net*, 020 7607 7852 for more details.

Can you buy it secondhand or at a cheap auction? Check charity shops; eBay; *www.loot.com*; *www.exchangeandmart.co.uk*; local small auctioneers; car boot sales; garage sales; local papers; or put an ad in your local freesheet newspaper or in a sweet-shop window for about 60p: remarkably effective and under-used.

HELPFUL HINT

When searching for phone numbers, the Phone Directory books are still free. So is *www.192.com*. Or if it's a company, evade the more costly corporate phone numbers that begin 08, by putting its name into a search engine like Google and finding the head office, then phoning in and asking to transfer to the service team.

Auction News is a monthly magazine detailing auctions carried out by Official Receivers and the Police at which you may net anything from a house to a washing machine, for a song. *www.auctionnews.co.uk*, 01332 551300.

Government Auction News is a monthly newsletter devoted to over 100 UK auctions per month including Ministry of Defence vehicles and Customs seizures. *www.ganews.co.uk*

Greasby's of Tooting, 020 8672 2972, sells at around a third of their value, things like pushchairs, musical instruments and camcorders which have been left unclaimed in London Transport's lost property section. *www.greasbys.com*

www.auctionguides.co.uk lists lots of auctions.

HELPFUL HINT You don't have to attend an auction to bid. You can leave a written bid – but phone and get the item immediately or you rack up storage charges. Ask what the auctioneer's rates are. They add a 'buyer's premium' or small percentage to the winning bid which you have to pay on top of the price, so take account of that when deciding how much to bid.

Charity shops often have specialist branches. Oxfam – 0870 333 2700, *www.oxfam.co.uk* - now runs individual shops specialising in books, music, including sheet music, furniture, Fair Trade food and gifts and bridal wear. The British Heart Foundation also has larger stores selling furniture, plus books and music. *www.bhf.org.uk*, 0870 1204141. For a list of second-hand bridalwear shops, see p. 268.

Specialist charity shops

Use your initiative and ask people. I wanted four tables to accommodate people attending day courses at Jane Furnival's School of Life. Cheap shops like Ikea didn't have anything suitable. I saw some in a catalogue, but at nearly £1,000. Eventually I decided to buy cheaper trestle tables. Trestles, new, cost £120. By calling around local catering firms and asking if they had any tables to sell, I bought them at £40 each.

Can you get someone else to buy it for you? Do you have a birthday coming up, or can you feign illness so effectively that someone will buy you something nice to your specification?

Can you get your employer to buy it for you on business expenses? You may be able to make a case for books, magazines or stationery or computer equipment. See my section on tax perks in 'lumps and bumps of life', You can get computers, mobile phones for all the family, bicycles, food and more tax-free.

Can you get it through the State? (I said the State, not the States! Don't venture to America to buy things. The travel costs a fortune and you may have to pay customs duty.) What I mean by the State is:

- If it's a book, DVD or CD, you can order it from your local library. If they can't get it for you, you pay a few pence and they will buy it for you. The advantages of this include not having to pay for expensive shelving at home to store it permanently.

- Many local authorities run toy libraries. Like a book library, but for toys. Aimed at childminders, they are often open to everyone who asks.

- Join a local college of further education, even for an evening class, and you will be able to use, free, their internet and broadband facilities, library and read their newspapers and magazines.

I don't do second-hand. It's dirty

People use this excuse to buy something more expensive and clean in a new carrier bag. Don't make me laugh. Stuff in antique shops, sales, etc. is often lovingly cleaned. If not, all you have to do is polish it.

On the other hand, many well-known and expensive shops lend their stock, including bras and knickers, to fashion models and favoured clients for the evening. I have seen girls receiving bags of stuff, trying things on and concealing the price-tags down their backs as they wear the dresses for the evening, then discarding them on the floor afterwards. The next day, those dresses and underwear are replaced on the shop's rails for customers to buy. I have been offered underwear and shoes to borrow, in department stores, just to make sure that an outfit would 'look right' when I tried it on. *That* is what I call dirty. Especially if the dresses in question are bridal and lent for photographic use and worn by the all-comer for a bit of a laugh.

> 'I bought my fridge-freezer at a local auction house for
> £25. It just needed a clean-up.' *Joan, Oxshott*, one of
> the most elegant and fastidious people I know.

Have you checked your local dump? Things there are not always dirty. Before taking things away, you may have to give the staff a small sum. I gave £3 for a William Morris fabric-covered Chesterfield chair recently.

Gardeners, you can sometimes get free compost at dumps, if you take a bag and cart it away yourself.

Have you looked in skips? Skip-hunting is not what it used to be, but you never know, especially in classier areas. Up-and-coming areas are also good, as are business streets just after office hours. It is against the law to take anything without the owner's consent, of course.

'Been there. Done that. I really do need to buy something'

Can you wait for the sales?
Can you wait till tomorrow? And tomorrow?
Before searching the shops, research.

Look at specialist magazines – free in the library, colleges or clubs – and see what is around.

Look it up on the internet. Check frequently asked questions from users.

Ask friends what they think of different makes.

Scan the papers to see if new technology or rules will affect your purchase. For instance, if you need a car, think about dual fuel cars or which ones evade company tax rules or congestion charges. Likewise with new televisions and radios, there are huge changes afoot to phase out terrestrial channels so don't buy a model that will shortly be obsolete. Appliances like washing machines have to carry EC ratings for their power and water use. Aim for A or green.

For personal expert up-to-date advice on which products to buy, try the Good Housekeeping Institute, 09067 529 070, 9am–5 pm Monday to Friday. Unfortunately this costs 75p per minute but if it saves you hundreds, it is a worthwhile invest-ment. Or try emailing me on *jane@smartspending.co.uk.* I will pass on any advice I have about specific brands. That's free but I can't be responsible for your ultimate choice.

A survey for *Which?* Magazine (2005) threw up the fact that readers felt Bosch and Miele were the most dependable washing machines and Miele also made reliable cylinder vacuum cleaners.

It is always worth phoning a manufacturer's head office and chatting to their marketing people about a large purchase before making it. You may discover find esoteric facts such as the fact that they sell reconditioned machines from the factory at half price.

Try to buy top quality at half the price by finding a company's secret sales shops. Any smart spender can buy last season's half-price furniture, say, in a sale – but seek the shops carrying this season's stuff at half price or less. These are things that good mainstream companies like M&S and Laura Ashley have perhaps over-ordered, or customers have returned. For instance, Trade Secret in Middle Aston and Noke, Oxfordshire, sells furniture from such brands but is not allowed to advertise, so keep it under your hat that I told you! *www.trade-secret.co.uk* Unit 5, Hatch End Industrial Estate, Middle Aston, Oxfordshire, OX25 5QL. 01869 347720 and Lower Farm, Noke, Oxfordshire, OX3 9TX. 01865 378166.

HELPFUL HINT

One company makes many brands. This is particularly true for sofas and kitchen appliances. Some machines are virtually identical, but come with different logos or badges; others are still different designs, but owned by one company. Before buying an appliance it is worth asking a good independent repair man, found through your local newspaper small ads or Yellow Pages, which machines he recommends. He will tell you which machines are made by the same companies and which ones have virtually identical innards. This can save you several hundred pounds.

If you live further North, National Brands Aintree, Britain's largest discount furniture warehouse, stocks even more including conservatory and freestanding kitchen furniture, at a minimum of 50 percent off. Nelson Business Park, Long Lane, Aintree, Liverpool L7 2PD, 0151 521 8907, *www.national-brands.co.uk*.

Southern Domestic Electrical Services, 4–6 Bridge Road, Woolston, Southampton, Hants SO19 7GQ, 0238 032 8428.

Can you buy a cheaper alternative?

You don't need a luxury carpet when you can paint the floor with floor paint and put down a mat. You just need conviction and style. I once knew a couple who kept their food in an old filing cabinet. The 'B' drawer was for bread, 'C' was for cakes and so on.

Buy only by internet.

This has many money-saving advantages. You tend to get discounts. You evade parking charges, petrol, incidentals like ice creams and coffee and save time on going shopping. Check shops' websites for bargain deals that aren't in the shops. *www.allshopsuk.co.uk /shops/offers* has a handy directory of online deals.

Price comparison websites

www.pricerunner.com
www.dealtime.co.uk
www.abcaz.com
www.kelkoo.co.uk
www.thesimplesaver.com
www.abargain.co.uk

www.planetonline.com
www.pricemonkey.co.uk
www.mysimon.com
www.compare andreview.co.uk.

If you intend buying something expensive, you might sign up to *www.greasypalm.co.uk*, a discount website offering cash-back – usually up to five percent – every time you shop online through it, at all sorts of well-known high street and discount eShops. Other benefits include money off coupons and £7 for referring others. I understand that the minimum sum you must earn is £25 before they send it. There is nothing to say that the companies signed up to this are the cheapest, so do your sums rather than be seduced by the thought of money back.

www.couponsrule.com gives you money-off vouchers and other money-saving tips, like the current best buys to earn the maximum loyalty points from stores like Boots.

HELPFUL HINT

Can you download a discount voucher or find a discount code to use before you buy? Try *www.wishvalue.co.uk*, *www.instantcoupounz.com*, *www.couponmountain .co.uk*, *www.offers.co.uk* and *www.freebies .co.uk*

The extra money-saving advantage of buying by internet or by mail over shopping is that if you have not seen and touched an item before buying it, you can claim a refund (not just a credit note) if you then open the box and don't like it – a stronger legal position to be in, than if you merely hated your new shop purchase when you got it home.

HELPFUL HINT

You should return anything within seven days of receiving it to be sure of getting a refund. I always send things by registered post or recorded delivery, in case the company claims they got lost.

All this is great, as long as you don't become a mail-order junkie, buying everything using your credit card.

Beware of buying things from abroad. You may have to pay additional shipping costs and custom charges, and if you want to return something, it becomes costly and time-consuming, with your legal rights being harder to establish and pursue.

www.letsbuyit.com allows buyers to group together to get a bulk discount on electronics. It works on economies of scale; so everyone enjoys a lower price created by bulk-buying.

HELPFUL HINT

If you want to buy something from America, it may be easier to ask a friend out there to buy it for you as a gift. You reciprocate with something from here.

I don't recommend using TV auction or lowest bid channels. If you're feeling tired or weak especially, I think it's too easy to get carried away by the feeling that everyone else is buying an item and so must you. Then you can become a shopping addict.

'I chose my new washing machine on the internet but phoned the shop, Curry's, to order it. I got money off the shop price by not going in to buy it at the shop, as they could deliver directly from the warehouse.'
Jacqueline, Clapham

JANE'S GOLDEN RULE.
Check delivery charges before agreeing to buy. Try to get delivery free, saving typically £30. Companies may appear to offer good deals but the delivery charge makes them more expensive.

Don't assume eBay is the cheapest website

People become very boring about eBay, as if it were an all-purpose solution to every need. If you have weaned yourself off going to the shopping centre, please don't become an eBay addict instead. New things can be just as expensive there as elsewhere. eBay is good if you need something obscure, like a wheelchair, or spare parts for obsolete cars or motorbikes. Regular internet traders may offer better deals, so shop around using price comparison sites like the ones listed above.

JANE'S GOLDEN RULE.
eBay is a collector's paradise, but if you're trying to save money, you shouldn't be a collector.

'The time I looked, the price between a chainsaw on eBay and one from the shop was so close, that by the time I added postage, it was cheaper to go to the shop.'
Andy, Peckham

Getting the best from eBAY

Get up early on Mondays. Few people bid in auctions ending then. Avoid popular times like Sunday nights.

Try to buy from UK-based sellers. It is harder to get satisfaction from traders overseas.

Shop out of season. Buy ski-wear in July when few people want it.

Avoid the words 'as in' in the small print. These mean the item has flaws and you have no right of return.

Don't confuse buying a product with bidding for information about how to buy a product, sometimes called secret sites'. These are famous scams.

Enter every spelling variation you can imagine, including abbreviations and removing spaces between words. Others won't bother.

Get to know the site. The shops page *www.stores.ebay.co.uk* has a directory of specialist microsites which are shop windows with their own unique web addresses within eBay.

Spend some time visiting the various eBay chat-rooms and find out what established users are saying about other buyers and sellers. You can learn a lot just by listening, it may even put you off buying an item altogether.

HELPFUL HINT *www.fatfingers.co.uk* will automatically look up misspelt variations of any keyword and search eBay on your behalf.

'I hear what you say Jane, but I need to choose something personally in a shop'

There's still time not to go shopping. Try mail order catalogues, either the various small specialist traders who advertise in the back of magazines, or the big ones that give you money back on your purchases. The traditional stalwarts of people on tight budgets, don't forget these catalogues also sell things like insurance on instalment plans. Try Littlewoods, *www.littlewoods.co.uk*, 0845 707 8810, and Freemans, *www.freemans.com,* 0870 606 6099. If you are a Freemans 'finest' customer, your commission on catalogue sales starts at 10 percent, with other benefits. Check 'Amber to Platinum' tiers on the website. *www.kaysnet.com,* 0870 1510 541, offers £10 back for every £100 you pay, or £12.50 in goods.

As with internet shopping, don't buy more than you bargained for.

'My sister really irritates me. She doesn't have the ability to colour-match an outfit for herself, so when she buys clothes from a catalogue, she buys exactly what the model is wearing, from hat to shoes. It makes a small purchase into a major expenditure.'

Charlotte, Petersfield

OK. *www.shoppingvillages.com* will give you the latest information on factory shops and other discount centres. But I want you to take someone with you who hates shopping, and can't stand a marathon shopping session, like your grandad. That way your wallet might come out of the experience still alive. Don't fritter while you're there!

'Jane, I need, need, need, need to check colours with my own eyes and try sitting in a sofa before I buy it ...'

How to be a smart shopper

HELPFUL HINT

Consider whether you would be better off buying it in France. DIY items are near enough a third cheaper and getting your car serviced at a franchised garage can save £108 on average, according to a 2005 survey by *Auto Express* magazine. A day return to Calais is as little as £9. For more information, check *www.day-trip-per.net*.

Try it out first. Can you borrow your intended purchase? Before buying a particular garden shredder, I hired it and saved over £100 by finding out that it wasn't up to the tasks I had in mind.

Allow yourself enough time to choose. Have a good idea of what you want before you leave the house. If you get panicky, you end up throwing money at the problem.

Don't take children. They distract you. You have to buy them stuff.

Don't buy things when visiting people or on holiday. Research shows that you buy more when your mental brakes are off in unfamiliar territory. Bright orange kaftans, giant donkeys and shell-covered mirrors look great in the sunshine when you are in a fun mood, but soon end up in a cupboard. 'Tripperish' is a wonderful dismissive word. Someone used it, rightly, to describe a light in a conch shell which I brought back from some outing, as a student. I was crushed. I still have the shell, in the garden. Waste not, want not.

Visualise. Take measurements with you. Don't join the clowns who turn up at the shop and buy a TV the size of a tractor, without checking where it will go in the room, or thinking how it will overwhelm everything else in it, including themselves. Taking measurements stops you from buying ready-made curtains, trousers, or even a plug in the wrong size.

If you are searching for something to match an existing item, like a hat for a suit or cushions for a sofa, take a colour swatch, even a near-match colour torn from a magazine picture or anything, or the item itself if possible.

Don't expect the salesperson to tell you the whole story.

> **JANE'S GOLDEN RULE.** *The more expensive your proposed purchase, the less the salesperson wants to discuss it. They often expect – or hope – that you know little or nothing, but just want to admire the most superficial details.*

When I bought my car, I chose it because it is considered one of the safest and least likely to break down. The salesman was surprised that I was not interested in its colour. This was something

I had no choice about anyway, as it was secondhand!

Buy the best quality for your purpose. If you buy cheap, you buy twice.

Buy to last. I have in the past lived for years with tables made from packing cases and cardboard removal firms' wardrobes, until I could afford the one lovely antique item. You can always re-sell a good quality item if you need some cash.

Don't let your heart rule your head. Huge white sofas look beautiful in showrooms, but at home, they don't mix with toddlers and Marmite sandwiches. How many times, as a teenager, did I go out looking for a sensible skirt and come back with a party dress?

Don't shop when you are hungry or tired. A survey by Somerfield supermarkets concluded when we are hungry, we spend up to 20 percent more. We buy sausage rolls, pork pies, crisps and sweets to eat while walking up and down the aisles and on our way home.

Buy nothing except what you need now. Don't collect other purchases which might come in handy at some mythical future point.

Don't rush to get everything you will ever need for a new house. There are sob-stories about people buying whole rooms of furniture for new homes – only to find the house chain collapses. You don't need to furnish your home in five weeks. One good item in a room, with some obvious makeshift bits and pieces, says more about your taste than fifty cheaper ones.

> **JANE'S GOLDEN RULE.** *If you fail to buy something big from a salesman, he will come back later with a better discount.*

Don't buy anything in a fashion colour if you want it to last years, like a fridge or a business suit. Why do Labour politicians insist on wearing white shirts? Because they want to spend many years in office! Classic styles are never wrong.

Avoid complicated items with too many features. Does it do the thing you need it to do? If in doubt, you will have to wade through some impenetrable instruction manual and probably give up.

Is it meant to change the way you live or go about things? Because it won't after the first fortnight. How many keep-fit devices or kitchen appliances have you got stuffed in a cupboard? I can think of a cream-making machine which I once thought would provide endless cheap cream from butter and milk. One go, and it was discarded.

Will it need love and attention which, after a time, you won't want to give because you are the kind of person who likes new things all the time? Be honest. I once read a sad email ad from a woman who wanted to give away the family's giant pet rabbit because a new puppy had taken his place. The rabbit, once allowed to roam as a house-pet, was now stuffed in a cage.

Consider the on-costs

Does it need dry cleaning?

Is it fur, and will it mat or go peculiar after a time?

Does it need special cleaning or resurfacing, like a waxed jacket?

Will it require accessories, updates or add-ons?

Will there be heavy repair costs?

Will it be obsolete soon and can you live with having to restock with new-sized disks or whatever when the next model comes along?

Is it made a long way away, or by a small factory, and therefore spare parts will take a long time to arrive?

Encouraging you to change from one perfectly good product to another is called 'churning' in financial sales circles. Beware being sold a new extra-deep mattress, or an antique French bed. As you can guess, I speak from bitter experience. Both items will probably require extra-deep sheets or specially made bedding, forcing you to discard perfectly good linen. The salesman will not tell you that though.

Now *really* consider the on-costs.

Things are always more expensive than you think

For example, you buy a garden table and chairs. Shops, magazine articles and social pressure (everyone else has it') tell you that you now 'need' the following:

Cushion pads – at over ten pounds each, these have become a fashion accessory you 'should' change each year.

A large plastic box to keep the cushion pads in, when not in use.

A tablecloth.

Decorative weights to keep the tablecloth from blowing off in the wind.

Mosquito-repellent candles.
A wasp-catching device.

A cover to protect it from the weather.

An umbrella to shelter you from the sun.

The 'lazy Susan' circular server you slot over the umbrella hole so guests can turn the salt round to them without anyone passing it.

A heater to keep guests warm at night when sitting round it. Why stop at one heater?

The matching ice-box – a glorified vacuum picnic box at £800.

Jingly bells to hang nearby to drive the neighbours and local cats to distraction.

Then there's wood treatment to keep it all from rotting each year ...

Think laterally. You can make tables from circular wooden cable drums you can beg from the dump or from industrial sites, or from packing cases. I once saw an excellent built-in garden table and chairs which its owner had made of concrete with broken bits of china – everyday family breakages – embedded smoothly in like a mosaic.

... or do without. At Glyndebourne Opera in Sussex, everyone sits on the grass, including duchesses in their family tiaras, and *that* is considered the epitome of chic.

My husband insists that I add the following confession here. Boo, my Bouvier des Flandres puppy – a combined birthday and wedding anniversary gift from him to me – has cost a considerable unlooked-for sum in on-costs, mainly because he has chewed up three crash helmets, most of our best shoes, hats, any number of soft toys, books and puzzles, four watering cans, many plants, all my make-up case and other things that puppy love has blotted from my memory.

On the subject of on-costs, there's a trick of the trade to watch out for. Price gouging is when you are offered something at a bargain price – but once you have it, you have to pay nearly as much for repeat purchases like batteries to make it work. There are mutterings about iPod batteries among my teenagers at home, but from my own experience, computer printers are an example. Some cartridges cost £16 and contain just an ounce of ink. The latest ruse is putting all colours into one cartridge, to be replaced even more expensively when only one colour has run out. You can refill a cartridge up to12 times per colour for the cost of a new cartridge. Ink refills cost under £1 with free delivery from *www.cartridge-monkey.com*, 0870 240 5518.

Finally, will the item you intend to buy have any value to sell on, when you no longer need it? This is particularly important with things like cars but also, when house-hunting, I have seen rooms ruined by expensive fitted wardrobes which made the place look too small.

Try to buy only from shops with a relaxed exchange policy that returns your cash. Oh, the dog-eared tokens I have carried around in my handbag till they fell apart, given in exchange for something I have taken back! Thanks, Argos.

But shops are not legally obliged to give you a refund just because you didn't like your buys when you got home. You saw them and touched them; if you're lucky, they will give you a credit note or the dreaded tokens.

If something is faulty, that's different. Within a reasonably short time of buying it, you are entitled to a refund or exchange, and don't have to accept a repair. In fact, don't accept a repair because when, inevitably, it goes wrong a second time, you are stuck in a circle and the shop does not have to offer you a new item. Ask for a replacement or say, 'After this, I have lost faith in this make of steam iron: can I have a different one please?'

Think you will fall foul of temptation to spend too much if you go into a shop? Here's a swanky way to shop. Large department stores employ personal shoppers to guide confused people. They tell me that they will select anything for you, down to one egg cup. Call and make an appointment, telling them what you want to buy and your budget. Arrive and swan off to their personal shopping suites, where you normally find free drinks, including wine, while the shopper brings you what you want. Pay, looking neither left nor right at other things, and exit swiftly as if pursued by a bear.

Cheap tricks to save yourself money

Take your own carrier bags with you and insist the shops put things in them. This is reverse psychology in action. That expensive face-cream just does not seem worth buying when carried in a much-used supermarket plastic carrier, does it?!

Don't buy basics that are packaged in gimmicky ways. You pay more for the drink with the funny nozzle or the pump toothpaste, so stick to a bottle and a tube.

When buying major things, don't pay upfront if you don't need to. Put down a deposit if you have to. If you have second thoughts, it's easier to backtrack than to reclaim cash – and it encourages the shopkeeper to come up with the order too.

Be suspicious of bargains that are too good to be true. They are and there is a reason. In late summer, it may be because the item is about to be withdrawn from sale in time for a newer improved Christmas model.

FUNNY MONEY. *I overheard a couple in T.K. Maxx asking the manager for a further reduction on some outfit in the sale 'because it's really very naff'. (They didn't get the discount.)*

Getting a discount on anything

Elton John may be famous for his high spending habits, but Geri Halliwell, the former Spice girl, once confessed to a newspaper that she loves asking for discounts as her father was a car dealer, adding that the worst that can happen is that the shop says no. A splendid attitude. Lots of well-off people do this, even in the smartest shops. One personal shopper told me that she is embarrassed and hides behind coat racks while her millionaire client negotiates discounts.

Be friendly when asking for a discount. Look a salesperson in the eye and strike up a relationship.

Ask for money off in return for paying cash. Find the manager, not the Saturday assistant, or any assistant with a bitter and mean mouth (you'll recognise what I mean). Speak quietly as they won't want other customers to hear. You need not carry the cash around with you there and then, but showing a few notes tends to have a magical relaxing effect on shop managers.

JANE'S GOLDEN RULE. *Don't feel second best or that the shop is doing you a favour. On the contrary, you should be treated like royalty. The shop makes a sale, so meets its sales targets – usually unrealistic sums dreamed up by head office honchos. And it saves the savage cost of processing credit cards or cheques, without waiting for the money to clear into their account*

Suggest a reason for the discount. Are you buying lots of things? An unpopular colour, which would be left on the shelf? Can you take your purchase away there and then? We bought a cheap but large trailer for this purpose, but my husband has also been known to use a wheelbarrow to take things away from shops. Offer to buy a damaged or torn item, for a larger discount. You have to build up the inconvenience to you and the impossibility that it will ever be quite perfect. Are you a regular shopper? Thanks to my local Budgen who once asked, 'would you mind accepting a 15 percent discount because you shop here a lot?' Would I mind?!

Shop near closing time or during inclement weather. If it is very hot, or there is a storm, they will have had a bad trading day and are more amenable to negotiating.

Don't look well-off. A great antique-dealer's trick, this. A friend of mine had a job designing holiday apartments for Arab princes. Most of her time, she had to source identical bedrooms in different colours for their various wives, but she once decided to refurbish a bathroom in the plushest style. She was in a shop looking at solid gold bath taps and had forgotten her rather shabby attire, when the assistant conducted her away, saying, 'Madam could *never* afford those prices: here are the cheaper ones.' He made the mistake of judging by appearances. The irony is that she was trying to spend as lavishly as possible rather than save.

Make a proposal. 'I don't want to pay *that* for a sofa,' said one smart shopper at a large warehouse-style furniture shop. 'I want to pay *this*.' They accepted his offer. But he was a literary agent, used to brokering multi-thousand pound deals, so perhaps he exuded an air of authority.

Shop with an OAP. They sometimes get a sympathy vote but can be wily or winning when it comes to asking for money off. Incentivise them by offering to split the discount you get as a result of their fronting the deal. Among shops which give over-60s a discount are Wyevale Garden Centres, 0800 413 213, *www.wyevale.co.uk* and Focus DIY centres, 01270 501555, *www.focusdiy.co.uk*.

It's always worthwhile to make a complaint, as long as you don't make it fruitlessly.

Know your cut-off limits. Have in your head an idea of how much your time is worth.

Effective complaining

Don't waste money-making hours and your phone bill hanging on, particularly if you are self-employed.

Alternatively, keep a notebook and pencil by the phone to record all the times and dates you called; who you spoke to and what they said. This kind of detail is invaluable when complaining, especially if you have to take the company to court.

Know what you want before you begin: a refund, credit note, extra money? If you are fed up with call centres, obtain the headquarters phone number of the company and ask to speak to the Managing Director's personal assistant. They normally get things done.

If you have reached an impasse, consult your local Trading Standards Officer, available through your local authority, free. I have always found them jolly helpful.

Goods bought from a shop must be fit for the purpose for which they were bought, match any description that is given and be of satisfactory quality

If you are getting nowhere with a company's call centre, a new service called Registered Call records conversations (10p a minute) to help you to claim compensation for shabby treatment. You sign up for the service and dial a special number before phoning the call centre. Recordings can be heard later by phone, over the Internet, or emailed to company complaints departments. One man received £150 compensation after Lloyds TSB's insurance call centre apparently tried to wriggle out of covering him for a skiing trip as he is in a wheelchair. 0871 550 2929, *www.registered call.com.*

When complaining, I have found it worth quoting The Sale of Goods Act 1979/1994, Trades Description Act 1968 and Consumer Credit Act 1974, a recital which seems to unnerve shop staff. I can't imagine why. For more details on these, visit *www.dti.gov.uk* or ask the Citizens Advice Bureau.

Trade Associations usually act, in the last resort, for their members who pay them rather than you. Even if they say they have complaints procedures, don't expect much and you will be pleased if you get more.

If you want to complain about services like the phones – and who doesn't? – look up the ombudsman for your particular service at your library, in the phone book or on the web. They are slow but free. Don't involve a lawyer before dealing with them or you will have spent money and the ombudsman may say they can't deal with your case.

www.bbc.co.uk has useful information including, in the Watchdog section, how to complain and letters to download and personalise.

www.howtocomplain.com is a free, independent site which claims that over 76 percent of complaints made through it have been resolved, mainly in the consumer's favour.

www.financevictims.co.uk offers help on complaining about financial institutions. Also try the Financial Services Authority, *www.fsa.gov.uk*, 0845 606 1234.

Before buying legal advice, check your home insurance policy and your union, which often have advice lines free.

For consumer advice, I recommend the **Which?** Legal Service, *www.which.net*, 0845 307 4000 or 01992 822800, £12.75 for three months' membership, with £3 off for **Which?** Magazine subscribers, or check for special offers.

Citizens Advice Bureaux, *www.adviceguide.org.uk*, have leaflets on consumer rights and may offer specific help. The Office of Fair Trading, *www.oft.gov.uk*, 08457 22 44 99, also offers leaflets on consumer rights. I have found them unwilling to offer specific advice and get the impression that they tend to concentrate on the larger legal issues of trading in Britain.

www.haveyoursay.com is a shining example of direct action. Its founder had problems with his Land Rover and was unimpressed with the way they were handled. He began a 'blog', a kind of web diary, of complaints which turned into a consumer discussion site so influential that Land Rover ended up asking him to take a new car, as long as he would remove the site. The site remains and is worth looking at for those who would follow suit

Blogging – the up-and-coming consumer power tool

12. Smart Spending on Food

To save money this month, I want you to use up the food you already have at home, rather than shopping for more food. *All of it.*

> **JANE'S GOLDEN RULE.** *You can tell an expensive food shop without going in. Check for a stripped wooden floor.*

Is this you? I have found that the worst overspenders tended to have two freezers full of food, even if they were a household of two. They still went shopping every week in supermarkets, which they treated as a social jaunt. They also had extras like meat delivered. Another characteristic that overspenders share is a high use of takeaways and ready-prepared food. Often, they have given up the effort (or pleasure) of cooking proper food, or as one girl put her addiction to microwave meals, 'I only cook it if it pings'. Once they rediscovered the joys of food, they saved loads.

An easy way to save? Stop eating out for the month and *take away the takeaways*. You can feed a family for a week for the cost of one moderately-priced restaurant bill.

Try not to overstock with food as if your life depended on it. Even on Christmas Day, shops still sell food.

If you have a freezer the size of a stretch limo, sell it. It takes money to run, you tie up cash stocking it up – and unless you live deep in the country, it is healthier to buy fresh food more often. Since I moved into our new house last year, I have fed a family of five using a tabletop freezer inherited from my mother. It has not affected the quality of our life one jot.

If children complain that their favourite things aren't always available under your new smart spending regime, point out that you are not a short-order chef running a restaurant for them.

Give them responsibility. Ask what they would do in your position. Which they would rather have? Luxury ice cream all year at £3.59 a tub or a nice toy at Christmas for £186.68, the cost of the ice cream? But not both. You could use beads or tokens, or even pictures cut out from magazines, to get them to understand that there is only one pot of money to be spent. They can still have a cheaper ice cream, but it is not their birthright to have Ben and Jerry's, delicious though it is – or anything else – on tap.

HELPFUL HINT

Keep fruit and veg fresher for longer by storing in Stayfresh bags, (£3.25 for 20, *www.lakeland.co.uk*, 015394 88100)

If they give you smart answers, repeat this technique until it begins to sink in. And it will, if they see you practising what you preach.

Buy the food you really eat, and eat what you buy

Sixty-one per cent of households confessed to throwing away a soggy lettuce each week because they thought they would eat more salad than they do.
(Source: Prudential survey, April 2004)

If you throw stuff away, take the hint and don't buy any more of the same.

Have a freezer audit. Go down to the bottom and use what is lurking there. Take the opportunity to defrost your freezer. It will save electricity if it doesn't have more icicles growing in it than Santa's grotto at Harrods.

Make food shopping into a game. Challenge yourself, or who-ever is food shopping for you, to buy an entire week's groceries only buying special offers or marked-down things. It is strangely satisfying to succeed. Or make shopping into an inter-family contest each week: who can buy the same basics and come home with the lowest bill? Display each person's bill on the family notice board or fridge.

Don't be a supermarket snob. It's a bit Hyacinth Bouquet to care where you buy your things, and in my price comparisons, the most prestigious stores averaged 50p extra per pack on basic things like cat food, compared to more down-market stores.

> *'But I'm a Waitrose kind of person.'*
> *'I shop at Sainsbury's to impress my friends.'*
> *'I don't want my friends to see me shopping for meat at this cheap market.'*

The above are all comments I have heard from various silly spenders whose money I have tried to save.

Shall we grow up here? No one who is worth impressing gives a brass farthing about where you buy your food. These are not prestigious restaurants. They are warehouses full of goods to sell.

I am not against shopping at supermarkets. There is a current idea that we should shop at old-fashioned little shops which are portrayed as beacons of perfection with fresh produce and helpful assistants. Well, I recall the time before big supermarkets when the local little food shops were far from helpful and stocked mainly suet and gravy powder, plus battered old tins and bruised peaches.

Supermarkets have some unpleasant habits, as I hear from small suppliers, but they have transformed our eating habits and the quality of the food and service we expect, and we would be silly to forget it. You can get bargains from them. But they are too successful at selling. You always pick up more than you intended. If you are trying to economise, use sparingly or avoid a weekly 'big shop'.

Iceland is cheap for non-freezer food cupboard standards, so don't ignore.

Smaller supermarkets often try harder on prices and special offers.

The Co-op is both cheap and keen on ethical policies towards food and suppliers.

Shops like Aldi and Netto don't have familiar British food brands, but their own – and they are wonderfully cheap. Take cash because some don't take credit cards, and your own carrier bags – they charge for these.

www.fixtureferret.co.uk is a brilliant site with all the latest cut-price supermarket offers and two-for-one offers. You can sign up listing the products you are most interested in buying cheaply – in our case, Ben and Jerry's ice cream – and it emails you when it has a good offer to let you know about, and even which freebies are around.

Small and local shopping

Small local shops have to be competitively priced compared to supermarkets or they would be blasted off the high street. My local butcher and greengrocer are about a third cheaper than supermarket prices and bring in fresh produce daily. My greengrocer buys B-grade produce which may not be the identikit size and shape the supermarkets demand, but children delight in finding bird-shaped potatoes and carrots that resemble a little man.

Stock up with things like jam at events like local fetes, the Women's Institute sale or horticultural shows. You are benefiting the local economy.

HELPFUL HINT **When shopping at a market, never stop at the first stall offering a bargain price. You will find the ones in the middle offer the best value because they occupy a less convenient space and have to compete.**

Ethnic food shops are wildly cheaper – buy nuts, noodles, rice and spices. Have a wander round local ethnic areas.

Old-fashioned gorblimey open-air markets tend to be cheapest of all.

You can order basics like flour by the small sack from health shops. I find a sack enables me to feed my five-person family for months.

Don't forget 'pound shops' in less-grand neighbourhoods. They sometimes operate on what is called the grey market, snapping up bargains left in foreign docks because someone can't pay the duty for instance. Usually, food, soap powder and kitchen rolls are sold three for £1, but you must take cash.

Check local specialist shops near supermarkets. If a supermarket is offering three cat food boxes for the price of two, the local pet shop will probably come up with a better offer, and may deliver it free.

Buy eggs and veg from local farmers' markets if you can. My local one sells free-range eggs at 40p a dozen cheaper than the supermarket. But don't be romantic about these farmers' markets. They are sometimes not cheap and I have known them boast about selling on inferior quality produce rejected by stores, which people assume is organic and pay through the nose for.

If you have many mouths to feed and want to buy in bulk, investigate joining a wholesale club like Makro *www.makro.co.uk* or Costco, *www.costco.co.uk*, 01923 213113. Both require that you are a bonafide business owner or equal partner to apply for membership. I know a woman who got her membership by claiming to be her friend's lesbian partner! Don't go to warehouse clubs if you don't need to. That is falling into the discount diva trap, over-shopping, tying up cash on bulk buying which you don't need to do, when you could use that to pay your bills.

If you are giving a party, try your nearest wholesale fruit and veg and meat market, which normally sells larger quantities for cash. You have to get up early!

For large amounts of meat, try a catering butcher – get your nearest from Yellow Pages.

Some people like boxed fruit and vegetable delivery schemes from local farms. These provide fresh seasonal produce. But they're not cheaper, in my experience. The only saving advantage is that you don't go down to the shops where you are tempted to buy more than you need.

Pick your own food. This is much cheaper, with added attractions like tractor rides to keep children happy. Plan what you are going to do with all those sweetcorn in advance, though. For your nearest pick your own farm, farm shop or home delivery scheme from farms, check *www.farmshopping.com*, 0845 45 88 420.

Save jars and bottles to make your own jams and preserved vegetables. Get a book from the library or try *The Basic Basics: Jams, Preserves and Chutneys* by Marguerite Patten, £6.39 from Grub St Publishing.

You can get bargains at supermarkets and I don't diss them. Follow my insider secrets for saving money here.

How to save money on a big supermarket shop

One of my clients used her supermarket shop on Fridays as the highlight of the week. She would have a coffee after shopping and treated the whole thing as a social activity in itself. Supermarkets love this. That is why they often place their cafes at the end of the shop, when you're hungriest and buy more food.

It is natural to want to reward yourself for spending what I see as 'downtime' – when you're out of serious action – in a supermarket by adding a few extra treats; but an electric toothbrush, a DVD, some coloured candles and a potpourri can soon add £50 to your bill.

If you have to shop at supermarkets, **avoid the smaller convenience branches** – often labelled things like Metro or Express – which can charge higher prices.

Shop at supermarkets in cheaper areas. Supermarket prices tend not to be fixed across the country. They can vary according to local conditions.

Take your loyalty card. The average family saves over £26 a year on food using it.

Buy food from the back of the shelf. It has the longer sell-by dates so you won't have to throw away anything uneaten by tonight.

Don't buy pre-packed fruit and vegetables. Put things in a bag yourself. You will save considerable sums.

Look high and low on the shelves. I don't mean make a long search! The items in the middle of the shelves, at eye-height, are the supermarket's most profitable. Cheaper things are placed on the top and bottom shelves.

Never pick things up from the ends of the aisle. They are put there to tempt you. A lot of expensive research goes into finding new things you might pick up, as this is a real profit hotspot.

Don't shop when you are hungry or tired. As I said before, you will increase your spend by up to 20 percent on average and all you will get is fatter.

HELPFUL HINT

If you must have a snack, don't buy nuts from the snack counter, but the cake-making section where they are unsalted and tend to be cheaper.

Hungry? Don't sit in the café. You know the food is the same stuff you are buying, but with a massive mark-up. Instead, go to the deli counter and ask for a free sample of cheese to keep your taste buds quiet, or graze on an item from your trolley (that's supermarket speak for eating it!). This is technically illegal so make sure at the checkout to show the empty wrapper and pay for it, saying 'I suffer from sugar imbalance and needed something to eat quickly or I would have collapsed.'

Don't buy ready-to-cook meals. My tests found that they can be up to eight times more expensive and you get less in the packet than the raw ingredients bought from the same store. Raw ingredients are just as easy to cook – steak, jacket potato, boiled broccoli, or omelettes take a few minutes. No one needs to buy ready-cooked pasta.

Try not to buy ready-prepared anything. Business schools will teach marketing pupils the lesson of the 80p grated cheese packet. They are selling you perhaps two minutes of your own time at a massive mark-up. What would you do that's so valuable with that time? Watch TV? Is it worth it?

Don't assume anything on a shelf or dump bin that looks a bit tatty, is actually a bargain. It might just be put there to LOOK like a bargain but at the normal price, in order to shift annoyingly lingering stock.

Don't buy three for the price of two offers unless you wanted the thing to begin with. They will clutter your kitchen, you will eat them, need big costly American fridges to accommodate them, and get fatter.

Don't assume that larger boxes are best value. I once heard a soap powder executive boasting that this isn't the case. It isn't the case with my pets' favourite cat food either. Check the small print on the edge-of-shelf labels to see the price per item/weight and compare this price with a different size box to check it really is good value for money.

Shop later in the day, when prices are marked down.

Supermarket delivery services are convenient if you get special offers which waive the £5-ish delivery charge. You can always share the charge by combining a shop with a neighbour or two, though all food will be dropped off at one address of course.

> **JANE'S GOLDEN RULE.** *Talking of coloured and/or scented candles, which I was earlier, you can save loads of money painlessly by ignoring these (not least because they stain your table linen too). Instead buy cheap plain white household candles and sprinkle aromatic oil on your lightbulbs or paper napkins or base of glasses to scent the room instead. Also buy plain and basic paper napkins and towels instead of expensive coloured ones, and decorate your table in more interesting ways with flowers I use ivy entwined around glass stems in the winter, for instance. This is free.*

If you find a special offer has run out, ask for a 'rain check' voucher entitling you to the same offer, even after it has expired in the shop. Tesco offers this. 'I used to work in a Spar shop and we did this, but if you gave out too many, you got fired,' a checkout assistant told me.

You have favourite food, but don't assume that all the variant flavours cost pretty much the same. In my local supermarket, identical sized packets of Ryvita Original cost 42p, but Dark Rye is 54p and Sesame, 78p.

Knowing prices of basics like milk and bread does help you to think quickly in shops when comparing prices. To help you compare accurately, supermarket websites supply prices per kilo which you can use to check up, even if you don't order home delivery. Particularly useful when buying meat.

Buy turkey instead of chicken. It's cheaper.

Buy chicken pieces with the skins on and remove these yourself. They are about half the price of skinned chicken pieces.

You get about three slices more bread for your money by buying medium-sliced rather than thick-sliced loaves.

HELPFUL HINT

If the item has one of the supermarket's own screaming orange 'reduced' stickers on it, and it was a two for the price of one offer before they stuck the sticker on, ask for both reductions. I have done this successfully.

Buy dried pasta rather than fresh. You can save over £1 per pack and the dried stuff serves more. Some top chefs say that they prefer dried anyway.

Chop everything finely, the Chinese way, when you cook. Vegetables and meat go so much further and you use less.

Make friends with local supermarket staff. They may pass on their staff discount. It has happened to me.

Money isn't everything when buying food. Stick to your principles and pay more for ethically-farmed food.

Organic food is more expensive. Is it worth it? You have to make your mind up. Farmers I have talked to mutter grimly that chemicals like sulphur used on organic crops can be more harmful than synthetic, non-organic chemicals.

As I have already said, you can pick up nibbles at deli counters. You can also sample wine, free, at Majestic wine warehouses *www.majestic.co.uk*, 01923 298 200.

You can find that day's leftover food – things like lettuce still in its plastic bags – thrown into bins outside some supermarkets and also dumped by market traders at the end of the day. I have seen groups of people known as 'freegans' waiting outside supermarkets and taking these with great delight.

More than two-thirds of homes buy bagged salad at well over £1 a time, rather than buying the ingredients for a fraction of this, cutting them up and putting them in a bowl. Yet factory-washed salad is dipped in chlorine, said to destroy some of the nutrients.

Last year, I reclaimed a small area of our garden for growing vegetables and although a rank amateur, this summer I did not buy vegetables for my family of five for two months, relying on my new harvest. According to a recent survey by BBC *Gardener's World* magazine, people who grow vegetables at home save up to £10 a month, especially growing them from seed. This is easy in a heated propagator – the cheapest I found was at B&Q for £12.99. I have also grown tomatoes from seed in the plastic boxes which grapes and tomatoes are sold in.

Think ahead when sowing crops and don't sow all your seeds at once or you have a glut of the same thing. Go for cut-and-come-again vegetables. Chard is one of my favourite crops. A cross between salad leaves and spinach, it tastes great raw and also steamed, and you can keep picking the leaves each day, and new ones grow all the time for months.

I can't say that growing fruit and vegetables is entirely free. You have to factor in the cost of seed and feed, plus your time. You can spend a fortune on gardening equipment, too. Try to borrow or swap as much as you can and get friendly with the local park staff, who will give you booty like bulbs they don't want for next year.

The money-saving plus of growing and making your own food is that these make excellent gifts for friends, who are delighted with your home-grown garlic or onions, at the fraction of the cost of a shop-bought house plant or bunch of flowers.

Even if you don't want a full-scale vegetable farm in your garden, grow seeds on your windowsill. Organic suppliers Jekka's Herb Farm sells ready-mixed salad seeds you just stick in a pot, water and wait to grow in four styles including Tuscan and Provencal, at £1.40 per collection. 01454 418 878, *www.jekkasherbfarm.com*.

Free gardening masterclasses

If you want to learn the skills, volunteer to help at any of the following:

Any one of the four Royal Horticultural Society's gardens: Wisley in Surrey; Harlow Carr in North Yorks; Hyde Hall in Essex; or Rosemoor in Devon. For more details call Elysa Rule: 020 7821 3120.

Any of the 200 National Trust gardens. Call the National Trust's Community Learning/Volunteering Advice Line on 0870 609 5383 or email them on *volunteers@nationaltrust.org.uk*.

HDRA, the organic gardening charity, has lots of sites and opportunities for gardener volunteers plus mentors to help support potential organic fruit and veg growers. Mentors get free training courses at HDRA's Coventry HQ plus newsletters, handbooks and seeds. For information, email Joanna Lewis on jlewis@hdra.org.uk

Cheap seeds. Harvest your own from flowers, usually by drying the heads in the airing cupboard and shaking into a plastic bag. Seed exchanging is the free way to get new plants. Search under 'seed exchange' for groups. Try *groups.yahoo.com/group/seedexchange*

I recommend Alan Romans, *www.alanromans.com*, 01337 831 060, whose packets cost from 50p, free p&p for orders over £5.

Join your local allotment society even if you don't have an allotment. This will enable you to purchase basics like fish blood and bone meal much cheaper than at a garden centre. The National Society of Allotment and Leisure Gardeners is on 01536 266 576, *www.nsalg.org.uk*. The National Vegetable Society is another useful mine of free advice and special offers for vegetable gardeners. *www.nvsuk.org.uk*, 0161 442 7190.

Join a local gardening club or horticultural society for free plants, swaps and equipment sharing. Your library lists these or try the Royal Horticultural Society – David Osbourne at the RHS can give you details of 3,000 affiliated clubs. 020 7834 4333 and membership on 020 7821 3000.

Do your research before buying fruit trees. The old adage, 'Plant pears for heirs' should tell you that they take a long time to bear fruit. Choose modern, fast-fruiting varieties and 'self-fertilising' trees rather than those that need a companion tree before they can bear fruit. Check the number on the label carefully in order to find the size of the 'grown-up' tree. This can be complicated. Seek advice.

HELPFUL HINT Local nurseries which grow their own plants tend to be cheaper than slicker garden centres.

You can find information about food growing wild or in the garden which you can eat – not just mushrooms – from Richard Mabey's classic *Food For Free*, published by Collins, in a pocket-size edition useful for outdoor forages. The cheapest I have found is £3.49 from *www.tesco.com* or order it free from the library.

Foraging and picking food can be a fun family activity. At the time of writing, we are drinking our way through elegant and delicious non-alcoholic elderflower champagne, made in a few moments from flowers outside the kitchen door, and I have also frozen enough elderflower cordial to last until autumn. For the price of a few bags of sugar and some lemons, we save £2.84 a week on soft drinks. I am about to pick rosehips and elderberries to give us an autumn soft drink for free. I am adding a few recipes to inspire you.

HELPFUL HINT

Floating slices of fruit in a jug of water in the fridge gives you flavoured chilled water at a fraction of the cost of shop-bought drinks.

Elderflower champagne

Assemble around six clean plastic screw-top bottles depending on size. Stir 1.5 lb of sugar into a gallon (eight pints, four litres) of cold water. Add two tablespoons (30ml) of white wine vinegar, the thinly pared rind and juice of a large lemon and ten to twelve elderflower heads, snipped fresh as described above. Cover and put in the fridge for 24 hours, stirring when you feel in the mood. Strain through clean boiled muslin or even a fine mesh tea-strainer into the bottles, squeezing the flowers to get their essence out. Pour into the bottles, leaving a gap of several inches at the top for the air to expand, otherwise they will explode. Stand for two to three weeks in a cool place and drink at once or it goes a bit tangy.

Elderflower cocktail

This is an old country drink. Use this as a squash, diluted with water or tonic, or pour it over fruit salads, plain yoghurt or ice cream to flavour. Start looking out for elderflowers in late May. Not near roads where they will be polluted. Wait until the flowers have just opened don't use flowers that are past it and about to drop. Gather them on a dry morning when their perfume is most intense.

Have five sliced lemons to hand and loads of old bottles or containers, glass or plastic. Boil two pints of water in a pan. Pour a bag of sugar into it (1kg/2lb). Leave it to dissolve and turn the hob off to save fuel. Now snip your elderflower heads off the bush so that you use them when they are really fresh. Use between 20 and 30, the more the merrier. Rescue any insects, then holding the flowers over the pan, snip them off from the stems. I use embroidery scissors for this as you can get between the little stems. The stems and leaves are bitter and poisonous so don't get them in the water – I have to add this warning, though I have never heard of anyone dying from elderflower poisoning.

Add the lemons and taste. If you want a very lemony drink, add a 1.5 oz small packet of citric acid, about 70p from chemists. Cover the pan or bowl and leave in the fridge for five days, stirring when you remember to. Strain through clean boiled muslin (from kitchen shops or £2.95 a metre from fabric shops) into sterilised bottles (very hot from a dishwasher usually does the trick). Keeps up to a year in the fridge. Or freeze.

Fans of the TV series *Smart Spenders* still tell me how amused they were at the delightful family who owned an orchard but bought apples from Asda as they felt they were cleaner. I helped them make better use of their apples using a wonderful juicer by Vigo, *www.vigoltd.com*, 01404 890262. This is expensive, but I have convinced a well-off friend to buy one, which I share, on the understanding that I will juice their apples too. I don't think I have tasted anything so delicious as juice that has just been made, and it can also be frozen in waxed juice cartons which you have saved from shop-bought juice.

Making your own apple juice

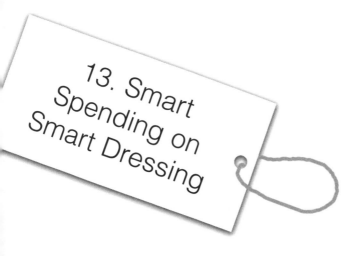

13. Smart Spending on Smart Dressing

Each home spends an average of £22.30 per week on clothes and shoes: £3.50 in supermarket chains, £6.70 in chainstores and £12.10 in other stores.

Take a silly spender, and you will find they have several wardrobes (never one) bursting with clothes. Clothes tend to 'creep' out of the bedroom until they take up the spare room wardrobe and even the garages of some people's homes.

> **JANE'S GOLDEN RULE.** *If you feel like buying new clothes or shoes, search the back of your wardrobe or shoe store first. You will find a forgotten similar dress or pair of shoes to the new ones you fancied.*

Leaving the price tags on clothes they buy is also the mark of a silly spender – or a person with a serious spending problem who is not interested in wearing the things, just the process of buying them. Do they do it because they plan to wear the outfits then return them to the shop? (Illegal and immoral. Assistants check the back of the neck and the cuffs for giveaway perspiration marks.) Or are they trying to remind themselves what a 'brilliant bargain' they bought, when they haven't even got an occasion to wear the outfit? I say 'outfit'' because it never stops at one item of clothing. There are shoes and accessories to match, all bought ready for some non-existent occasion.

Marketing talk for buying expensive clothes is 'investment dressing'. This ignores the fact that unlike an investment, you can't usually sell your clothes for more than you paid for them.

There are two kinds of expensive clothes. Good quality, that lasts and lasts – and clothes with the labels on the outside which advertise a fashion house to the rest of us. Buy the former, wear things for years and eventually they become fashion classics. If they are very distinctive and stylish, like Biba clothes, they do become very valuable. But this is an exception.

Clothes that make their wearers act as walking advertising for the manufacturer, on the other hand, are worn only by socially unsure people who don't have eyes to judge what they look like, but think that anything bearing a designer label must say the right things about the wearer. And like the emperor's new clothes, they tell onlookers that you have more money than sense.

You buy clothes to help you play a part. You may want to appear cool and efficient in a suit or a traditional country gent or lady in a Barbour coat. However, when you are next tempted to splash out, remember that clothes do not transform you into something you are not. An advertising designer I once worked with remarked to me, that a fat lady watching TV and eating chocolates on the sofa may think that by buying a certain brand of chocolate, she is transformed into a sophisticated, svelte diplomat's wife. But actually, she is now a fatter, poorer lady eating chocolates on the sofa.

Worth its weight in gold is one eye-catching piece of jewellery. Not expensive, preferably handmade in some way – the V&A Shop at the museum of the same name sells one-off pieces at reasonable prices. This is a conversational godsend, as others who don't know what to say to you can latch onto it and say how much they like it.

You buy a smart suit for a wedding. The reality is, the only person we're looking at closely at a wedding, is the bride. For the rest of us, the chances are that after a cursory glance at each other – probably without our glasses on anyway, at my stage – we are thinking about how much older everyone looks, how uncomfortable our shoes are, what time the bar will open, whether the parking meter will run out and whether Aunty Molly will bring up that old family row about the garage. We are not thinking about your suit and how much it cost.

I once wrote a series of articles on the best-dressed business-women in Europe, interviewing people like Paloma Picasso. They all said they mixed couture labels with funky finds from anonymous cheaper shops.

Kate had lots of elegant evening dresses and matching shoes and bags which just hung in the wardrobe going nowhere. I persuaded her to sell loads to a dress agency, which re-sells good quality clothes, and she made around £800 towards clearing her credit card bills.

Giorgio Armani told me that he drove around Chelsea looking at the street fashion for inspiration. The street fashion comes from charity shops. Shop at those in the most expensive areas near you for the best bargains, or try Oxfam's special designer shops Oxfam Originals in very trendy locations like Covent Garden and King's Road, Chelsea.

Charity shops

> **JANE'S GOLDEN RULE.** *The top people buy what they like, whether from charity shops, Top Shop or top designers. People who are secure and who like themselves don't need expensive labels or brands to seem as if they're 'worth more'.*

SHOP HORROR. *I was once asked to work for a few days at the offices of a major newspaper where I noticed a hunched-up woman shuffling around aimlessly, clutching a used coffee cup and dressed in baggy black garments and a shapeless hat. 'Poor old soul,' I whispered to a colleague. 'Does the paper employ her out of charity, to do menial things like collect the empty coffee cups?' 'No,' came the reply. 'That's the Fashion Director.'*

These are great ways to get some money back on expensive clothes you no longer wear, which the agency sells for you at a commission. You can also buy good-as-new clothes, shoes and accessories at prices which begin where charity shops leave off. For local to you agencies, try *www.localuk.com* and *www.fashionfizz.co.uk*.

Dress agencies

Pandora Dress Agency, London's most famous dress agency in Knightsbridge near Harrods, is at 16–22 Cheval Placer, London SW7, 020 7589 5289, *www.pandoradressagency.com*. Also try The Dress B, 020 7589 2240 and Salou, 020 7581 2380.

Sheila Warren-Hill is the doyenne of dress agency experts. She holds Sunday sales in North London with no pressure at all to buy, but with free food and wine. She only sells the couture clothes of ten extremely rich and well-known people. These clothes may have been worn, or not, as millionaires tend to order clothes they like in several colours, then try one outfit on at home, decide they hate it after all, and discard the others untried. Sheila sells accessories including shoes and jewellery too.

'I'm a great believer in not having too many clothes,' she says. 'Most of us are not big film stars. Don't pay up to £450 in a high street for something in a cheap fabric when you can get the best quality for £200 or £300 from me (and other dress agencies).'

Sheila's wardrobe advice

Fashion trends always die. Wear navy, black and cream. You will look chic and natural. Get (from a dress agency, not new!):
One good suit, preferably Chanel or Yves St Laurent. (Note from Jane: Sheila's advice, not mine!!)
Four jackets.
Four pairs of trousers.
A selection of evening and day tops – stretchy if you have a small waist and loose if you don't.
A pearl necklace, pearl earrings and a good watch.
Good shoes. People judge you on your shoes.
Then you need cheaper running-around clothes – trousers from M&S, jeans and tops.
Wear quality.

For details of Sheila's Sunday sales, call The Warren-Hill Agency, 020 8348 8282. Sheila donates couture clothes to *All Aboard* charity shop, 3 Porchester Street, London, W5 5DP. 020 7229 0048. *www.allaboardshops.com.*

Also try Designer Warehouse Sales, 020 7837 3322, *www.dwslondon.co.uk*, or the last day of London Fashion Week, at which you will find wonderful bargains for women, men and children as all the major fashion houses sell off their samples, and accessories including luggage. This fashionfest happens several times a year. *www.londonfashionweek.co.uk*; info/ticket line is 0870 890 0097.

> **JANE'S GOLDEN RULE.** *You can never go wrong with antiques. Clothes, shoes, bags – they do not have to be expensive, but anything old is always right and is unmistakably classier than anything new. (Apart from food.)*

FUNNY MONEY. *When I was a journalist, I once covered a glittering party in New York. The guest of honour, the elegant Princess Elizabeth of Romania, politely admired my evening bag, which was faded floral chintz with a silk cord. 'Where did it come from?' she asked. 'I'm afraid you can't buy one,' I replied. 'I got this from a skip in London, thrown away among an old lady's personal effects. I'm sure that old lady is pleased that it was rescued and loved.' She was delighted and intrigued.*

You can buy vintage clothing from Steinberg & Tolkien, 020 7376 3660 and Rellick, 020 8962 0089. Trend-setting mags such as *Dazed & Confused* and i*D* often source vintage clothing for their fashion shoots from *Rokit*. Brighton 01273 672053, *www.rokit.co.uk* or *www.pop-boutique.com* with stores around the UK. Liverpool 0151 707 0051 or Manchester 0161 236 5797.

The real meaning of glamour

In the 1980s, I was lucky enough to interview Giorgio Armani. As I entered his glass and stone palazzo in Milan and was greeted by Amazonian blonde assistants in flowing clothes, their tops half open, I thought I had never seen anything so glamorous.

A charming man with a warm twinkle in his eye, Armani showed me a huge tableau of all his personal friends in his office. He was too polite to mention my personal fashion disaster – my handbag had fallen apart on the plane! He taught me one of the best lessons in my life. When he was first asked to design clothes for a film, he was incredibly excited. At last, he felt he had left his 'normal' world and found glamour – Hollywood, the cinema and all that.

The director of the film was equally excited to meet Armani. Eventually Armani realised that this major film man thought he was entering the 'glamorous' world of couture fashion because his world of film was to him, just workaday and ordinary.

Armani drew the conclusion that glamour is non-existent. It lies somewhere in your imagination – and in the eye of the beholder.

However, we all need to escape. Glamour is a delightful myth, even if it is responsible for selling more uncomfortable shoes and pull-you-in-tight knickers than anything else.

14. Christmas

A survey by Somerfield on 'the stress of Christmas' revealed that many women take glossy Christmas magazine photos as their standard of perfection and reproach themselves if they can't do as well. They wouldn't if they saw the other side of the camera. Lighter fuel is used to get a pudding or log fire to flare, and to get all the candles burning simultaneously on a table usually involves people hiding under it and split-second timing, especially if sparklers are involved. So buy ready-made gravy if it gives you more time to play with the children and admire their new toys.

> **JANE'S GOLDEN TIP.** *The principle of Christmas is 'something to make their eyes light up'. Their eyes will not light up if you have beggared yourself and are stressed out and exhausted. They will light up if you put sparklers on everything.*

Write a list here of the presents you bought last Christmas which have either been put away virtually unused or broken within a few hours.

_____

_____

_____

_____

_____

_____

_____

Some original gift ideas

Don't go 'Christmas shopping'. You will get into a panic, caused by others being in a panic, and overspend. Most mail-order gift companies will dispatch wrapped presents for you, so you can shop from the phone or on the internet in one fell swoop. The additional advantage is that some will send you reminders in time for next Christmas, so you don't even have to compile a gift list!

Never enter an 'I can give more lavish gifts than you can' contest. The loser will feel a failure. A book, even if funny and crass, is an 'intellectual' gift whose price is irrelevant, so find one book and give it to all. My current all-purpose gift for young and old of all tastes is *The Secret Life of Cows* by Rosamund Young, £14.99, published by Farming Books and Videos, *www.farmingbooksandvideos.com*

Scratchcards, enclosed with a card, are a great way of sending an acceptable but cheap gift and avoiding postage. The recipient, in my experience, is delighted – and several people I have sent cards to have won money and still purr about it when they see me.

Send everyone the same gift. That way, you don't spend time wandering round the shops buying gifts on a 'one for me, one for you' basis, and thinking what people would like.

One year, my husband gave everyone, male and female, pearl-embroidered skull caps from an Indian shop. I like to give bottles of wine or champagne, bought on a three for the price of two basis.

Personally I think store vouchers are a waste of money. You may have to pay extra for the gift card and people forget to use them. You can always make your own voucher for your time or skills babysitting, gardening or whatever. People really appreciate that.

Don't give teachers lavish presents. Get the children to choose them. My son Charlie once chose an Action Man for his teacher on the grounds that the poor woman must 'need' this essential.

> **JANE'S GOLDEN TIP.** *Put your money where Christmas should be and buy everyone you know a gift which is not for themselves, but a donation to a needy person.*

Two charities offer practical help to people in this country and far away, from buying a fishing net for £5, to stocking an entire farmyard for thousands: *www.sendacowgifts.org.uk*, 01225 874 222 and *www.goodgifts.org.uk*, 020 7794 8000. The gifts are witty and unusual and you can (secretly or overtly) theme them to the recipient, for instance a pig or bees to make honey. The recipient receives a card telling them what you have bought in their name and a warm glow. They cannot say they don't like what you have bought them!

Hawkin's Bazaar catalogue contains the best range of cheap, silly Christmas gifts. *www.hawkin.com*, 0870 4294000. Also look at *www.letterbox.co.uk*, 0870 6007878.

Anything home-made or home-grown is more 'valuable' than anything bought in a shop. Make your own chocolates, biscuits, bread, jam, bottled fruit …

If you must buy something posh, make it inexpensive. You still get the expensive-looking wrapping if you buy a nail varnish from the Chanel shop or a tiny handbag spray from Penhaligon's. Fiona Temple at the *Daily Mail* gave me this hint.

A survey by Populus revealed that most people spend over £500 on gifts and one out of ten Northerners spends over £1,000.

We are not in a food crisis. Don't buy too much food. The shops are open even on Christmas morning. Most people put on 5lb in weight over the Christmas holidays. No one will shoot you if you forget brandy butter or bread sauce.

Write a list here of the things no one eats at Christmas which you still buy.

_____

_____

_____

_____

_____

_____

How many bits of toffee and obscure spiced sauces are still lurking in the back of your fridge since last year? Hmmm.

Don't buy a Christmas cake if no one eats it. Nor a pudding. Nor a large Stilton cheese. Nor double-thick cream. Nor liqueurs. Don't buy a huge turkey. You spend all night and day cooking it and then everyone complains. Get turkey steaks. If your family prefers steak, or egg and chips, cook that instead. It's meant to be a celebration not an ordeal.

If you are going to buy a turkey, leave it as late as possible. You will find birds marked down especially in places like Iceland. I once served chicken instead of turkey and no one noticed!

Crackers. Buy cracker pulls, mottoes and tiny gifts from *www.absolutelycrackers.com*, 01908 604751. Save loo roll cardboard tubes or bits of thin card for the body of the cracker, and use paper napkins and sparkly bits of leftover wrapping paper to tie each end of the cracker. 'Make your own' cracker kits with cardboard outers are in my experience a waste of money as you cannot pull cardboard easily.

Giftwrap. You *do* save bubble wrap and all sorts of paper through the year, don't you? The alternative is to ask a florist if you can buy a huge roll of florists' wrap. I bought mine, which is very pretty, three years ago from a florists' wholesaler and it is not even half used up. Alternatively, use newspaper or plain paper of any kind, even begged, clean, from the local chippy, or from printers who always seem to have surplus free or cheap paper, and spray with gold and silver paint.

Cards. Get your children to draw these. Or download images for cards free from websites. Dover Bookshop, 020 7836 2111, *www.doverbooks.co.uk*, sells wonderful books of instant clip-art that are copyright-free Christmas images to photocopy or cut and colour, such as '*Christmas Drawings*' (£8.99)

I am told that there is little or no difference between posting first or second class these days – things get there pretty much at the same time. Don't blame me though ...

FUNNY MONEY. *My family are well-known among our friends for home-made spoof Christmas cards. One year our card consisted of an outrageous round robin claiming that our son Charlie had been sponsored by Action Man to lead an expedition to Everest and that I had won the Daily Mail's 'I'm even thinner than Catherine Zeta-Jones after giving birth' contest. To my delight, someone in the Daily Mail took this claim seriously and started to check ...*

Table decorations. Cover the table with paper from a roll of lining paper which you don't have to bother to launder later. Scribble festive messages all over it, or if you have time, stick down images cut from magazines. Or cut long strands of various types of ivy – easy to find in gardens – and trail around glass bases, etc.

The tree. EC regulations regarding subsidising European imported trees have changed and there is expected to be a shortage of trees for the next few years. The best-value and cheapest trees will probably be from members of The British Christmas Tree Growers Association, 0131 6641100, *www.bctga.co.uk*.

Buying a root-balled tree to keep in a pot over several years may be a good idea. As an alternative, use long branches from a bush, sprayed or painted white, gold or silver, or buy these from a florist and hang with pretty things.

238

Decorating the tree. This is not the time for expensive shop-bought decorations. Trees are a kind of sentimental family record of your evolving life. Go back to the original Victorian German tradition and hang anything that you find glittery or interesting, even little dolls or teddies or walnuts sprayed or painted gold; souvenirs you brought back from holiday. Anything home-made should take pride of place.

HELPFUL HINT Cut a few inches off the bottom of the tree before putting it on its stand and keep it liberally topped up with fresh water to make it last. I add a little plant food.

FUNNY MONEY. *I was once asked to decorate a Christmas tree for fifty pounds and another one for five pounds. The newspaper involved accidentally transposed the images and labelled the cheap one as the expensive one, including a fetching snowman made by my son from cotton wool at school, labelled as £15 from Harrods. No one noticed! The snowman still has pride of place on our tree.*

HELPFUL HINT Don't hang all your decorations on the outside of the branches. Start from inside, to give the tree visual interest and depth.

15. Wastes of Money

Don't waste your money!

Each year, on average, each of us wastes seven percent of our income on fritterations – things we don't use or need. That is £1,725 on average – nearly as much as the average credit card debt. Men admit they waste £240 more per year than women, mainly on gadgets, hobbies, sports, nights out and their cars. (Source: 2005 survey, Prudential)

I am astonished at how people court money trouble by buying the same item again and again – and usually a useless one. Sometimes they have a fixation, like a girl I met who couldn't stop buying carnival pierrot masks. (A few well-chosen words sorted that out, especially as I was wearing a tiger mask at the time and gave her a bit of a turn.)

Another form of waster can never find something when they need it, so keep buying the same thing. Recognise yourself? Well, smarten up and save your money!

I am here to tell you that you or members of your household, only need one of the following:

- drills
- nail varnish remover
- nail clippers
- skateboards
- strimmers
- calculators
- Scrabble and Monopoly sets
- any camping accessory
- picnic baskets
- umbrellas
- pairs of wellington boots
- tins of white emulsion paint
- pretty notebooks with blank pages

Add your own or your family's double-up purchases to this list.

> *Mary was a keep-fit machine fanatic. Her spare room bulged with equipment of all kinds – exercise balls, rowing machines and fearful-looking things I didn't like to ask the use of … She explained that she bought so many keep-fit aids because they worked well in the shop, but by the time she got them home, something had gone wrong with them and they didn't seem to work.*

This story reminded me of Miss Piggy's notorious excuse for buying more clothes – that they shrink in the wardrobe.

Here are things that you need *none of*. (Feel free to disagree but don't come crying to me when you've spent all your hard-earned cash!)

- bottled water
- fizzy drinks
- keep-fit machines, unless you are a saint
- expensive trainers

Add your own non-essential items to this list.

SHOP HORROR. *I once bought a stainless steel sink that came with the instructions 'Wipe down after each use. Water may stain the surface.'*

The Money Generation Game

Imagine you are a contestant on TV's *The Generation Game*. You stand behind a moving mechanical belt like the ones at supermarket tills. Think of all the useless things you have bought in your life and mentally place them on the belt. Imagine how embarrassed you would be if millions of people saw your collection of glass ornaments, dusty gadgets and tools you have never unpacked.

Wastes of money items	What I paid for the item	What they were worth to someone else	Losses

Make a list below of the most useless items you have ever bought.

Now find them and sell them. *This week!* Note down here how much you paid for each item. After you sell them, in the second column, note how much they were 'worth' to someone else. Finally, add up how much money you have lost and note it here.

Think what you could have spent that money on. Don't do it again!

EXTRA HINT. This game is more revealing if you fill out the list and also get your partner to list your wastes of money. Then do the same 'service' for your partner. First you must agree not to argue afterwards about whose wastes of money were 'justified'.

Tim and Debbie, overspending clients of mine, 'invested' in a timeshare apartment in Florida. But once they paid the £1,000 annual maintenance charge and the managing agent's charges for letting it, they made a loss. I found a similar holiday on the internet for less than half the price of the timeshare, so I told Tim and Debbie to sell the apartment. Then they confessed they had been trying to do this for several years. And they had a second timeshare I didn't know about!

Timeshare apartments and holiday clubs

Don't be lured into timeshare presentations, even by the offer of a free weekend away. While I'm on the subject of thinking you will get something for nothing, don't believe scratchcards, phone calls, letters nor calls that say you have won a holiday. Always ask yourself, 'What's in it for them?' The answer is, they want to sell you something

Holiday clubs are a variation of timeshare holidays which promise a selection of holidays in return for a membership fee. At the time of writing, the Office of Fair Trading is investigating 40 clubs.

How to save money on holidays

'Holidays are heavenly, but going on holiday is hell. Going on holiday is not to bask in the blissful oases of repose we are promised by the advertisements. It is like moving house for a fortnight, only to a foreign country … before returning to fifty more weeks of work and worry. And why? To pay for the holiday, of course. Best of all, stay at home! Holidays are the perfect opportunity to do nothing.' *Lionel Hilary Qadosh Fanshawe, The Chap magazine*

So often, I hear that people's financial troubles began when they couldn't resist a cheap deal to Dubai or New York, where they *had* to shop as it is so cheap. This ignores the cost of getting there and the fact that you are supposed to pay customs duty on your purchases from the USA, making those bargains rather less attractive.

For most people, according to a survey of over a thousand holidaymakers for Adnams Brewery (Summer 2005), the benefits of a break wear off within 24 hours. Personally I rather resent going away on the grounds that I haven't spent time and money on making my home comfortable, in order to transport the family to live in two cramped rooms and pay hugely for it.

To save money this year, stay at home and go out for weekends and days or stay with friends. Even camping can be expensive by the time you pay for the kit. At home, you won't have to endure tummy trouble, other people, crime, stupid souvenir shopping for all and sundry, and exhausting flights.

If you insist on travelling, Thomas Cook's *2005 Cost of Holiday Living Index* lists Goa as top value for living costs – you pay £5 for a three-course meal. Next comes Tunisia (£7.20), Turkey (£7.50) with Spain and Florida costing over £10. Also look at Bulgaria, Croatia and Cyprus for cheapness.

Stay away from home free, and meet congenial people, by joining *www.staydontpay.net*, 01227 470780. Members earn 'credits' by giving others free b&b in their homes.

My favourite places for cheapness are the Youth Hostels Association, who have palatial places, taccommodate all ages with cars, serve excellent meals with wine and don't ask you to do cleaning. Internet-only offers can net you extra savings. YHA is on 0870 770 8868, *www.yha.org.uk.*

Also check the Landmark Trust for amazing places to stay at reasonable rents, from a banqueting house to a castle in Scotland. 01628 825 925, *www.landmarktrust.org.uk.*

If you are skint, avoid 'buy now pay later' travel deals. You are unlikely to be able to afford them later, if you can't now.

Be aware that some websites automatically add travel insurance unless you specifically click to take it off – a ruse called passive selling.

Don't click through from one travel website to another. Exit and go again to the second site. You may find the prices are cheaper as they don't include commission paid to the first site.

To calculate the real costs of your holiday, include pre-travel spending like vaccinations, equipment for skiing or water sports, insurance and clothes, toys and suncream. Then there is spending at the airport and transfers to the hotel.

Don't bother with travellers' cheques whose service charges, or whatever they call them, can range from £12 to £21. Take a Nationwide debit card on holiday, as it has no foreign exchange or fee for using a cash machine abroad.

Use *www.oanda.com* for fast currency conversions. Make a written exchange rate table for yourself and family and carry it for rapid calculations in shops.

SHOP HORROR. *Years ago, on holiday on a houseboat in Kashmir, I accidentally ordered a boatload of flowers, instead of a bunch. I got a decimal point wrong in my currency conversion. It pays to check how many zeros are on your credit card voucher, too – an extra one, in a foreign currency, turns £10 into £100.*

A bottle of Johnny Walker whisky works wonders in a crisis. I always carried one when I travelled for *The European* newspaper. It can get you tables in restaurants and rooms in booked hotels.

Don't change money in the hotel. You usually get a poor exchange rate. Use a proper bureau de change. Don't let the foreign restaurant write your credit card bill in sterling, either – they will 'load' the exchange rate.

Leave your mobile at home (if you can). You may have to pay for incoming calls. If you want to use your phone abroad to phone your friends or family who are there with you, buy a travel sim which enables you to pay local prices. *www.sim4travel.com*, 0905 335 0336 a phone line that charges you 40p a minute.

www.dh.gov.uk is the Government website containing the latest health advice for travellers anywhere, help with getting medical treatment and information about the E111 form which gets you some medical care in most European countries.

Save money by bartering. Think of the local conditions – the weather in off-season, and any shortages. Take a stock of tee-shirts with slogans in English and anything good quality, like thermal gloves, condoms and glossy magazines, to barter for goods and services and give as tips and small thank you gifts. Battery-operated goods are not a good idea as they rust.

HELPFUL HINT Always book tickets in the exact name written on everyone's passport or you may not be allowed to travel. Also remember to renew your passport at least ten months before it runs out. Many countries, including the US, won't let you in with six months or less on your passport.

Tell your credit card company that you are abroad. A friend was left without the means to pay, when his card was refused in South America as the transaction seemed 'suspicious'.

Hotels. Booking and paying the hotel yourself may be cheapest. Check reviews of destinations and hotels at *www.tripadvisor.com* and *www.hotelshark.com*. *www.nextag.com* and *www.laterooms.com* allow you to make discreet internet-only offers of up to 40 percent off room rates for over eighty nice hotels all over the UK. For cheap hotels, try *www.laterooms.com* or *www.lowcostbeds.co.uk.*

Personally, I prefer a real person to arrange everything for me. Then I know who to blame. Internet travel agencies include *www.travelsupermarket.com*; *www.opodo.co.uk*; *www.expedia.co.uk*; *www.allcheckin.com* and winner of October 2005 travel awards *www.short-breaks.com*, 0870 027 6002. The advantage if you book a package through them, and the airline goes bust or something goes wrong, they have to reimburse you and help. If you click through from airline to hotel to car hire, you have not bought a package and no agency will take responsibility if things go wrong.

For cheap flights. check *www.skyscanner.net* or *www.wegolo.com*, *www.airline-network.co.uk*, then check the airline's website.

HELPFUL
HINT

You may get cheap air tickets and be paid about £15 an hour plus accommodation to take casual work as an air courier, carrying business papers. Contact your local branch of a courier firm, or check free magazines given out at stations intended for Australians or South Africans, or for good advice, look at *www.aircourier.co.uk*; *www.courierlist.com*

Know your rights within EU countries. If you are delayed over two hours by a cancelled flight, you are entitled to claim up to £415 or a full refund if you choose not to fly. This depends on the journey length and delay.

Cars and ways to save on them

A car takes a quarter of the average family's income – around £100 a week including fuel and servicing. (Source:RAC/Deloitte and Touche 2005)

Zoomy cars cost a lot more, and so do cars you think you are going to do up and sell for a fortune. So before you 'invest' in that Caterham, check the sell-by date. You can actually lose money by selling a 'classic' car after a certain time.

Buy a diesel car which holds its value better and gives you more miles per gallon than petrol.

Save £10 a week on a typical car by converting from petrol to LPG using a government grant to subsidise the initial work. Then save 40 percent on petrol, up to £10 on road tax and in some cases, evade the Congestion Charge. Find out more from *www.greenfuel.org.uk*, 0845 490 0189.

HELPFUL HINT

Cutprice car websites include *www.broadspeed.com*, *www.oneswoop.com*, and *www.virgincars.com*.

Remove luggage racks and boxes, empty picnic boxes and any other surplus you carry. They can slow the car down and use more petrol.

HELPFUL HINT

As a rule of thumb, supermarket garages are cheapest for petrol.

Develop money-saving driving habits. Don't warm the engine up when it is standing but drive slowly for the first few miles, and don't speed or brake a lot. Switch off air-conditioning. You use up to one extra gallon of petrol in every 140 miles (two litres per 100km).

Open the air vents rather than the windows. You use 4 percent extra fuel driving at 60 mph with the windows open.

Check your tyre pressure. Low pressure uses more fuel.

Car share. If the Inland Revenue says the average car costs 40p a mile to run, you can halve that using a service like *www.liftshare.co.uk*, 0870 011 1199 which aims to match drivers with passengers to share journeys to work, school runs or wherever you might be heading. The matching service is free and you share petrol costs directly with sharers. Or join a security-checked car share scheme at *www.roadpals.com*, £20 p.a. Or become a passenger yourself and save on vehicle wear-and-tear too.

Many local councils are also starting to set up similar schemes so ask at local libraries.

- Honda's Civic Hybrid 1.3 does over 60 mph per gallon (£16,000).
- Toyota's Prius, £17,500.
- Lexus's new RX400H is the world's first electric and petrol-powered 4 x 4.
- G-Wiz costs £7,999 and 1p per mile to run, does up to 600 miles per gallon (that's £40 for 4,000 miles) with no road tax, congestion charge, free parking in most central London car parks and Group One insurance – saving up to £8,000 annually – but it can't go faster than 40 mph. *www.goingreen.co.uk*, 020 8574 3232.

New ecological, economical cars

MOTs

If you think your car is OK, call your local council to find the name of your nearest Government MOT test centre to save up to £500 on needless 'faults' found by garages which also offer repairs. This tip from a chat forum, was passed on by *www.moneysavingexpert.com* which is a good place to start for the latest deals on cheap rescue services and insurance too.

Insurance

Get some quotes direct using a typical insurance comparison service like *www.confused.com*, then ask a broker for quotes. They know obscure insurers and if you have a ding, will help by handling the insurance company for you. I saved hundreds on my car insurance – with exactly the same insurer – by going through a broker rather than phoning direct.

You can also save money by insuring with the woman as principal driver, if you both share equally.

If you are a young driver, I recommend taking the Institute of Advanced Motorists' Advanced Driving test, available via most driving schools. Your insurance bills will be discounted.

If you drive into central London a lot and clock up huge fines because you forget to pay your Congestion Charge, *www.eightpounds.co.uk*, 020 8536 4019, is an excellent money-saver. You pay £5 to join – refunded if you display their window sticker. You also pay £10 a month per vehicle.

Save on the congestion charge

For this, they pay your charge automatically. You don't need to tell them when you drive into the charging zone. And you pay £7 not the normal £8, receiving the bill at the end of each month. If you pay your congestion charge in advance monthly, you receive three free days, rising to 12 free days for paying annually. *www.cclondon.com* or 0845 900 1234 or for those who have call-charge plans, 020 7649 9122.

It is not true that the more expensive the cream, the more magical the effect. I used to think up the names of magic ingredients for expensive creams, in my early career as an advertising copywriter. Research told us that the key age for remortgaging the home to buy a pot of hope is when a woman hits 30.

Beauty creams and cosmetics

Some would pay a hundred pounds for a pot of strawberry yoghurt if it were relabelled 'makes your bottom smaller and your skin younger'. When the Shangri-La effect doesn't happen, the pot joins the rest on the bathroom shelf, and it's back to the beauty counter for the next expensive 'treatment'. Or should that be 'treat'? If this is you, recognise the signs and remind yourself that Marilyn Munroe's beauty secret was a layer of Vaseline, then a layer of powder, building up the layers to give her skin a translucent look.

How to look a million pounds on a fiver a month, if that

Direct Cosmetics offer discounts of up to 70 percent on toiletries, cosmetics and perfume. If you can't find what you want, ask. *www.direct-cosmetics.com*, 0870 746 0040. Also try Stonelake Ltd in Guernsey, 01481 720053.

www.cheap-perfume.co.uk has a guide to discounts including shops that sometimes sell off unused tester bottles at £1.

Find any department store cosmetics counter or Space NK (020 8740 2085, *www.spacenk.com* for branches) on a quiet day like Monday and say, 'I don't know what to do about my skin/lipstick/foundation' (not sticky-out ears though, nothing they can do about those). You will receive offers of free makeovers and samples.

Get top quality beauty treatments free or for a few pounds, electrolysis, manicures and massage, from supervised beauty students at your local College of Technology or Further Education. You usually have to book ahead. It is nice to tip the student. For colleges of further education visit *www.direct.gov.uk* and then search for FE colleges.

Have a hair-do free or very cheap by becoming a 'model' for trainee hair-dressers. Ask at any trendy-looking local salon or try Saks, 01325 380333.

Make your own beauty aids – though remember 'natural' things like strawberries can cause allergies and always test ingredients on your skin 24 hours ahead. My favourite recipe book is *Hints and Tips from Times Past*, published by Reader's Digest, which you can order free from the library. The Women's Institute also has Simple Solutions, a booklet with beauty and cleaning recipes, for £1. 020 7371 9300, *www.womens-institute.org.uk.*

Glycerine from your chemist for a few pence is a simple moisturiser.

Soften your hands the Victorian way by rubbing them with almond or olive oil, putting on a pair of cotton gloves and sleeping in them.

Baking soda – a few teaspoons in your bath – softens your skin, apparently. The herbs or other magical ingredient contained in expensive bath salts can be in negligible amounts to be of any real medicinal value so strike those off your money-saving shopping list.

Baby oil or almond oil from the chemist – perfumed by yourself if you wish – is a cheap alternative to expensive bath oils.

Make lipstick and eye-shadow last longer by using the tricks of the TV stars. Mac's Matte Creme Matifiante is a no-shine base that is applied before anything else. Powder over this with Studio Fix on a damp sponge, or use the moisturising cream version. Makes rouge, eye colours and lipsticks stick like glue. Expensive but last for ages. Compare prices for various suppliers at *www.dealtime.co.uk* or try Cosmetics Direct Cosmetics Direct as above before paying full price in a department store.

Use spray-on, leave-in hair conditioners rather than stuff you rinse out. They have the same effect but last a lot longer as you only need a few squirts each time. My favourite is Fudge's One Shot spray-on which is costly at £7.95 but lasts months. From *www.glamguru.co.uk*, 01228 562777, which offers free p&p on cosmetics, saving several pounds per purchase.

Some typical wastes of money

Couture baby clothes. A survey by the Prudential (July 2005) found that 80 percent of British babies have designer clothes from Versace, Prada and similar. 12 percent have designer luggage. One mother was pictured in the Daily Express saying she would pay £3,500 for her one-year-old's clothes that year.

Babies can't read and giving them expensive clothes does not prove you love them more. They just need to be clean, warm, dry and cuddled.

Baby clothes are only the beginning. Research pinpoints 180,000 British children whose parents spend £20,000 on fashions and luxuries for them each year. Wardrobe favourites include £250 leather jackets and mini-Porsches that work.

A TV series, *Britain's Spoilt Kids*, featured the parents of a six-year-old who confessed that they regretted lavishing gifts including an electric guitar and scooter and a wardrobe of designer clothes on their son; he threw himself on the floor when he didn't get his own way and told a psychiatrist that he wanted new parents who could buy him everything.

Personalised number plates. Vulgar and a dangerous distraction to other drivers. A titled friend bought a matching pair of number plates proclaiming MILORD and MILADY for himself and his wife. He was teased about them so badly – teasing was perhaps an understatement – that within a few weeks, he 'lost' them. If you have this amount of money to waste, see my comments about charity at the end of this chapter.

A wine rack stacked with bottles. Do you think this signals to your friends that you are a wine connoisseur? More like prize plonker. Most supermarket and off-licence wines are chosen to be quaffed around the time when you buy them. The longer you leave such bottles, the more the flavour can actually go off. If you want to collect wine, you need expert advice and proper temperature-controlled storage.

Warranties for appliances. One electrical chain used to make more profit from these than from selling appliances. Staff are keen to push warranties if they earn commission on them. These guarantees offer to repair your purchase free, and may add protection against accidental damage or theft.

However, most appliances come with a year's guarantee from the manufacturer, free. You are also protected by consumer legislation that states you can get a refund or a new item if the item is not of satisfactory quality or fit for its purpose for a 'reasonable' time, though the law never states what time that is. You may also have accidental damage cover through your house contents insurance policy. Your local council's trading standards officer will advise you.

A warranty will only save money if the appliance is likely to break down many times and cost a lot to repair, in which case, don't buy it. A recent Office of Fair Trading survey found that the average washing machine repair cost up to £65, but a 2002 *Which?* survey for the Consumers Association reported that 81 percent of washing machines did not break down in the first six years.

If you buy a warranty lasting over a year and costing over £20 and change your mind within 45 days, you can get a full refund if you have not made a claim. You can cancel after this time but only get a partial refund.

Clubs you attend once in a blue moon. Golf clubs, smart clubs where vodka costs £200 a bottle … Don't tell me! You're a member of a gym – and I expect you bought the tee-shirt – but you never go.

I am here to tell you that joining a gym – and paying for it – does not equal becoming healthy.

An average annual gym membership costs £372 in the UK.
(Source: Sainsbury's Bank)

One in five people uses their gym less than once a month.
(Source: Mintel market analysts)

Do some sums and work out how much it costs you per visit. If it doesn't make financial sense, leave or scale down your membership to a cheaper level – deals for using it in the evening are usually the most expensive, but if you are too tired, be realistic! Cancelling a gym membership is costly: normally, you are locked in to giving three months' notice. But by stopping your £50 a month gym membership, you save £600 a year.

Local authority-run gyms can be just as nice, and allow you to pay per visit – typically, around £5 – with no membership fee.

If you want to get fit, walk up escalators or walk instead of driving. Play tennis for peanuts in your local park or go to the local baths for a few pounds a time.

If you feel like a little pampering from time to time, all gyms hold regular free open days and the most luxurious offer free trial memberships. Ask, or keep an eye on the local papers.

Vitamin tablets. In 2004, we spent over £360m on nutritional supplements (Well I didn't. I don't know about you). Ignore pressure to take more of these from America and from beauty and health writers, who might as well witter on about this as anything else.

Children, pregnant women and elderly people, or vegans on diets may need specific supplements. See *www.nhsdirect.co.uk* for advice or ask your GP or health visitor. For the rest of us, supplements don't replace healthy eating, nor are they a quick fix. Personally, I can't see how they can help you deal with stress or pollution, as some claim. Some supplements take weeks to have a significant effect.

HELPFUL HINT

Your body absorbs about 15% of a vitamin supplement if you don't have a specific deficiency, so if you take an 'insurance' dose a day, you are producing some very expensive urine. You can overdose, as well as overspend on these things.

HELPFUL HINT

'Beauty vitamins' are said to contain skin-improving ingredients like vitamin C – at a premium. One thing is sure: they can cost even more than 'ordinary' vitamins.

Advice from *www.dietician .com* says that you don't need a multivitamin supplement if you eat normally, unless you consume under 1600 calories daily.

The body is a wonderful thing. Take vitamins with a pinch of salt. If you feel ill, see a doctor and get tests and the right treatment. If you simply feel low, go for a walk or do something for someone else.

White carpets and white sofas. Talk about the victory of hope over experience! I know they look nice in adverts, but we are now in the real world.

Natural woven floor coverings. I speak from experience, having moved into a house covered in these. How I wish the previous owners had saved the money and put down dried rushes! They would have been less rough underfoot and easier to keep clean.

> **JANE'S TRUE CONFESSION.** *When five foxes invaded my bedroom, coming in through the cat door when we were on holiday, I got rid of my sisal floor coverings. It was an interesting insurance claim, including steam cleaning a chaise longue where we found one fox lounging among the cushions, eating chocolates and watching the telly. (I lied about the telly, but the rest is true. OK, not the chocolates either but they had eaten enough cat food.)*

Gadgets and gizmos. These are typical Saturday afternoon shopping purchases, often made by bored couples out together who want to go home with a toy. You won't understand the instructions. The only person who can, is the one who wrote them. Or perhaps not. Years ago, I wrote ads for Kenwood and read a research report that said people stop using machines once they put them in a cupboard. *Use it or get rid of it!*

Expensive and elaborate kitchens. When househunting, I lost count of the number of kitchens I saw, which I would describe as 'footballers' wives' kitchens. Invariably, the wife would spiel on about how she loved to cook. She may have talked the talk, but her kitchen did not walk the walk. Set amid burnished acres of empty worktop, was one tiny sink – when any family cook needs two deep butler's sinks. Backlit cupboards displayed gleaming crystal, when I needed space for food and everyday dishes.

There are basic points to check when buying a kitchen, like the quality of the drawers and hinges – which in an ideal world, I should swing on with all my weight before buying, as my kids do at home during 'ordinary' use.

My experience is that a kitchen is not better because it costs more. It is only as practical as the designer who planned it. Some young man purporting to be a designer once said to me, 'You don't really need a place for the kitchen bin, do you?'

Investments and collectors' items. For 'exclusive' read 'expensive'. Nothing advertised in a mass publication is a collector's item or collectors who know what they are doing would have already bought it. Including bits of jewellery.

Computers. Do you need to buy one at all? If you only use it occasionally, ask to borrow someone else's or ask that someone else if they will look something up for you and ring you with the answer, saving a huge amount of extra hassle. If you rotate round your friends, like King Lear round his daughters' palaces, you won't outstay your welcome.

You can use a computer, free, at your local library. If you enrol for any course (even if only half an hour and you didn't turn up) at a College of Further Education, this also entitles you to use the computers in their library. Or ask a friend if you can use theirs. Call Learn Direct for advice on colleges near you, 0800 100 900.

There are also internet cafes in most places – check in Yellow Pages – which charge a fixed sum for access per hour. The advantage to you is that you pay no overheads, have no tiresome helpline to hang on to, and no broadband costs. *This tip will save you hundreds if not thousands of pounds and hours of heartache.*

OnSpeed says it accelerates your access to websites, making it up to five times faster to connect, without broadband. A subscription costs £24.99 a year – saving around £20 a month charge for broadband. *www.onspeed.com*, 0870 758 5859. NB: Make sure you have good anti-virus software – dial-up connections are targets for fraudsters who re-route you through premium numbers.

Nights out and entertainment

Lydia earned £900 a month and had few outgoings, as she lived at home, but was always overdrawn after the first week, as she spent so much money on clubbing. I advised her to sign up for an evening class in DJ-ing which cost a few pounds a week. She loved the course, saved money and developed a new interest.

Check your local library or your local authority on the internet for its adult education classes. They usually offer everything from fashion to French, with discounts for students, OAPs and those on benefits.

Tickets for shows or matches are expensive, with ticket agencies and even auction sites like eBay adding extra sums from 30 percent to 600 percent of the price. Top agencies Keith Prowse, Ticketmaster and See Tickets charge £4 and upwards *per ticket* plus £5 postage.

Many theatres sell cheap tickets on the day, sometimes from £5.

The Society of London Theatre's half-price TKTS booths in Leicester Square and at Canary Wharf sells tickets for London shows. You can see what is available at *www.officiallondon theatre.co.uk/tkts/today*. Savings can be as much as £30 per seat.

HELPFUL HINT Find a booking agency that charges a fee per order, not per ticket.

TV and radio recordings are free – a brilliant alternative to paid-for shows. Ask your local stations, or for all channels, including satellite and pilot shows, Applause Store offers free seats. 0870 024 1000, *www.applausestore.com*, or try BBC Audience Services, 020 8576 1227, *www.bbc.co.uk/tickets*.

HELPFUL HINT Cinemas are cheapest on unpopular nights like Mondays. Orange phone users can get two tickets for the price of one on some weeknights.

If you like going round National Trust houses, you might like to know that there is always a free entry day each year. It varies from place to place so call your desired place and ask.

Entertaining children. People complain about the cost of keeping children amused. Don't forget stuff on your doorstep like organised bicycle rides or walks. If you live within striking distance, London Walks – 020 7624 3978, *www.walks.com* – offer a huge variety of guided walks seven days a week; mornings, afternoons and evenings. Children under 15 are free provided they accompany a paying adult (£5.50 or £4.50 for concessions). Buy a discount Walkabout card and it's even cheaper. After all that walking, and education, they're too whacked to demand the usual complement of naff souvenirs and MacDonald's.

Swap your unwanted films for money or for other films at any large chain like Blockbuster. Check with smaller local shops in case they offer a better deal. The same applies for Playstation and other games.

DVDs and videos

To get cheaper DVDs, buy from Europe where they are 25 percent cheaper on the whole. They are even cheaper in America, but you need to buy a multi-region DVD player rather than a Region Two (Europe only) model – I found the SumVision N808 at £32.84 plus £7.50 p&p from *www.microdirect.co.uk*, 0870 44 44 456.

If you want to stay in, a postal DVD service may be cheaper than buying or renting DVDs. Pay a monthly subscription and order as many films as you like.

HELPFUL HINT

You don't have to see the newest releases immediately. After four months, DVD prices drop to under £10 in ordinary shops.

www.screenselect.co.uk, First five rentals free, no late fee, no postage to pay, £9.99 per month.

www.lovefilm.com, First two weeks free, slightly more titles, otherwise the same as above.

www.tescodvdrental.com, 0845 310 5003, £7.97 per month, fewer titles available, two week free trial

Finally, don't you dare to waste more oney after reading this!
There are kids in Britain who have little to wear and raid dustbins for food, yet are not considered badly enough 'in need' to be taken into care. Their parents are drug addicts and inadequates.

Please stop wasting your money and instead, donate it to a charity* that tries to feed them one meal a day. They are always desperate for new Christmas presents so each kid gets one.

* Kids Company, 1 Kenbury Street, London SE5 9BS, 020 7274 8378, *www.kidsco.org.uk*

16. Planning for Life's Lumps and Bumps

If few of us plan ahead properly for Christmas, imagine how foggy we are about major life changes. Getting married, giving birth or retiring is rarely seen through anything but a golden haze – with little thought given to what might lie beyond.

In the short term, taxwise, you lose money. In the long term, you gain emotional and financial stability especially (sorry to say this) if you are a woman with children and you divorce.

Getting married

Engagement rings. These days the average ring costs £1100, according to a recent survey by the Woolwich. That is ridiculous. Engagement rings cease to be important once you have a wedding ring; and to walk around with a glittering, expensive and easy to remove accessory is a come-on to thieves.

When I wrote jewellery TV advertisements, research revealed that people buying engagement rings positively avoid trying to get good value. Like sending flowers and arranging funerals, it's not considered 'nice' to haggle over the price. I say: fooey to that.

Save money and add sentimental value to a ring, by asking members of your family if they have any rings they would like to see passed down.

Buy a secondhand ring – except they won't call it that, they'll call it 'antique' because that sounds a lot more valuable, and so should you, when you present it to your girl.

Or if you want something new, go to London's Hatton Garden, Birmingham's jewellery quarter or any similar concentration of trade jewellery-makers or wholesalers near you and browse around the shops. Ask a few to quote on the cost of making you a design 'inspired' by the ring design you like. And save a lot of money.

Cutting the costs of the wedding, or any party
Buy beautiful, but don't bankrupt yourself or Dad in the process.

Have small nibbles of food that go into the mouth without needing a second bite, or they ruin peoples' clothes and guests can't talk while they are eating.

Ignore ice sculptures. They are expensive and vulgar.

You can get away with simple food if you have as your centre-piece an eye-catching chocolate cake – my faves are by Choccywoccydoodah whose 'ordinary' cakes begin at a mere £22.50 mail order, but they will do you a cake taller than yourself covered in chocolate cherubs – and they don't melt even next to radiators. Guests talk about those cakes for years afterwards and you can mention that all sorts of Hollywood celebrities have them. *www.choccywoccydoodah.com*, 01273 329462.

Saving money on bridal dresses

Don't panic-buy. Make an appointment and shop on Mondays, when shops are least busy.

Choose a dress which needs no alterations, but if you do need extra work, always take your wedding shoes – or the dress may look too long or short on the day.

Talking of shoes, no law says you have to spend a fortune on shoes worn for perhaps four hours. Find cheap sequined slippers or ballet shoes for a few pounds.

A plain dress will be cheaper and more chic. A wonderful bouquet is better value because it will enhance the dress.

Find a dress you like in a magazine. Take it to a local dressmaker and ask them to copy it. But don't let the seamstress buy the fabric.

To buy online, try *www.fabricsite.co.uk*. My favourite suppliers are MacCulloch & Wallis Ltd. *www.maculloch-wallis.co.uk,* 25 Derring Street, London, W1R 0BH, 0171 629 0311 and Allans of Duke Street *www.allans-of-duke-street.com*, 75 Duke Street, Oxford Street, London W1M 5DJ, 0044 (0)20 7629 5947.

Buy accessories like tiaras and posies at a craft shop like Hobbycraft, *www.hobbycraft.co.uk*, 0800 027 2387.

Hire a bridal dress for half its shop price, and the brides-maids' dresses too – that means you may be able to afford a

HELPFUL HINT Phone around charity shops in posh areas asking them to let you know if they have any good dresses – they are quickly snapped up.

couture frock and anyway, they won't be worn again.

If you buy, don't bother to tell yourself that you will sell the dress on. The most you will get for a designer frock is a few hundred. Ignore silk – it is hugely expensive and may show every crease. You can find lovely inexpensive frocks at websites like *www.DirectDresses.com.*

Oxfam sells new and second-hand bridal wear from full-scale wedding dresses to all accessories for everyone involved in the big day at its dedicated bridal wear shops.

Here is a list
95 Corporation Street, Birmingham 0121 236 7376
54/58 Darley Street, Bradford 01274 306700
5 The Bridge,Chippenham, Wiltshire 01249 447061
300 Walsgrave Road, Walsgrave, Coventry 024 76 448909
258/258a Telegraph Road, Heswall, CH60 7SG, 0151 342 8416
17 Terminus Road, Eastbourne, 01323 640731
22 Market Street, Leicester, 0116 2556455
358 Rayners Lane, Pinner, 0208 8669616
76/78 High Street, Shirley, Southampton. By appointment only. Call Sue Hutchings on 07969 668939

Flowers

For the room where the ceremony is happening and the reception.
Check with the wedding and reception locations to see if more than one ceremony is happening that day, and make sure you're the second couple in. In which case you may find the previous couple say, 'Keep the wedding flowers'. Or propose sharing the cost of flowers between all the couples being married that day.

For the bride and bridesmaids, groom and ushers. Choose flowers that are in season to save hundreds. Get a gardening-mad friend or relation to grow special flowers for you. Ask for double what you need, in case of mishaps. Tie simply with raffia or ribbon to match an outfit, but taper the ends of the flowers for elegance. Or buy flowers to make your own bouquet and buttonholes, and add greenery from the garden. Practise making it by finding a book or going on a short floristry course at your local college of education which may well have an 'arranging flowers for weddings' course.*

Visit a wholesale florists' supplier – for which you need a business card or letter on business headed paper explaining that you are buying for a large party – or wholesale market like New Covent Garden (£4 entry charge, add VAT to prices, call the information officer on 020 7720 2211 ext 201 or email *info@cgma.gov.uk* or visit *www.cgma.gov.uk.* to discuss your visit before turning up). It is up to individual traders whether they will sell direct to members of public – not many are so inclined unless you are placing a really decent size order.

If you don't feel confident, ask at the local church, horticultural society or Women's Institute. There are lots of talented amateur flower arrangers who would arrange your bouquet for a small consideration or a contribution to an organisation's funds or charity.

Keep table settings small and low or people won't be able to see each other. A round margarine tub sprayed or covered in fabric or silver paper is fine as a base. Or save on flowers by decorating tables with photos of the bride and groom in the past. Run a caption competition: presenting a prize for the wittiest will give the best man something to say apart from telling scurrilous stories about the groom.

* (See Wedding Flowers by Paula Pryke, pub by Jacqui Small, £15.00, second-hand copies available from *www.amazon.co.uk*)

To help preserve buttonholes, use 50 cm water tubes and caps which are like tiny vases you wear, concealed, at the base of the flowers. £1.75 including p&p for five, Orchids for You, 01934 623626, *sales@orchidsforyou.co.uk* *or visit www.orchidsforyou.co.uk.*

Getting the best prices from locations and caterers

For the best catering prices, don't marry on a bank holiday. For the best location prices, marry on a weekday between October and February.

JANE'S GOLDEN TIP. *Weddings are not an exam in perfection and having all the bits like 'favours' on the table (favours? Inedible silver almonds do my teeth no favours, I don't know about yours.) You can do no wrong on your wedding day even if things go wrong around you so keep it light.*

JANE'S TRUE CONFESSION. I have been married twice. The first time, I had all the trimmings and was married in pink silk at an Oxford college. Years later, I remarried. This time, it was a ceremony for us alone rather than a social come-one-come-all. We had very little money, so married mid-morning and asked the local Café Rouge to open early for us, without charge, on the grounds that we would be bringing loads of guests. We ordered what guests wanted from their normal menu: buck's fizz, capuccino and chocolate croissants. A real wedding breakfast! We didn't have to pay thousands for a venue or pay florists and caterers and then clear up. Everyone was happy, and the early start gave us plenty of time to travel to the honeymoon hotel and enjoy the lovely surroundings, rather than arriving tired and late.

An excellent short guide is *Fresh Start: A Practical Guide to Separating your Finances When a Relationship Ends* by Alison Steed, free from the Yorkshire Building Society, 0845 1200 100, *www.ybs.co.uk*.

Legal arguments cost you money. Resolve everything and then get a court to rubberstamp it. Resolution, 01689 820272, *www.resolution.org.uk* used to be called the Family Law Association and is a group of lawyers committed to helping you divorce as 'peacefully' (i.e. without inflating the legal bill) as possible.

Buy the best place you can afford in a 'good' area rather than a good place in a 'bad' area. You make your home easier to sell, and having lived in all sorts of 'good' and 'bad' areas, I can say from experience that a good local authority will offer things free for which you would otherwise have to pay, saving you hundreds on 'grudge' purchases that bad local councils make you pay for. Free wheelie bins, free bin bags for recycling or garden rubbish, free children's activities, all sorts of grants and clean, well-lit streets are valuable extras that you don't get in deprived areas.

The average cost of moving home in 2004 was £5,551, according to the Woolwich. Half of this went on stamp duty. When you are looking at houses and arranging a mortgage, take this extra sum into account or you will find yourself short of money.

Stamp duty rates

Under £60,000	nil, as long as this is not part of a linked series of transactions (i.e. you are trying to evade tax).
£ 60,000–£250,000	one percent of the price
£250,000–£500,000	three percent
Over £500,000	four percent

JANE'S GOLDEN TIP. *If you are selling or buying a house, you will make it more attractive by pitching the price just underneath the next stamp duty band, e.g. £245,000 and adding a sum for things like curtains and carpets which will not be taxable. But tell the truth. You may be checked up on.*

HELPFUL HINT

Buy or lease for under £150,000 in certain 'deprived' areas and you don't need to pay stamp duty.

If you house swap with someone else, and the difference in value is under £60,000, you don't have to pay stamp duty.

But you have to find this out before buying the home – it seems they won't refund it if you pay in error (which strikes me as wrong – surely mispaid tax can be reclaimed and this is no exception?). However, to find out, phone the Stamp Taxes Helpline, 0845 603 0135 or see *www.hmrc.gov.uk*, enter the potential home's post code and use the Disadvantaged Areas Relief Search Tool.

Removal firms, solicitors and estate agent fees are all negotiable. You should always get several quotes and haggle. 'So and so offered me less' usually produces the desired result.

HELPFUL HINT **Never buy homes in new developments at the quoted price. Negotiate.**

When you move into a new home, you don't know what horrors are in store, so it is well worth buying an insurance policy that sends workmen round to clear drains and deal with emergencies. I suggest buying one policy rather than individual ones from the water company, gas company, etc. as it seems easier and better value.

Direct Line Home Response costs from £7 per month, 0845 246 1999, *www.directline.com*, or Home Call from £7.95, 0800 195 20 33, *www.homecall.co.uk*.

JANE'S GOLDEN HINT. *Keep the policy number and phone number somewhere outside your home. If you lock yourself out, you will know who to call to get a glazier to take out the window so you can climb in.*

Student bank accounts. Ignore introductory bribes (sorry, I mean 'free gifts'). Go for the account that gives you the largest interest-free overdraft.

Being a student

How to save money on student rent. Buy a property as a student let. Afterwards you can hope to sell it at a profit.

I know someone who found a rundown property on the internet at bought it, for £40,000, on various credit cards. His son paid him rent to live there when at university, his friends moved in too and their rent covered the costs.

271

Graduation

Many banks automatically swap your student bank account to their 'graduate account' but shop around, ideally for an account lasting three years with the largest interest-free overdraft. If you're earning and don't need an overdraft (this may be a fantasy but bear with me), you can use the 0 percent credit card trick of taking the 'free' overdraft money and plonking it in a cash ISA that enables you to make and take all the interest, tax-free. You can make several hundred pounds this way. Make sure that the ISA is a flexible one that allows you draw money out and that you repay the overdraft money in plenty of time. Allow two weeks.

Pregnancy

The key to claiming any pregnancy-related benefit is form MATB1 which confirms your pregnancy. Your doctor or midwife can give you this when you are 20 weeks pregnant.

You are entitled to 26 weeks' maternity leave, even if you have only worked for your employer for a short time. If you have worked for one employer for at least 26 weeks by the 15th week before the baby is due, you may also qualify for another 26 weeks, making 52 weeks or a year.

Listen carefully. I can only say this once. If you have worked for 26 weeks or more by the 15th week before your baby is due, and are still employed by the same company, even if you are off sick or part-time, *and* your pay is at least £77 per week before tax in the eight weeks before the 15th week (or two months if you are paid monthly) you are entitled to Statutory Maternity Pay. This is 90 percent of your average weekly earnings for the first six weeks of your maternity leave. Then for the remaining 20 weeks of your maternity leave, the pay falls to either £100 per week or if you earn under £100 per week, 90 percent of your average earnings.

For more information, check your phone book under 'benefits centre' or try *www.jobcentreplus.gov.uk* or the Maternity Alliance, *www.maternityalliance.org.uk*, 020 7490 7639. Or see leaflet NI 17A – 'A Guide to Maternity Benefits' from the Job Centre Plus.

If you don't qualify for Statutory Maternity Pay because you are unemployed, changed employer recently or are self-employed, you may qualify for the Maternity Allowance for up to 26 weeks. This can be up to £106 a week starting from the 11th week before your baby is due to the day after the birth. You need form MA1 from your Job Centre or Benefits Agency.

HELPFUL HINT **Sort out your claim as soon as possible, or you risk hitting cut-off dates especially if the baby comes early and you are in hospital and can't think straight. If information-giving staff are impossible – as some can be – don't argue: phone again another time.**

If you or your partner are getting benefits or allowances including income support or pension credit, you may be eligible for an extra sum called a Sure Start Maternity Grant. You can claim from the 29th week of your pregnancy until your baby is three months old. If you are adopting a baby, claim within three months of the adoption, as long as the baby is still under a year old. You need form SF100 Sure Start from the Jobcentre Plus office.

> **JANE'S GOLDEN TIP.** *Check with your local benefits or tax office that your National Insurance is credited free for each week you receive maternity benefits.*

Fathers can take two weeks' paid paternity leave paid by their employers at the same rate as Statutory Maternity Pay at the time of writing. If your weekly earnings fall below £75, you may be able to get Income Support whilst on leave. For advice, phone DTI Employment, 08457 14 31 43, *www.dti.gov.uk*.

Copy the sample in the leaflet *Working fathers – rights to leave and pay (PL517)* which any of the offices listed here can give you. Once you have done this, employers are not expected to hassle you for further proof.

Child benefit

For the eldest child, Child Benefit is £17 per week and £11.40 for all other children. One of the glories of the welfare state, this tax-free benefit is paid for each child up to the age of 16 or 19 if a full-time school student. Download or complete an application form online at *www.hmrc.gov.uk*. Or pick up IR ChB form from post offices, Job offices, Local Authorities, Inland Revenue Enquiry Centres or the Citizens Advice Bureau.

Nine out of ten families with children, including carers who are not parents, can get tax credits. Child Tax Credit can be paid to those earning up to £66,000 per year with a child under one or families with incomes up to £58,000. The 'family' payment is worth up to £545 and the sum paid per child is up to £1,690 at 2005–6 levels. There may be more for those with babies or disabled children.

The other tax credit you may be entitled to, if either you or your partner is working, is called Working Tax Credit and if you and your partner work at least 16 hours each a week, the credit gives you up to 70p in tax credit for every £1 you spend on registered or approved childcare up to £200 a week.

For more information, try *www.inlandrevenue.gov.uk/taxcredits* or 0845 300 3900 or *www.direct.gov.uk*.

You may find yourself looking after your children and your ageing parents or relatives. Or you may be in need of care yourself.

The care sandwich

Having cared for my late mother, and helped care for a terminally ill friend, my feeling is that if you can care for someone at home, at your own home or near to home, with bought-in nurses and carers, they are happier and it makes money go further. Don't try to be a saint and do everything. You will work yourself to a frazzle. Try *www.caredirections.co.uk*

> **GOLDEN TIP.** *Hospital social workers can be mines of information about good care homes.*

Sheltered accommodation is preferable to care homes. Sheltered developments have wardens who check on you daily, or will come when an alarm is rung.

HELPFUL HINT **Ask your local social services for their 'approved' list of care-providing companies. These tend to be cheaper.**

The cost of *care homes* varies greatly but is crippling – starting from £310 to £500 weekly.

Nursing homes – with medical care – start at around £450 a week. Shared rooms cost less, but sharing with strangers can be distressing for the people involved. If the person needing care is suffering from dementia, you may have a long search. These homes can be hard to find, and can be even more expensive, especially if the person is violent.

Check with your union or the union and any charities involved with the former work of the person needing care. They may have places in sheltered, care or nursing homes which may be more comfortable and cheaper than average.

It is a truth universally acknowledged, at least in my home, that if you go away for the weekend leaving an elderly person who seems OK, they will fall off a chair whilst cleaning windows because they didn't want to bother anyone. So I suggest getting from social services, free if you're lucky, or buying from *www.ageconcern.org.uk* 0800 77 22 66, a wearable alarm which connects with a manned phone centre which can hear them and summon you or the emergency services. This involves a monthly subscription. Tell the wearer never to take this off, even at night. Show them these words as a warning.

My own mother lay helpless overnight until her condition deteriorated too far to help her, because she took her alarm off and could not reach it on the bedside table.

Who pays for residential care

One old lady remarked to me how galling she found it that, while she scrimped and saved in her life, and now had to use her savings to pay for her care, others in the same care home simply spent all their money and then got the State to fund their care.

To get Social Services to pay for your care home fees, at the time of writing you need less than £20,500 in savings or capital and/or a regular income that would not cover the care bill that Social Services would pay. If you own a house, there is a twelve-week 'property disregard' or something called a Deferred Payments Scheme. You need to check carefully – figures can change.

When trying to work out how much you can afford for a care home, distinguish between 'continuing NHS health care', 'funded nursing care' (FNC) and ordinary everyday care (i.e. help getting out of bed, etc.). The National Health Service will fund nursing care for someone who is ill in a home, but that does not include paying for carers to help with 'ordinary' activities like washing or dressing. That is extremely unfair if the person has dementia and needs help with every activity.

To get FNC, an assessing nurse decides whether you need low-category help, medium or high. The National Health Service then pays the care home a sum to cover this – £40, £75.50 or £125 weekly at the time of writing. That is taken off the fee for accommodation, food and personal everyday care.

If you are going to stay in your own home or have a granny flat in someone else's home, it is possible to get an occupational therapist to come, free, via the NHS, to make a list of helpful adjustments to be made to your home, like rails and bathing aids. If you have reasonable savings, don't imagine you will get these for free and hang on, waiting. Eventually they write saying that you will have to buy these for yourself.

The first £30,000 of redundancy money is untaxed. The rest of your money will be taxed at top rate, unless the redundancy money is 'part of your contract'. You need specialist help from a tax expert

Retirement age for men is 65 and for women, 60, but this will rise to 65 for both sexes between 2010 and 2020. The average man lives 18 years after retiring and saves £123,948, while women live 21 and a half years and save just £59,393.

Can you afford to retire? Find your pension statements. Request a Retirement Pension Forecast telling you how much you can expect to receive when you retire from the Retirement Pension Forecasting and Advice Unit (RPFA) at 0845 3000 168 or by filling in form BR19 online at *www.thepensionservice.gov.uk* and then using the search engine to get to the forecast service.

The Basic State Pension currently pays £131.50 a week for a married couple and £82.05 for a single person. If you didn't pay National Insurance contributions for a time, you won't get it all. You have to pay for 44 years for a man and 39 for a woman.

The Second State Pension (SERPS) is a top-up to the State Pension which you may get if you are someone's employee.

Pension Credit tops up your pension. Apparently if you are sixty for a woman and 65 for a man, you are guaranteed at least £109.45 weekly or if you have a partner, even if under the age-limit, £167.05 a week. The information adds mysteriously that 'you may be rewarded for saving for your retirement' but don't expect a funny hat: you get up to £16.44 if you are single or £21.51 a week if you have a partner. This can be backdated a year if you did not know you could apply. For information try *www.thepensionservice.gov.uk*, 0845 60 60 265.

In April 2005, according to the Prudential, £100,000 might buy a joint-life annuity that would give a man aged 65 with a wife of 60, a join income of £6,200 per year. A widow's pension would be two-thirds of this.

Conventional pension wisdom advised one to aim for a pension of two-thirds of your final salary. This is unlikely, these days, unless you are a civil servant. By mid 2006, the new Self-invested Personal Pensions or SIPPS allow you to add life insurance, shares and buy-to-let and business properties which you lease back to yourself, into a pension pot, with considerable tax advantages. *www.taxcafe.co.uk,* 01592 560081, gives clear explanations.

HELPFUL HINT **Can't find or can't remember an earlier company pension? Try the Pension Schemes Registry,** *www.essential pensions.co.uk*

When you retire, you can take 25 percent of any pension fund as a tax-free lump sum and use the rest to buy an annuity, which is an income paid for the rest of your life. You pay tax on this annuity.

Alternatives to conventional pensions

Pension plans may give you tax relief, adding value to your savings, but they have performed abysmally. Look at alternatives. Investment bonds, ISAs, houses, or other forms of solid investments can be part of your retirement savings. You can invest, currently, up to £7,000 per year in ISAs and use the proceeds free of income and capital gains tax. You don't have to buy an annuity with this, unlike pension plan funds.

HELPFUL HINT **The University of the Third Age is a charitable trust that encourages lifelong learning for retired people. Most courses are free. 020 8466 6139.** *www.u3A.org.uk*

The family home

Or if you are over sixty, you can stay there and look at a Home Equity Plan, a loan based on the idea that eventually when you die, the house will be sold and the money repaid to the loan company.

If you need repairs, improvements or changes made to your home, check with Houseproud, run by the Home Improvement Trust through your local authority. This helps anyone who is disabled or over 60 to get building work done and loans with a no-repossession guarantee. 0800 783 7569 for details.

HELPFUL HINT **Private medical insurance** can make a lot of difference to your comfort. Exeter Friendly Society says it is unique in not increasing premiums as you get older. This could save you thousands. *www.exeter-friendly.co.uk*, 08080 55 65 75.

Personally I intend to milk the idea of being a frail old lady for all it is worth. Take advantage of special offers like those from Help the Aged for the over-60s including travel insurance and savings accounts to benefit grandchildren. *www.helptheaged.org.uk*

HELPFUL HINT **RIAS insures the over-50s and offers savings but I really like the sound of its Home Help Benefit at £1 a month, at the time of writing. It gives you a cash payment towards getting help at home if you break a leg or something in an accident. 0845 6501333 or 0845 234 0011, *www.rias.co.uk*.**

See Help the Aged (Seniorline on 0808 800 6565) or:

England 207–221 Pentonville Road, London, N1 9UZ
Tel. 020 7278 1114

Wales 12 Cathedral Rd, Cardiff, CF11 9LJ
Tel. 02920 346 550

Scotland 11 Granton Square, Edinburgh, EH5 1HX
Tel. 0131 551 6331

Northern Ireland Ascot House, Shaftesbury Square Belfast, BT2 7DB
Tel. 02890 230 666

Can you speak the language? No? You will never get a plumber to do what you want. You would be better off looking at the cheap rates for two-month-long holidays somewhere warm, and shutting or letting your home while you are gone.

Thinking of retiring abroad

As an EU member you can live anywhere in the EU. Consider exchange rates and currency restrictions abroad. Although you will receive your state pension, it may not go up if you live outside full member countries of the EU or if you are not covered by EC social security regulations so check. The upside of living abroad is that you may be able to claim extra benefits from your host country, and we have agreements with unexpected places like Barbados and the Philippines, although you can't claim things like housing benefit as if you lived in Britain. See leaflet GL29 from the Department of Work and Pensions.

To get free or discounted state medical treatment abroad, you need form E121 from the DWP as above.

You still pay UK tax, but some countries have a 'double taxation agreement' with the UK enabling you to pay less. Check leaflet IR121 from the Inland Revenue.

For more information, ask the Foreign Office – *www.fco.gov.uk*, 0870 60 60 290.

Offshore banking can minimise the tax you pay. All the big banks and building societies offer offshore accounts: HSBC is at *www.offshore.hsbc.com*, Barclays at *www.wealth.barclays.com* and Abbey at *www.abbeyinternational.com.* To find the web address of any UK bank or building society go to *www.financelink.co.uk*.

Specify how you would like to be buried in your will. It saves so much trouble. For inspiration, the best guide is *The Natural Death Handbook*, which has loads of cheap but lovely ideas. Free online at *www.ac026.dial.pipex.com/naturaldeath/publications.htm* or as a book, around £14.99 from the Natural Death Centre charity, 0871 288 2098.

The useful IR45 leaflet 'What to do when someone dies' is free at post offices and GP surgeries, or can be downloaded at *www.hmrc.gov.uk/pensioners/tma* or call the helpline, 0845 30 20 900.

HELPFUL HINT

The moment you die, your assets are frozen and this can prove inconvenient if there are immediate bills to pay until your house is sold, etc. An elderly lady I know has put some money aside in a 'secret' savings account to cover her funeral and other expenses, in the name of a younger person she can trust. That way, they can pay her expenses without waiting months to be reimbursed.

Cutting the cost of medical care

If you have a chronic condition like asthma or eczema, you are entitled to buy aids to your health without having VAT added by the shop. This applies to anything from organic cotton sheets to adjustable beds and is 'self-certifying', i.e. the shop gives you a simple form to fill out, and keeps and deducts VAT at source. The only place I have found which insists on a doctor's note is Dreams, the bed superstore, which charges VAT and makes you jump through hoops by filling in forms, unnecessarily in my opinion, before it refunds later.

For a full list of zero-rated VAT products, and a simple declaration

to download and sign for buyers and sellers, look at
www.hmrc.gov.uk or call 0845 010 9000.

Dentists

All UK residents are entitled to NHS treatment. Contact NHS
Direct on telephone 0845 4647. Or the website *www.nhs.uk* can
give you your nearest NHS dentist. You may have to wait
months for an appointment. Adults still have to pay 80 percent
of fees up to a maximum of £384 per course of treatment.
Children, those on low incomes and expectant mothers get free
treatment up to 12 months after the birth with form FW8 from your
midwife or GP. In Scotland you can ring 08454 24 24 24.

Private charges vary hugely and it is worth phoning around and
asking. A check-up can cost £15 or £90 and there seems no rhyme
or reason why. I queried one dental quote, for the suspiciously
round figure of £3,000, and was told 'You wouldn't understand'.
So I left.

Before signing up with a dentist, check their opening hours,
emergency and weekend cover too.

Schemes you pay into each month. Denplan is the largest of
these. You pay a fixed monthly fee in return for regular examinations
and any treatment including a hygienist. *www.denplan.co.uk*,
01962 828000 and enquiries 0800 401 402.

Dental insurance plans

These pay a smallish amount for regular dental work and a larger
amount for emergencies. Quotes vary spectacularly. In my
sample, I was quoted £34.12 (WPA) or £11.60 per month
(Universal Provident) to cover a family of two adults and two
children. Compare prices at *www.insuresupormarket.com*

Cash plans

Often offered by non-profit-making companies, these refund much of the cost of dental or optician's charges, medical treatment, screening for cancer, diabetes and heart trouble and a little cash if you are admitted to hospital. You can make a profit if you take out the right plan, as you are entitled to payments for having a baby, dental and optical treatments, health screening and physiotherapy, osteopathy, chiropractic, acupuncture and homeopathy, chiropody and allergy testing. You can cut premiums by around 20 percent by persuading your union or employer to offer a plan.

Association of Friendly Societies, 020 7216 7436, *www.afs.org.uk.* British Heath Care Association, 0153 651 9960, *www.bhca.org.uk.* HSA, 0800 072 1000, *www.hsa.co.uk.* Westfield Health, 0114 250 2000, *www.westfieldhealth.com.* Healthshield, 01270 588 555, *www.healthshield.co.uk.* Bupa, 0800 600 500, *www.bupa.co.uk.*

Going abroad for medical and dental work

Luxurious, clean and air-conditioned hospitals staffed with well-qualified smiling staff and working equipment ... it seems like a dream. If you go down this route for an operation, you have to add travel costs, not to mention the cost of getting up-to-date vaccinations and anti-malaria drugs before travelling, which can be a good few hundred pounds. *www.worldhealthcare.net* is a useful site to consult.

For instance, Jaipur Dental Hospital, www.jaipurdentalhospital.com in India quotes savings of 90 percent on prices in America. For instance, a crown can cost $600 in the USA, but $70 in Jaipur.

Try an established medical tour operator. For India, *www.meddicaltourism.com* has links to all the main companies offering medical treatments and recommended travel agents.

Choose a destination that is not too hot and stuffy during the time you are there. Bangalore's Manipal Hospital is considered a good choice in India, offering a health check for a sixth of the price of a British private hospital.

Take someone with you – hospitals usually offer an adjacent bed free, unlike British private hospitals, which charge sums such as £80 a night to sleep near the patient. Airlines may say that they will not carry post-operative convalescents without a companion.

Many foreign hospitals have tie-ups with British private hospitals for aftercare which may add to the cost, but the NHS will still come to your rescue, wherever your original operation was performed.

Apparently, the Inland Revenue only aims to get three out of four tax calculations right. Check your bill before paying. If you are an employee, rather than self-employed, the Instant Tax Refund's software (priced at £29.95) helps you reduce tax and claim obscure allowances, backdated up to six years if you have to work from home at least one day a week, with no form to fill out. *www.instanttaxrefund.co.uk*. 0800 0640270. Save an average of £400 for a successful tax claim.

Tax allowances: the bare bones

Figures change each year and these are those for 2005–6.
Everyone is allowed the first £4,895 of their earnings tax-free. If you are blind, you get £6,505. Those between 65 and 74 get £7,090; over 75s get £7,220.
Then we pay:
10 percent on the next £2,090 of earnings (you pay up to £209)
22 percent on the next £30,310 (you pay up to £6,668.20)
and 40 percent beyond that.

On top of that, if you earn over £4,264 p.a. you pay National Insurance.

If you are contracted in to the state pension scheme, you pay 11 percent on weekly earnings between £94 and £630 and one percent on all earnings above that.

If contracted out, you pay 9.4 percent plus 1 percent on earnings over £630.

Find out if you are contracted in or out by asking your employer or tax office. For more advice, seek an independent financial adviser.

It is worth running your tax bill past an accountant or tax adviser, even if you are employed and it is all done for you at work. Tax experts know the latest ways to avoid tax and will aim to save you money, their fee at least.

Saving on your tax bill if you're self employed

The way to save most on tax is to go self-employed and/or form a limited company. Consult an accountant first. Self-employed national insurance rates start at £2.10 a week on earnings of £4,345 p.a., rising to 8 percent on profits between £4,895 and £32,760 and one percent after that. To avoid paying national insurance, pay yourself a low income and take dividends on your company shares instead but watch the papers – a current court case is being fought which may change the legality of this.

Being self-employed involves saving all your till receipts and bills. Before you calculate your 'taxable income', you may claim expenses on everything from using your home, phone and car to newspapers and accountancy advice. Claim enough expenses and your taxable income dips so low that you pay a fraction of the tax which an employee on a similar income would pay. If you register for VAT, you reclaim this on office equipment, etc. too. On the other hand, by going self-employed, you lose holiday and sick-pay, entitlement to benefits and other safety nets.

One of the biggest savings is claiming, as a tax-deductible expense, the use of part of your home as an office, including utility bills. But to avoid paying capital gains tax when you sell your home, be hazy about which room it is. Make sure you put a sofa-bed, a box of Christmas decorations, or anything not connected with the business into the room too.

To calculate the cost of a home-office, work out how many rooms you have, excluding kitchen, bathrooms and hall, then add together annual costs of utilities, council tax and insurance (both buildings and contents). Divide by the number of eligible rooms. 50 per cent of this sum is the amount you can offset against tax.

> ### The construction industry: a special case
>
> *Simon was a fireman, about to take a second legitimate job as a decorator. I advised him that he could save considerable sums by refusing to allow his employer to treat him as an employee.*
> *The construction industry has special rules about self-employed people and if he did not want to set up his own company, he could at least ask his employer for a 'registration card'. That enabled him to pay only 18 percent tax on his earnings, deducted by his employer at source, some of which he could ultimately reclaim from the Inland Revenue when he submitted expenses including car, mileage, tools, travel, protective clothing and laundry. If Simon managed to get an 'exemption card', he would get all his earnings paid to him at source and pay tax later. It was vital to get professional advice.*

How employed people can save tax

Do not assume that 'they' work out your tax and national insurance correctly. Mistakes can go on for years. If you are employed, check your tax code. The usual code is 480L. If you have an 'x' or 'month 1' written after your code, you may be on emergency tax rates, which can be higher. Phone the Inland Revenue tax helpline and ask why.

Tax benefits you can get from your employer (if only anyone knew …)

Bicycles. The Cycle to Work Initiative saves employees 40–50 percent of the total cost of a bicycle and accessories. The company buys the bicycle for you and then leases it on to you, usually for 18 months. When the lease ends, you buy the bicycle for about the cost of one month's lease, you don't pay VAT on the bike, and as the repayments are taken out of your gross monthly salary (ie before tax), you save 22 percent in income tax and 11 percent on National Insurance contributions for that sum.

Free meals and drinks. As a further perk, employers may provide free meals and drinks to employees who cycle to work. As long as the benefit is provided on a specially designated cycle-to-work day, meals provided as an incentive to employees who get on their bikes are free of tax. Employers can offer these days as many times as they like. Every day if they want.

Travel expenses. People who travel for business – other than to the office – should keep a mileage log. If your employer does not reimburse the costs, you can claim these off your tax bill. 40p per mile for the first 10,000 miles and 25p per mile after that.

Uniform. Wear a tee-shirt with the firm's logo on it to work. (It can't just be a pin-on badge.) Then you can try claiming up to £60 a year off your tax bill for laundering a 'uniform'.

Childcare. £50 weekly in Childcare Vouchers is exempt from Tax and NI. Although there is a service charge, they actually cost less than giving cash.

Mobile phones. The employer provides a phone for the employee and pays his mobile phone bills, taking the cost back from your earnings before tax and NI, which both employer and employee save paying. You do not have to use the phone for work. You can have two phones yourself and three for family members – a number agreed with the HM Revenue and Customs.

Financial planning. Employers can provide financial information and advice up to a value of £150 per worker, without landing the employee with a tax bill.

Personal computers. You accept a cut in your gross annual salary ('salary sacrifice') in return for the use of a loaned computer costing up to £2,500. At the end of a given period, you buy the computer – which will not be worth much by then. ... Combining the maximum annual tax exemption with a salary sacrifice can save you a third on the price of a computer, 41 percent for higher tax payers. VAT should be deductible from the cost of the PC.

Season tickets. Here, the employer will loan you the money you need to buy an annual season ticket. You pay the money back each month via a deduction in your salary. The loan is interest-free.

17. The Cash
Crisis Section

For those whose credit cards have
exploded

People you owe money to, do not want to pass your debt to debt-
collection agencies or to see you go bankrupt. It's expensive and
they won't get all their money back. They will try to work something
out with you.

Things are always better if you take control of the situation. So promise yourself that nervous breakdown tomorrow. And then the day after that. You haven't got time for one now. Here's what to do.

Make one entire list of where you owe money and payments you think you can stick to.

Don't go on using your credit cards up to the last limit and running up more debt. You will weaken your credibility when you talk to the credit card companies – they will probably think you are a bit of a chancer and try to pressure you to repay more faster.

Contact the relevant credit card or lender and tell them the problem. Show your complete budget or repayment plan to everyone with your proposals to sort out their particular debt, e.g. 'I will pay you £20 on 10th March.' Seeing the whole picture, and that you have thought things through, should make them willing to agree to a proposal to, say, freeze the interest on a debt. Don't allow non-essential creditors to pressurise you into increasing payments to them. The Citizens' Advice Bureau has examples of typical letters you can write. Check *www.adviceguide.org.uk* or find your local branch through the phone book or library.

HELPFUL HINT

Offer token £1 or £2 payments for the moment to each creditor, just to show them that you will repay.

Don't make up a sob story to get out of paying, like saying you can't work because all your arms and legs have been amputated or your hamster's died. The credit card companies can check up on you – and if you are a serial sob story maker-upper, they will keep notes. I remember this from a brief spell I once spent in the 'credit control' department of a multinational company selling books and tapes. They were kindly to hard cases, unless they received a letter from one of their regulars. However, in exceptional cases, they will 'write off' or draw a line under your debts.

Keep them informed about changes. If necessary, re-negotiate the whole repayment package.

Barclaycard told me that they don't have a general policy for all defaulters, and assess each case on its merits. If someone phoned and confessed they can't pay that month, lots of things can be arranged before they take legal action. They may offer a payment holiday, or to freeze the interest on the outstanding debt and ask you to pay back the minimum. Never stop talking to them.

Not paying your bill will affect your credit rating after three months (usually) but that doesn't mean that you can never get a card again.

If you feel too traumatised to do this, talk to a credit counsellor. A free one, not one of the pay up-front debt agencies. Credit counsellors are there to help.

HELPFUL HINT **If the first person you speak to is unhelpful, simply say goodbye and ring back and speak to someone else five minutes later, or ask to speak to a more senior person.**

'Dear Sir, I am dying. Can you send me £10, and so consummate your many kindnesses to me?' The writer Hazlitt to Francis Jeffrey, having forgotten that they had not spoken after Jeffrey had written a cruel review of his work. **Jeffrey sent him £50.**

There is no need to pay for help in dealing with debt. You can get the same advice and help for free – see the list below:

Where to get free advice

- National Debtline: A free, confidential and independent service funded by the Department of Trade and Industry and the credit industry. Tel: 0808 808 4000, *www.nationaldebtline.co.uk*
- Debt Solutions Company, 0800 716239, *www.fcl.org.uk*
- *www.debtadvicebureau.org.uk* (internet only service)
- Business Debtline: Provides a free telephone debt counselling service for self-employed and small businesses, funded by banks. Tel: 0800 197 6026
- Consumer Credit Counselling Service (CCCS): Funded entirely by the credit industry, the service offers practical help and advice to people in debt. Tel: 0800 138 1111, *www.cccs.co.uk*
- PayPlan, 0800 917 7823, *www.payplan.com*, has had good reports from my readers.
- The Money Advice Association (trade service only), 01476 594970 in England and Wales; Money Advice Scotland, 0141 572 0237, *www.m-a-a.org.uk, 0113 270 8444*
- Citizens Advice Bureau: Offers free, independent and confidential advice from more than 700 locations throughout the UK. Look up the number in your local phone book or try *www.citizensadvicebureau.org.uk*
- AdviceUK (formerly the Federation of Information and Advice Centres), 020 7407 4070, *www.adviceuk.org.uk*; in Northern Ireland, the Association of Independent Advice Centres, 028 9064 5919.

HELPFUL HINT To save time, assemble all your bills before contacting any of these debt counselling services.

Sell your house. This may be traumatic but at least you will be able to pay your debts. If you don't want to take on another mortgage, explore buying through housing associations who have new schemes to help you back on the housing ladder. These might involve buy-lease schemes, or the association paying half. See what is available.

National Homebuyers, *www.nationalhomebuyers.co.uk*, 01444 257 111, guarantee to make a no-obligation fast cash offer for your house below its market value. I do not recommend getting less than a house's value, but if you need to move quickly for some reason, like paying off out-of-control debts, a quote from a company like this is an option.

HomeSave is the Central Institute of Housing's scheme to provide tenants with a stake in their home without the pressure of buying it outright. *www.cih.org/policy/hmesave.htm*, 024 7685 1700.

www.keyworkerliving.co.uk tells you whether your job falls into this category, e.g. teacher in an inner city state school, and if it does, lists various lending schemes to help you buy a home.

If you rent, have you checked whether you are paying a fair rent? Ask your local authority for the Fair Rents Officer. I once successfully challenged a moorings rent increase, when living on a houseboat in the Thames. Then I introduced a health and safety inspector to the communal facilities, for good measure, and the landlord wished he had never put the rent up!

Don't give up, hand back your house keys to the mortgage provider and walk away. Too many people have seen their hard-earned homes sold at auction for a low price. Years later, when they are in a better position to pay, mortgage companies present them with a bill for the balance between the house sale-price and their mortgage. It's heart-breaking to see them back in debt. Some have had arguments about interest building up over all that time, too.

Steer clear of ...

Last-ditch loans. Especially those who sell door-to-door in the poorest areas and prey on the most vulnerable. Those advertising in small display ads in newspapers may charge you exorbitant interest rates. You will be even worse off.

Agencies that charge money to take the debt off your shoulders. Some of these advertise as if they will offer you a last-ditch loan. Once you phone up, and admit how much debt you owe, they hard-sell you to send them a large sum of money upfront to reschedule their debts.

> What happens when you contact a debt advice service?
>
> 'We aim to pick up the phone promptly and talk to you. We send you an information pack. Many people use that to try to help themselves out of debt, but 40 percent of those can't and come back to us.
>
> 'We also offer a free counselling session which lasts up to an hour and a half. Afterwards, we offer you best advice on the way forward. For some it is a plan to repay as much debt as you can afford. We normally arrange to schedule an interview in seven days.
>
> 'People with just one big debt might do well to go direct to the creditor and talk. These days it's rare. The typical person we help owes £28,000 with ten or eleven different lenders.
>
> 'You are better off if we talk to your creditors rather than you. They virtually always accept our proposals because we put the whole picture in front of them, not just one debt.
>
> 'It takes four to five years to get the average person out of debt, but many people's situation gets better before that, as half of these cases are caused by relationship problems like divorce. Eventually their situation stablises and they can pay things off more speedily.' (*Malcolm Hurlston, founder and chairman of CCCS* which receives around 250,000 calls from people in money trouble each year)

It is definitely not nice to receive a letter from one of these. But they have absolutely no more powers than the people you owe money to. They are not allowed to harass you, only to write or telephone. They are just trying to embarrass or frighten you into paying by holding out fear of court action, possibly leading to bankruptcy. They must take court action against you before they can carry out any threat. If you try to come to payment terms with the creditor, the threatened court action won't happen as it is so expensive.

'I refused to pay a cleaning firm who had done an inadequate job on my house before I moved. They became abusive and sent a debt collectors' agency letter within a week. I wrote back, listing all the places they hadn't cleaned, including the bath and fridge, and offering a proportion of the money.

They sent their cleaning employees to my home. A big man and a youth. I wasn't in, but they spoke to my teenager, saying, 'You are rich and we are poor. Please pay us.' They walked all round the house, including the garden. When I heard of this, I was extremely worried. They could have come back to burgle the house or even damage my car and cause me thousands of pounds in bills.

I consulted the Police. They said there was nothing they could do, even though I said it was trespass, but advised me to tell the debt collection agency and the cleaners that if they came to my door again, the Police would come and check that that they were legally employed, and if necessary go back to the agency and go through their papers.

I decided to pay the bill in full, even though it amounted to hundreds.of pounds. When the debt collection agency phoned and sneered that I had backed down, I was quite bullish and superior. I said I couldn't be bothered with them and didn't want to go to Court. I didn't tell them that what worried me was that if I lost, for any reason, it could affect my credit rating.' (Julia, Mitcham)

A large agency which hoped I would invest in its shares told me it charges £250 to collect most debts, crowing 'this is highly lucrative as it can often be earned with a single telephone call'.

If you have a debt of £750 or more and it is not secured against your house, a creditor can take you to court and ask them to make you bankrupt. But the court may not agree.

It is traumatic if anyone to whom you owe money then decides to take you to Court. But a court is not there to punish you. It is more like going to a referee. You may end up with a CCJ (county court judgment) but you will be allowed to pay the debt off at a reasonable rate. Recently, a couple successfully argued that their debt was unfair because the interest rate was too high. Don't take this as the go-ahead to run up debts and argue the same as the case specifically did not set a legal precedent for judges to follow.

If you have a County Court Judgment made against you and your debts are under £5,000, you can request an administration order rather than going bankrupt. That means the court will work out what you can afford to pay and then administer your debts for you. But that will stay on your credit reference file normally for six years.

JANE'S GOLDEN TIP. *In England and Wales, if you have a judgment made against you, pay within 28 days or it will stand on your credit reference files for six years. If you repay after a month, you need to get a certificate of satisfaction from the court, for which you have to send the case number, a receipt or proof of payment and a £10 fee. The court sends the certificate to Registry Trust Ltd who pass it to the credit reference agencies. In Scotland and Northern Ireland, you need to write direct to Registry Trust Ltd with details and £4.50. Tel. 020 7380 0133, www.registry-trust.org.uk.*

Bailiffs are employed by people you owe money to, to collect it.

They can *only* come and do this, if your case has been to court and you have failed to pay. If you owe money on loans, catalogues and credit cards and a court bailiff appears, you can ask the court to 'suspend' the warrant and set repayments you can afford.

Private bailiffs are sometimes employed to collect council tax, child support or fines. Not only are they considered difficult to deal with – read what you like into that – but to add insult to difficulty, they may charge you for their 'services'. In some cases, you can challenge this and good luck to you – as the service was not commissioned by you, but by someone else, personally, I don't see why you should pay it.

If you can't give them cash or a cheque when they arrive, they may try to seize your possessions and sell them for payment.

JANE'S GOLDEN TIP. *Think carefully before letting a bailiff into your home. They are not allowed to come in by force unless you have already let them in when they came before to collect the same debt.*

If you let a bailiff in, they will probably ask you to sign a 'walking possession agreement' allowing them to take your things. But if you agree to make the repayments they demand, they will not take your things there and then.

They can't seize basic possessions, clothes, bedding or tools of your trade – which can include computers and books – though this is open to the individual's interpretation. See Jonathan Aitken's upsetting experience below. They can't take goods that belong to another person but they can take jointly owned goods, although they have to share the proceeds of selling them with your co-owner.

The Community Legal Service Direct, *www.clsdirect.org.uk*, 0845 345 4345, gives clear advice.

Between January and June 2005, over 40,000 people in England and Wales have gone bankrupt – the highest ever recorded total. Some experts predict that by the end of 2005, this will double.

You don't have to go bankrupt because you owe money. Look at all the other options first. The Department of Trade and Industry has an excellent website to explain more at *www.insolvency.gov.uk* The Consumer Credit Counselling Service says that people who go bankrupt tend to be either young or retired, though retired people resist advice to go bankrupt as 'they want to go out clean'.

The average student leaves university owing over £12,000 but with few assets like a car or home that can be seized, so bankruptcy carries less loss and upset – though please take note that you may have trouble getting the best lending deals afterwards. 15 percent of people declared bankrupt between March 2003 and March 2004 were aged thirty or younger. (Source: Survey, Pricewaterhouse-Coopers)

Going bankrupt has lost much of its stigma since the Enterprise Act of 2004 reduced the amount of time you suffer penalties ('the term') from three years to one.

You will free yourself from the immediate worry of overwhelming debt. But bankruptcy is not a holiday or like becoming a child again, with a court-appointed minder to do all your financial thinking and protect you against people you owe money to.

You have to pay your way and earn money after the bankruptcy – and pay your mortgage and living expenses, child maintenance, utility bills and transport costs. Meanwhile you and your family lose anything valuable, including your existing business and perhaps your good name and credibility for the future.

You can complete your bankruptcy application online. See *www.insolvency.gov.uk/doitonline* for the relevant forms, or there is a helpline, 0113 200 6066. At this website, you will also find details of official receivers, insolvency practitioners, records of people who have been or are bankrupt and an 'Enforcement Hotline' to report bankrupts who are still trading or behaving fraudulently.

You can also make yourself bankrupt by presenting your local County Court or the High Court in London with a debtor's petition. For details, ask your local court or Department of Trade and Industry for a leaflet called *Dealing with Debt: How to petition for your own bankruptcy.*

Or if you owe someone else £750 or more, they can present a creditor's petition to the Court. Don't ignore it, leave the country or think you can just refuse to go along with the court proceedings. It is easier to settle a debt out of court beforehand than to go back afterwards.

You may have an uncomfortable time explaining to the Court why you got into so much debt. If it makes a bankruptcy order against you, you must stop using all your bank and credit accounts immediately. The local Official Receiver or Insolvency Practitioner will check your circumstances and report back to the Court if they think you have committed criminal offences like fraud, or if they consider you have been dishonest. If you have overclaimed benefit, you will have to repay it.

They will give the news of your bankruptcy to your local authority, utility suppliers, other courts, bailiffs, National Savings and Investments, the Land Registry and anyone else with a professional interest in your finances.

They may also want to meet you, and will send you a form you must fill out beforehand, giving full details of your assets from banks; building societies; mortgage, pension and insurance companies; solicitors, landlords and anyone else, including people who have had held money or property jointly with you. You have to hand over all your passbooks and financial documents.

Then they take charge of all your money and property and distribute it to your creditors. You don't lose your home if you are living there and paying the mortgage.

You can't keep your bankruptcy private. It will be announced in *The London Gazette*, which is a legal publication, and a local and possibly national newspaper, and on the official bankruptcy website I have mentioned.

If you suddenly inherit, or get a windfall payment of any kind, including property, during your bankruptcy, you have to tell the administrators.

If you can see your way out of bankruptcy by paying your debts off in full, see a leaflet called *Can my bankruptcy be cancelled? Information on annulment of a bankruptcy order* from your Official Receiver's office.

SHOP HORROR STORY *(BANKRUPTCY AT 25)*

'I moved out of my parents' home, got a job as a receptionist and took out a bank loan to buy a computer. Then I celebrated my 21st birthday at the Taj Mahal – not the local Indian restaurant but the real place unfortunately – and paid with a credit card. It was so easy. I didn't think of it as real money. Suddenly, I was £3,000 in debt.

It was no use asking my parents for help – they have very little spare cash. So I got another card and used the balance transfer to repay some of the first one at 0 percent interest. But instead of earning money to repay what I owed, I blew the rest of the balance on shopping until I owed £20,000. I ignored the post, because bills came every day. I had trouble sleeping.

I saw TV adverts saying how easy it was to apply for a debt consolidation loan and pay off the credit cards at a lower rate of interest. I did that, then got another credit card. The crunch came when I was made redundant. My redundancy money didn't cover my repayments for even a month.

I found a debt management company who assured me they could take over my debts, in return for a large sum upfront, and a small monthly charge. I did not even need to open the bills – just send them on, and they would arrange for my interest payments to be frozen and reduce my monthly payments.

They spent months negotiating my bills down and meanwhile, I still had to pay everything, full interest and payment protection plans. I had less money to repay my debts as a result and realised it would be ten years before I would be clear.

I had not told the debt management people about a credit card and a storecard, and started using them again until my debts topped. £38,000.

I researched the idea of going bankrupt using the internet at my local library. It was the best option for me as I have no assets: I rent my flat and don't have a car. Now I'm back living with my parents.'

What it feels like to be bankrupt
(as told to me by Jonathan Aitken)

This famous high-flying and highly-paid politician became bankrupt after losing a libel case against the *Guardian* newspaper, and went to prison when he was found to have lied during it. Now a Christian lecturer and author, you can read more about his life as a bankrupt in his entertaining book *Porridge and Passion*, published by Continuum Books.

'The day you become bankrupt, someone is appointed as your Trustee [to pay your debts and administer your income]. They may be reasonably fair or very unfair to you. Being fair still means being tough.

My watch, my cufflinks and my computer were taken away immediately at my first meeting with my Trustee, so I would advise anyone in my position not to go wearing anything if it has sentimental value. They replace it with a cheaper one but you've lost your girlfriend's gift or whatever.

'Your furniture and everything you own is taken, except necessities. My books were taken away and so was my private correspondence because my creditors wanted to sell it as an asset to tabloid newspapers.

'Eventually I got my computer back, but I had to fight a court case to be allowed to keep my books as I said they were essential to enable me to earn my living as a journalist and author and the Trustee didn't believe I was a serious writer. The judge said I could keep them, as they were the tools of my trade. A Court also let me have my correspondence back, as the judge said it was morally repugnant to sell it. To go to Court to fight this wasn't free, but a young barrister who read about the case stepped in and said he would defend my right to keep my letters private without charging me a fee.

'They take your credit cards and close your bank account. It's difficult to get permission to re-open it. You live off a subsistence allowance. Mine was £3-400 a week – a comedown when I was used to £3-4000 a week.

'Bankruptcy is a big, big comedown in life. But people are very nice and helped me in all sorts of ways. For example one friend gave me a car. Another paid my fees at an Oxford Theological College. And when I was a student I learned to go to supermarkets after 11pm to buy things like half-price sausages past their sell-by date.'

Bankruptcy can last for as little as a year. During bankruptcy, the people you owed money to are not allowed to hassle you for payment. They have to go to the Official Receiver. But you can't get more than £500 of credit from anyone without telling them that you are bankrupt.

You must continue making mortgage payments to keep your home, or the lender will sell it and you may become homeless.

Although your utility bills run up till the court order, are paid from your funds by the Official Receiver, you will have to put down a deposit before you get any more supplies, or transfer the account to a partner. You still have to pay court fines, child maintenance, divorce settlements and similar.

You have to provide a list of everything you own, but can keep the following, unless they are expensive and can be sold and replaced with something reasonable for less money: tools, books, vehicles and other items of equipment which you need to use personally in your work; clothing, bedding, furniture, household equipment and other basic items you and your family need in the home.

If you foresee the bankruptcy and sell your home to a relative for less than its true worth, the court may reverse the sale. They don't normally claim an Inland Revenue approved pension fund. But payments you get from a pension may be shared out between your creditors, leaving you enough to pay your living expenses.

Your life assurance policies may be cashed in except if they are used as security for an endowment mortgage, for instance. If you have joint policies, your partner must discuss the situation with whoever the Court has appointed to deal with your case.

Your business is closed if you are self-employed and its assets claimed, as long as they are not needed to help you earn your immediate living. Your driving licence is not affected, but work-related registrations, licences and permissions can be sold – for instance a franchise agreement.

Your staff could make a claim to the National Insurance Fund if you owe them wages and holiday pay, payment in lieu of notice and redundancy, but if they don't get their claim paid this way, they can claim against you through the Official Receiver or whoever is handling your case. For details, call the Redundancy Payments Service, 0845 145 0004.

But you can start working for yourself again immediately, registering for a new VAT number. The Court may make an Income Payments Order against your wages, taking reasonable family needs into account first. The IPO can go on for up to three years from your bankruptcy order, even if you have been discharged from bankruptcy. An alternative is making an agreed series of repayments called an Income Payments Agreement for three years.

A note to say you have been bankrupt will stay on your credit status report for up to six years from the date of the Court order. This is used by lenders to check on your past repayment performance. Naturally it may hamper your chances of getting the best interest rates, or even credit cards.

Contact the credit-checking agencies Experian, Callcredit and Equifax to check what is on your record. Send each agency a copy of your certificate of discharge so that they can update their records if they are inaccurate and also check whether any debts which you did in fact pay, are still marked 'unpaid' in the records.

Experian/credit expert, 0870 241 6212, *www.experian.com*; Callcredit, 0113 244 1555, *www.callcredit.plc.uk*; Equifax, *www.equifax.co.uk*, Credit File Advice Centre, PO Box 1140, Bradford BD1 5US, 0870 010 0583 (use the phone number only for enquiries once you have your credit reference file).

Experian keeps search information for one year; Equifax and Callcredit for two.

HELPFUL HINT

Don't apply for credit to lenders whose company policy is not to lend to anyone until a bankruptcy is wiped off the records, i.e. six years. Check first before applying, or you will get several failed credit applications listed on your records – and you're going round in a circle because the more of these you have, the less your chances of getting credit.

If there were any unusual circumstances that caused your bankruptcy, like illness or redundancy, ask the credit agencies to add a Notice to your record explaining.

Try to avoid what are called 'sub-prime' lenders asking the highest interest.

Credit repair agencies charge for what can be poor advice. After a few years, the bankruptcy will vanish for things like credit cards and personal loans, but you may have to declare it to some mortgage lenders.

How to get a mortage if you have defaulted or been made bankrupt

You are called 'credit-impaired'. Expect to pay considerably higher interest – perhaps 2 percent or more than for those with a good credit record.

Also, many high street lenders won't consider you if you approach them direct. Chelsea Building Society will allow you to apply for morgages or remortgages but most others will only accept applications through brokers. A good broker will know who to contact and put your application in the right light – explaining how by misfortune, you had problems before. After a few years, you may be able to transfer back to the 'mainstream' market at much lower fees, so don't accept a deal which locks you in for years.

* London & Country mortgage brokers charge no fee. 0800 9530304, www.lcplc.co.uk

The
Congratulations
Zone

Go back to your budget planner in this book (page 12) and see how much you used to spend.

Write your savings here.

Daily total spent..

Weekly total spent...

Monthly total spent...

Total saved..

Now have that final chocolate/beer/bubble bath or whatever your treat is. But don't have the lot in one go!

I told you you could do it, didn't I?

Don't you dare to binge

If you haven't saved as much as you hoped – today is another day. Don't give up. Don't go shopping. You can only do your best. Analyse what went wrong and go from there. Email me if you want to.

At least once a month, read the personal money sections of any good newspaper for up-to-date news. Keep an eye out for better rates, especially for mortgages, including new ideas like the Euro mortgages which are supposed to take advantage of our strong pound, to give us better deals.

Don't stop now!

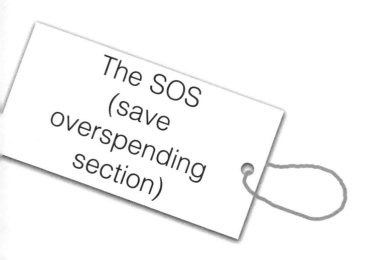

The SOS
(save
overspending
section)

Tempted to overspend?
Give me 30 seconds to stop you ... now!

Think. Even if someone has been disappointing or downright nasty to you, you are not a worthless person. You are trying to do something about your overspending and that takes guts.

Buying something will not make you feel better nor look better. It will not make any difference to the person who has upset you. You will feel guilty every time you look at your purchases because you cannot afford them.

Hold on to your self-control! Don't fritter! Don't binge! If you are throwing money down the drain, instead:

- Cut your credit card into tiny bits and throw it down the nearest drain.
- Fold your credit card in half.
- Take a small foil takeaway container or a sardine tin (not a plastic container – it's too easy to defrost) and fill with water. Wrap your credit card in cling film, submerge in the water and *freeze your spending*.
- Think whether you could spend that money on your children.
- Think how your heart will sink when the credit card bill arrives.
- Think how much work you will have to do, to pay for it.
- Put the item in the shop's basket. Admire it. For a moment, it's yours. Now put the basket down and walk out briskly out of the shop. Don't look back.
- Make a phone call. Not a text – that isn't personal enough. Talk to someone sensible, not a person who massages your ego and says you 'deserve' your proposed purchase. Usually a man will stop you buying something silly. Try your Dad.
- Walk away. Look elsewhere for five minutes. Now, can you even remember what the item you want looks like? Its colour, size, what it's made of, and the price exactly?
- Give yourself five good reasons to buy this. Good reasons. Five reasons. Four are not enough.
- Go home and check your cupboards or wardrobe. You probably have something just like it there already.
- Imagine that dress or bag in the window of a charity shop. That's where the latest must-haves end up, a season later. Now is it so tempting?
- Think how many other people have bought the same thing. Do you want to be one of the herd?

- Think who might have tried that dress/shoes/underwear on already. (They probably have.) Yuck!
- Do you have your tee-shirt on? That's the one that reads: *'Do not sell this person anything'*. If not, go home and find it.
- Imagine the shop as its owners see it. It is a warehouse, an'outlet'. Mentally turn off the soft relaxing music. Strip all the lovely decoration away – it helps to look at the shop's ceiling when you do this, which is usually pretty ropey. Remember, the smiling assistants don't need you to impress them with your spending. They probably earn less than you anyway. Once they have wrapped your purchases, they don't care what happens to you. There will be another lot of 'stock', as they call those seductive buys, along tomorrow. If you have trouble imagining all this, peer into the 'stock room' at the back of the shop. Remember, all those gorgeous purchases are being pulled out of tatty boxes under a Formica counter.

What would I say if I were just behind you in the shop? It's time to call your friend who has agreed to check your spending.

Finally, after all I've said, do you still feel like buying shoes? If you do, it's because you are not having enough sex, as I am sure a future medical study will prove. Surely you know what to do about *that* …

Should you be saving or investing?

Everyone, no matter how well off, thinks life would be better if they had 23 percent more money, Professor Mark Ritson of the London Business School tells me.

When you have sorted out your finances, try to save three months' salary as a comfort-cushion, so that you are not thrown into a panic by sudden blows like illness or job loss.

Don't just ask your nearest bank or building society for savings advice. Read the money sections of a few newspapers. You could start an investment club – put a few pounds in every month and play the stock market as a group of friends using the Proshare Investment Clubs, whose manual costs a princely £25. (Tel. 01227 878609, *www.proshare.org*). At least you know that your profits are not going to pay someone else's fat bonus.

Think about alternative investments. I don't consider race horses and becoming an 'angel' – investing in a theatre or film production – are a good idea unless you are an expert, in which case you will be rich already, but look at wine, stamps and art. They won't earn steady interest as you will in a savings account or bond, but they may give you pleasure and if you choose well, you can make spectacular profits. If you make the wrong choice, at least you can drink one and look at the others, and there may be tax advantages for you especially if you keep them a SIPP, self-invested pension plan (see my earlier comments about pensions, p.279).

Wine. I am not suggesting that you buy the next offer from the off licence and keep it in your garden shed (the one that used to be full of unused tools before you read this book). For independent advice, try The Wine Society, which claims to be the world's oldest co-operative wine club. 01438 741177, *www.thewinesociety.com* Premier Cru, 020 8905 4495, *www.wine-investments.co.uk* is one company offering a tax-free investment service.

Stamps. A stamp pundit tells me that mint GB Queen Victoria stamps have gone up in value by 19.6 percent in a year. Top sources of information include *www.stanleygibbons.com,* 020 7836 8444 (who also deal in autographs, memorabilia and rare coins), *www.churchillstamps.co.uk,* 01494 724948, or w*www.stampsforsale.co.uk*, PO Box 4167, Hornchurch, RM11 1ZP, 01708 440173; also *www.condorstamps.com,* 01252 623 710.

Art. A well-chosen piece of art can accumulate so much value that it outstrips conventional savings – and you have the pleasure of looking at it. Shortly, the tax rules will change to enable us to include art in SIPPs.

> **JANE'S GOLDEN TIP.** *Interest-free loans up to £2,000, repayable by direct debit over ten months, are available for anyone to buy a piece, part of a piece, or several pieces of 'innovative work' by living artists – painting, sculpture, photography, limited edition prints, jewellery, glass and ceramics – under the Art Council's OwnArt scheme. This is easy, according to my guinea pig, but you must shop at approved galleries, UKwide, and take ID like your driving licence. www.artscouncil.org.uk/ownart for details. Also try The Affordable Art Fair, www.affordableartfair.com, 020 7371 8787, and try www.londonartandartists.guide.com. The internet art price guides are www.artnet.co.uk and www.artsalesindex.co.uk, 01784 473136.*

For general advice about collecting art, including photography, try *www.artadvice.com/advice/article16.php* and *www.hwlondon artandartistsguide.com/consultancy.htm.*

For personal free advice, at least initially, try *hw.artlondon@virgin.net*, 020 7221 6983, who have a huge expert contact list of critics and historians too.

Read my previous book, *Mr Thrifty's How to Save Money on Absolutely Everything*, updated 2005, Michael O'Mara Books. Or have a look at my websites, *www.smartspending.co.uk* or *www.mrthrifty.co.uk*, are updated regularly with tips too.

More help

Come on a course. Jane Furnival's School of Life is based in Surrey, about 30 minutes by train from central London, and offers courses to interest and inspire you on money-saving matters and easy-to-acquire skills from keeping hens to chocolate- and wine-tasting. For more information, see *www.schooloflife.info* or write to Thriftyworks Ltd, PO Box 251, Sutton, SM3 8WU for a leaflet. 020 8641 9474.

Buy a tee-shirt. '*Please do not sell this woman/man anything*' tee-shirts cost £15 including p&p from Thriftyworks Ltd at the address above.

Invite me to yours. For more information about personal or group visits – or even surprise visits to get an overspending friend in order! – contact *jane@smartspending.co.uk.*

I am omitting books or webs which in my opinion duplicate my advice or which I know charge businesses for listings. My recommendations are not paid for.

Other stuff...

I recommend the 18 impartial free pocket planners issued by The Prudential on a variety of subjects from budgeting to pensions. Tel: 0800 000 000, or download from *www.pru.co.uk/plan.*

The Rough Guide to Ethical Shopping by Duncan Clark (Penguin, £6.99) has loads of contacts if you want to shop or invest ethically – which is not always cheaply.

Shopped. The Shocking Power of British Supermarkets by Joanna Blythman (HarperPerennial, £7.99) is fascinating for those who want to know more about what happens behind the scenes in retailing.

The Consumers' Association magazine *Which?* is always informative. For subscriptions and free trial offers, look on the website. *www.which.net*, 0845 307 4000.

- *www.debtfreeday.com* has easy to understand advice. www.debtfreedaily.co.uk 0845 2001845, is a newsletter with loads of suggestions and current best interest rates which you can sign up to.
- *www.moneysavingexpert.co.uk* isolates the best financial deals as they happen, with things like credit card rates and extra storecard points. *www.frugal.org.uk* is especially good for businesses. *www.Planabudget.com* is an American site with sensible advice. *www.msn.co.uk* has useful guides to most financial matters and helpful calculators.
- *www.fool.co.uk* is a lovely clear website for financial products and advice.
- *www.thefrugalshopper.com* has lots of sensible advice.
- For shoppers, Alison Cork's Really Useful Bargains column in the *London Evening Standard* is among my favourites. Her website, *www.bargainlondon.co.uk*, is useful. *www.shoppingvillages.com* lists factory shops and factory villages.

To know more, or get more involved, in the anti-consumerist movement, try *www.adbusters.com* and *www.buynothingchristmas.org*. The Adbusters magazine costs $40 for six issues.

Try *www.debtorsanonymous.info*. You can hear recorded information about the service on 020 7644 5070.

AND THE FINAL FUNNY MONEY. *The executive producer and one of the directors of a TV series drove hundreds of miles from their office to my home for a meeting. The tea I served them was the weakest I had ever made and I could not understand why. Later, I found the tea-bag, which I thought I had put in the pot, on the kitchen work surface. I had poured boiling water into an empty pot. They must have thought I was so mean!!*

All advice is given in good faith. However I am not a financial adviser, and readers must decide on their own course of action, taking expert advice for themselves

APPENDIX:
Family Spending

Mr and Mrs UK Average and their family

The average home has 2.4 people living in it and a disposable income of around £464. Each person spends £177.40 or (not 'and', my darling smart spenders!) each home spends £418.10 per home per week. This breaks down into:

Food and non-alcoholic drinks £43.50
Alcohol, tobacco, narcotics £11.70
Clothes and shoes £22.70
Housing costs, fuel, power £39
Household goods and services £31.30
Health £5.00
Transport £67.70

Communication (phones, post) £11.20
Recreation and culture £57.30
Education £5.20
Restaurants and hotels £34.90
Miscellaneous goods and services £34.90
Other expenditure £33.60

Mr or Ms Average

The average single working person spends £281.40 per week. This breaks down into:

Food and non-alcoholic drinks £21.80
Alcohol, tobacco, narcotics £9.20
Clothes and shoes £11.30
Housing costs, fuel, power £36.30
Household goods and services £19.90
Health £2.30
Transport £41.30

Communication (phones, post) £8.70
Recreation and culture £34.60
Education £2.20
Restaurants and hotels £23.80
Miscellaneous goods and services £19.80
Other expenditure £50.10

Working couples without children average weekly spending
£250.20 per person
£500.50 per home*
*Presumably the Government assumes they lost the other 10p down a manhole.

Food and non-alcoholic drinks £45.70

Alcohol, tobacco, narcotics £14.30

Clothes and shoes £24.60

Housing costs, fuel, power £41.50

Household goods and services £40.00

Health £7.40

Transport £80.20

Communication (phones, post) £11.10

Recreation and culture £69.90

Education £2.70

Restaurants and hotels £42.60

Miscellaneous goods and services £37.70

Other expenditure £82.60

Pensioners
Living alone, mainly dependent on state pensions.
The average pensioner spends £111.50 per week on:

Food and non-alcoholic drinks £21.10

Alcohol, tobacco, narcotics £3.70

Clothes and shoes £4.40

Housing costs, fuel, power £21.40

Household goods and services £7.30

Health £1.90

Transport £6.40

Communication (phones, post) £4.30

Recreation and culture £12.20

Education £0

Restaurants and hotels £4.80

Miscellaneous goods and services £12.60

Other expenditure £11.30

Married couple, mainly dependent on state pensions
The average married pensioner spends £101.60 per person, £203.30 per home weekly on:

Food and non-alcoholic drinks £39.10

Alcohol, tobacco, narcotics £6.60

Clothes and shoes £7.30

Housing costs, fuel, power £28.00

Household goods and services £20.60

Health £3.70

Transport £18.70

Communication (phones, post) £4.70

Recreation and culture £29.40

Education £0

Restaurants and hotels £10.10

Miscellaneous goods and services £14.90

Other expenditure £20.20

Retired married couple, not mainly dependent on state pensions
The average retired couple spends £174.20 per person, £348.30 per couple weekly on:

Food and non-alcoholic drinks £45.90
Alcohol, tobacco, narcotics £10.50
Clothes and shoes £13.20
Housing costs, fuel, power £29.70
Household goods and services £30.20
Health £9.20
Transport £49.60

Communication (phones, post) £7.20
Recreation and culture £57.80
Education £0.70
Restaurants and hotels £23.70
Miscellaneous goods and services £27.10
Other expenditure £43.50

THE NUTS AND BOLTS
Skim the ten income-groups here and choose the one closest to your weekly income. All households in the statistical survey tended to have two or three people living in them.

1. HOUSEHOLD INCOME per week UP TO £192
The figures per person and per household are not to be added together, allowing you to have a personal budget plus a household budget. They are just broken down to give you a clearer picture.

AVERAGE WEEKLY SPENDING
£105.80 per person
£173.30 per household

Average amount each household spent weekly on:

Food and non-alcoholic drinks £27.80
Alcohol, tobacco, narcotics £7.00
Clothes and shoes £7.80
Housing costs, fuel, power £28.30
Household goods and services £13.80
Health £1.80
Transport £16.90

Communication (phones, post) £5.70
Recreation and culture £24.00
Education £0.70
Restaurants and hotels £24.00
Miscellaneous goods and services £12.60
Other expenditure £16.20

2. INCOME per week UP TO £192
AVERAGE WEEKLY SPENDING
£105.80 per person
£173.30 per household

Average amount each household spent weekly on:

Food and non-alcoholic drinks £27.80
Alcohol, tobacco, narcotics £7.00
Clothes and shoes £7.80
Housing costs, fuel, power £28.30
Household goods and services £13.80
Health £1.80
Transport £16.90

Communication (phones, post) £5.70
Recreation and culture £24.00
Education £0.70
Restaurants and hotels £10.70
Miscellaneous goods and services £12.60
Other expenditure £16.20

3. INCOME per week UP TO £262
AVERAGE WEEKLY SPENDING
£115.10 per person
£224.20 per household

Average amount each household spent weekly on:

Food and non-alcoholic drinks £34.20
Alcohol, tobacco, narcotics £7.90
Clothes and shoes £11.90
Housing costs, fuel, power £31.90
Household goods and services £16.80
Health £3.10
Transport £23.30

Communication (phones, post) £7.20
Recreation and culture £30.00
Education £2.20
Restaurants and hotels £15.80
Miscellaneous goods and services £16.10
Other expenditure £23.90

4. INCOME per week UP TO £350
AVERAGE WEEKLY SPENDING
£153.70 per person
£298.30 per household

Average amount each household spent weekly on:

Food and non-alcoholic drinks £36.50
Alcohol, tobacco, narcotics £10.50
Clothes and shoes £14.10
Housing costs, fuel, power £34.90
Household goods and services £20.30
Health £4.60
Transport £40.70

Communication (phones, post) £9.00
Recreation and culture £42.80
Education £2.10
Restaurants and hotels £21.70
Miscellaneous goods and services £22.70
Other expenditure £38.50

5. INCOME per week UP TO £444

AVERAGE WEEKLY SPENDING
£152.70 per person
£361.70 per household

Average amount each household spent weekly on:

Food and non-alcoholic drinks £42.40
Alcohol, tobacco, narcotics £12.10
Clothes and shoes £18.40
Housing costs, fuel, power £42.00
Household goods and services £26.60
Health £5.10
Transport £48.00

Communication (phones, post) £10.70
Recreation and culture £52.10
Education £2.30
Restaurants and hotels £31.20
Miscellaneous Goods and services £27.90
Other expenditure £42.90

6. INCOME per week UP TO £557

AVERAGE WEEKLY SPENDING
£159.90 per person
£411.40 per household

Average amount each household spent weekly on:

Food and non-alcoholic drinks £44.70
Alcohol, tobacco, narcotics £12.30
Clothes and shoes £22.10
Housing costs, fuel, power £43.60
Household goods and services £31.30
Health £4.50
Transport £55.30

Communication (phones, post) £11.20
Recreation and culture £56.00
Education £1.70
Restaurants and hotels £32.40
Miscellaneous goods and services £34.70
Other expenditure £61.60

7. INCOME per week UP TO £672

AVERAGE WEEKLY SPENDING
£175.30 per person
£478.60 per household

Average amount each household spent weekly on:

Food and non-alcoholic drinks £48.80
Alcohol, tobacco, narcotics £13.70
Clothes and shoes £25.90
Housing costs, fuel, power £41.50
Household goods and services £34.20
Health £4.90
Transport £67.60

Communication (phones, post) £12.70
Recreation and culture £68.60
Education £2.80
Restaurants and hotels £43.90
Miscellaneous goods and services £41.10
Other expenditure £73.10

8. INCOME per week UP TO £827
AVERAGE WEEKLY SPENDING
£150.70 per person
£584.90 per household

Average amount each household spent weekly on:

Food and non-alcoholic drinks £61.00
Alcohol, tobacco, narcotics £14.30
Clothes and shoes £36.20
Housing costs, fuel, power £41.80
Household goods and services £42.00
Health £4.20
Transport £82.40

Communication (phones, post) £14.40
Recreation and culture £88.70
Education £5.10
Restaurants and hotels £48.70
Miscellaneous goods and services £50.60
Other expenditure £95.50

9. INCOME per week UP TO £1,091
AVERAGE WEEKLY SPENDING
£212.20 per person
£632.30 per household

Average amount each household spent weekly on:

Food and non-alcoholic drinks £60.60
[sic, same as last group]
Alcohol, tobacco, narcotics £16.60 [sic]
Clothes and shoes £35.30
Housing costs, fuel, power £42.80
Household goods and services £45.00
Health £8.30

Transport £104.00
Communication (phones, post) £15.60
Recreation and culture £88.40
Education £7.80
Restaurants and hotels £55.50
Miscellaneous goods and services £55.40
Other expenditure £101.80

10. INCOME per week ABOVE £1,091
AVERAGE WEEKLY SPENDING
£284.30 per person
£905.00 per household

Average amount each household spent weekly on:

Food and non-alcoholic drinks £67.80
Alcohol, tobacco, narcotics £16.20
Clothes and shoes £53.80
Housing costs, fuel, power £58.00
Household goods and services £71.40
Health £11.00
Transport £150.10

Communication (phones, post) £20.20
Recreation and culture £116.20
Education £27.10
Restaurants and hotels £77.40
Miscellaneous goods and services £74.70
Other expenditure £161.20

TWO-PARENT FAMILIES WITH CHILDREN
Mr and Mrs Average and their children spend on average £151.60 per week each, with a total of £580.00 per household per week. To work out budgets in more detail consutl the lists below.

TAKE-HOME PAY UNDER £192 PER WEEK.
AVERAGE WEEKLY SPENDING (including the children's spending)
£70.60 per person
£253.60 per household (that's right)

Average amount each household spent weekly on:

Food and non-alcoholic drinks £41.20
Alcohol, tobacco, narcotics £12.80
Clothes and shoes £18.90
Housing costs, fuel, power £34.10
Household goods and services £13.40
Health £3.00
Transport £30.10

Communication (phones, post) £7.40
Recreation and culture £29.70
Education £12.40
Restaurants and hotels £20.40
Miscellaneous goods and services £16.00
Other expenditure £14.30

TAKE-HOME PAY £193–£350 PER WEEK.

AVERAGE WEEKLY SPENDING (including the children's spending)
£85.70 per person
£334.80 per household (that's right)

Average amount each household spent weekly on:

Food and non-alcoholic drinks £50.60
Alcohol, tobacco, narcotics £12.30
Clothes and shoes £21.60
Housing costs, fuel, power £39.00
Household goods and services £25.70
Health £1.50
Transport £37.90

Communication (phones, post) £11.90
Recreation and culture £38.30
Education £8.10
Restaurants and hotels £26.40
Miscellaneous goods and services £26.30
Other expenditure £35.40

TAKE-HOME PAY £351–£557 PER WEEK

AVERAGE WEEKLY SPENDING (including the children's spending)
£112.60 per person
£434.70 per household (that's right)

Average amount each household spent weekly on:

Food and non-alcoholic drinks £51.90
Alcohol, tobacco, narcotics £13.80
Clothes and shoes £26.10
Housing costs, fuel, power £47.30
Household goods and services £31.30
Health £3.20
Transport £57.10

Communication (phones, post) £12.90
Recreation and culture £59.70
Education £3.20
Restaurants and hotels £34.50
Miscellaneous goods and services £33.60
Other expenditure £60.30

TAKE-HOME PAY £558–£827 PER WEEK.

AVERAGE WEEKLY SPENDING (including the children's spending)
£150.70 per person
£584.90 per household

Average amount each household spent weekly on:

Food and non-alcoholic drinks £61.00
Alcohol, tobacco, narcotics £14.30
Clothes and shoes £36.20
Housing costs, fuel, power £41.80
Household goods and services £42.00
Health £4.20
Transport £82.40

Communication (phones, post) £14.40
Recreation and culture £88.70
Education £5.10
Restaurants and hotels £48.70
Miscellaneous goods and services £50.60
Other expenditure £95.50

TAKE-HOME PAY OVER £828 PER WEEK.

AVERAGE WEEKLY SPENDING (including the children's spending)
£211.00 per person
£814.00 per household

Average amount each household spent weekly on:

Food and non-alcoholic drinks £72.70
Alcohol, tobacco, narcotics £13.50
Clothes and shoes £47.20
Housing costs, fuel, power £46.40
Household goods and services £63.70
Health £7.90
Transport £122.50

Communication (phones, post) £15.70
Recreation and culture £113.40
Education £30.40
Restaurants and hotels £61.50
Miscellaneous goods and services £75.60
Other expenditure £143.50

ONE PARENT FAMILIES WITH CHILDREN

Mr or Ms Average and their children spend on average £98.80 a week per person or £269.00 per week as a household.

TAKE-HOME PAY UNDER £192 PER WEEK

AVERAGE WEEKLY SPENDING (including the children's spending)
£63.80 per person
£166.30 per household

Average amount each household spent weekly on:

Food and non-alcoholic drinks £30.80
Alcohol, tobacco, narcotics £8.00
Clothes and shoes £14.70
Housing costs, fuel, power £22.10
Household goods and services £13.90
Health £0.70
Transport £12.40

Communication (phones, post) £7.40
Recreation and culture £20.70
Education £1.30
Restaurants and hotels £13.70
Miscellaneous goods and services £11.40
Other expenditure £9.10

TAKE-HOME PAY £193–£350 PER WEEK

AVERAGE WEEKLY SPENDING (including the children's spending)
£88.30 per person
£259.50 per household

Average amount each household spent weekly on:

Food and non-alcoholic drinks £36.10
Alcohol, tobacco, narcotics £8.80
Clothes and shoes £23.00
Housing costs, fuel, power £37.00
Household goods and services £17.10
Health £1.60
Transport £23.40

Communication (phones, post) £11.60
Recreation and culture £32.30
Education £3.10
Restaurants and hotels £19.80
Miscellaneous goods and services £21.00
Other expenditure £24.50

TAKE-HOME PAY £351–£557 PER WEEK
AVERAGE WEEKLY SPENDING (including the children's spending)
£134.10 per person
£360.50 per household

Average amount each household spent weekly on:

Food and non-alcoholic drinks £38.00

Alcohol, tobacco, narcotics £8.90

Clothes and shoes £27.10

Housing costs, fuel, power £42.90

Household goods and services £29.00

Health £2.00

Transport £39.60

Communication (phones, post) £13.20

Recreation and culture £46.30

Education £3.90

Restaurants and hotels £29.10

Miscellaneous goods and services £35.10

Other expenditure £45.40

TAKE-HOME PAY £558-827 PER WEEK

AVERAGE WEEKLY SPENDING(including the children's spending)
£182.40 per person
£488.60 per household

Average amount each household spent weekly on:

Food and non-alcoholic drinks £46.80

Alcohol, tobacco, narcotics £10.80

Clothes and shoes £26.40

Housing costs, fuel, power £40.70

Household goods and services £30.50

Health £5.80

Transport £68.70

Communication (phones, post) £14.10

Recreation and culture £69.00

Education £16.20

Restaurants and hotels £35.50

Miscellaneous goods and services £50.80

Other expenditure £73.10

TAKE-HOME PAY OVER £828 PER WEEK
AVERAGE WEEKLY SPENDING (including the children's spending)
£296.40 per person
£818.60 per household

Average amount each household spent weekly on:

Food and non-alcoholic drinks £52.00
Alcohol, tobacco, narcotics £10.00
Clothes and shoes £76.10
Housing costs, fuel, power £32.90
Household goods and services £90.80
Health £9.00
Transport £91.90

Communication (phones, post) £18.20
Recreation and culture £93.50
Education £46.90
Restaurants and hotels £46.40
Miscellaneous goods and services £80.70
Other expenditure £170.30

Factors to bear in mind

- Expect to spend most of your income, probably 20 percent, on your rent and mortgage.
- Students pay more rent than any other group, at £69.30 per week on average.
- The second largest bill is on transport (average £61 per week).
- Recreation and culture costs £57 and includes package holidays (£12), sports tickets, subscriptions and fees for classes like dancing and aerobics (£5), £2 for cinema, theatre and museums – and £4 gambling.
- Food and non-alcoholic drinks averages £44.
- Single people spend the most, at £281 on average, per week.

We hope you enjoyed this Hay House book.
If you would like to receive a free catalogue featuring additional
Hay House books and products, or if you would like information
about the Hay Foundation, please contact:

Hay House UK Ltd
Unit 62, Canalot Studios • 222 Kensal Rd • London W10 5BN
Tel: (44) 20 8962 1230; Fax: (44) 20 8962 1239
www.hayhouse.co.uk

***

Published and distributed in the United States of America by:
Hay House, Inc. • PO Box 5100 • Carlsbad, CA 92018-5100
Tel: (1) 760 431 7695 or (800) 654 5126;
Fax: (1) 760 431 6948 or (800) 650 5115
www.hayhouse.com

Published and distributed in Australia by:
Hay House Australia Ltd • 18/36 Ralph St • Alexandria NSW 2015
Tel: (61) 2 9669 4299 • Fax: (61) 2 9669 4144
www.hayhouse.com.au

Published and distributed in the Republic of South Africa by:
Hay House SA (Pty) Ltd • PO Box 990 • Witkoppen 2068
Tel/Fax: (27) 11 706 6612 • orders@psdprom.co.za

Distributed in Canada by:
Raincoast • 9050 Shaughnessy St • Vancouver, BC V6P 6E5
Tel: (1) 604 323 7100 • Fax: (1) 604 323 2600

***

Sign up via the Hay House UK website to receive the Hay House
online newsletter and stay informed about what's going on with
your favourite authors. You'll receive bimonthly announcements
about discounts and offers, special events, product highlights,
free excerpts, giveaways, and more!
www.hayhouse.co.uk